The Thought Awaits Us All

Daniela Calabrò

The Thought Awaits Us All

Essays on Jean-Luc Nancy

≝ Springer

Daniela Calabrò
Department of Humanities, Philosophy and Education
University of Salerno
Fisciano, Salerno, Italy

ISBN 978-3-031-75400-5   ISBN 978-3-031-75401-2 (eBook)
https://doi.org/10.1007/978-3-031-75401-2

© The Editor(s) (if applicable) and The Author(s), under exclusive license to Springer Nature Switzerland AG 2024

This work is subject to copyright. All rights are solely and exclusively licensed by the Publisher, whether the whole or part of the material is concerned, specifically the rights of translation, reprinting, reuse of illustrations, recitation, broadcasting, reproduction on microfilms or in any other physical way, and transmission or information storage and retrieval, electronic adaptation, computer software, or by similar or dissimilar methodology now known or hereafter developed.
The use of general descriptive names, registered names, trademarks, service marks, etc. in this publication does not imply, even in the absence of a specific statement, that such names are exempt from the relevant protective laws and regulations and therefore free for general use.
The publisher, the authors and the editors are safe to assume that the advice and information in this book are believed to be true and accurate at the date of publication. Neither the publisher nor the authors or the editors give a warranty, expressed or implied, with respect to the material contained herein or for any errors or omissions that may have been made. The publisher remains neutral with regard to jurisdictional claims in published maps and institutional affiliations.

This Springer imprint is published by the registered company Springer Nature Switzerland AG
The registered company address is: Gewerbestrasse 11, 6330 Cham, Switzerland

If disposing of this product, please recycle the paper.

Preface

Jean-Luc Nancy's *Thought-to-Come*

This volume shows how Nancy was able "to deconstruct" the founding sign of all metaphysics and all transcendence by redefining the concepts of existence, corporeality, and community, opening them up to the "disenclosure" of the outside, to the "excription" of the world.

In a time in which we are exposed to contagion with others, with everyone else, on the wave of globalization, a thought of the "exposed body," a reflection such as the one Nancy invites us to make on the "ex-peau-sition," on the fact that we are all, starting from the skin itself, exposed to and crossed by others, is as important and urgent as ever.

It is quite clear how much these reflections can influence today, even on a political level. The dimension of the community outlined by Nancy is not that of a substance that becomes a subject producing the world of meanings, values, and norms, but rather that of finitude capable of exposing itself to its own limit, of standing on its own boundary to grasp that excess, that disproportion of the Being-with that, when crossing it, breaks it and makes it impossible for it to dominate itself. This community is not made up of individuals, but of finite singularities that welcome the limit within themselves and do not leave it outside a presumed unity. Nancy outlines a community dimension that does not claim to become absolute, to assimilate within itself all the dimensions of man, but shows precisely what, by subtracting itself from the concept, from the total transparency of meaning, makes Being as an inappropriable other. In a multiple proximity of bodies, in which the "us" becomes palpable, touches itself and offers itself to be touched… the image multiplies, splinters, crashes, rejects itself. All this entails a radical reflection on where we come from and our trajectory; in short, on what we want to be "neither places, nor heavens, nor gods […] dismantling and disassembling of enclosed bowers, enclosures, fences."

To deconstruct. From Nietzsche onward, this seems to be the appropriate watchword to provide a new face to classical and traditional philosophy. To rethink the meaning of the world, the body, and existence; to thoroughly understand the terms of the emergence of biopolitics[1] and its tanatopolitical and eugenic implications; to rethink, therefore, the meaning of death—with the related questions of determining the "end of life" at the center of today's political debate—and the meaning of the ownership of life[2] (living will). To address and acknowledge all fundamentalisms and all identity madness. In other words, there is an urgent need to rethink our relationship with the world, with our body, with the other. There is an urgent need to understand the "weight" of thought: its materiality, extension, space, and boundary. To do so, it needs to remove foundations, ends, domains, and powers; in a word, it needs "to deconstruct." Nevertheless, here "to deconstruct" is not meant to be the negative, dialectically oppositional concept or meaning of "to construct." It is not about that, nor is it about being able to inhabit the "post-modern" or "the end of meaning," or to cope with the "nihilistic drift." Rather, it is about putting out, "dislocating," stripping away the "place" that has sealed the entire West within the meshes of tradition. "By sealing and self-sealing as tradition, which is normal, tradition walls up, closes and encloses."[3]

To deconstruct, then, has here to do with the "dis-closure," with the "reopening" of the founding places, to bring to light not only the foundations or fundamentals, but to make the "founding gesture (the impetus, the thrust, the fate) appear."[4] Such a founding gesture, in fact, in its appearing is—as Nancy puts it—"1) such that it had never grasped itself as such, 2) such that it ignored, by necessity, what it founded and that it was founder of as well, and that it sealed itself from itself."[5] This is why "to deconstruct" cannot be paired with or stand as the alter of "to construct," but rather means "to disclose" the ushering gesture; it means to enter into the "unheard-of."[6] "It is this returning to itself to discover that the 'self' is not and was never given, and therefore legs always behind all 'archaeological' counterthrusts, and is always ahead of one's own 'deconstructive' present. Ultimately, deconstruction is the autobiography of a subject who can only be found through this autobiography

---

[1] On the biopolitical paradigm, which has now become a central reference of any reflection both in the philosophical-political field and in the socio-economic, legal, and medical-scientific ones, in addition to the inevitable reference to Foucault's now classic texts, see the following at least: Esposito, R.: Bíos. Biopolitica e filosofia. Einaudi, Turin (2004); Bazzicalupo, L., Il governo delle vite. Biopolitica ed economia. Laterza, Rome (2006).; Amendola, A., Bazzicalupo, L., Chicchi, F., Tucci, A. (ed.): Biopolitica, bioeconomia e processi di soggettivazione. Quodlibet, Macerata (2008).

[2] On the subject, to give just one example, see the volume by Rodotà, S.: La vita e le regole. Tra diritto e non diritto. Feltrinelli, Milan (2006).

[3] Nancy, J.-L.: Il senso del mondo. Lanfranchi, Milan (1997). The quotation is from a Correspondence (attached to the volume) between F. Ferrari, T. Maia and J.-L. Nancy and can be found on p. 218 (my translation).

[4] Ibid. (my translation).

[5] Ibid. (my translation).

[6] We are speaking here of that "entry into the unheard-of" mentioned by Nancy when referring to Rimbaud, in "You ask me what it means today …" An epigraph for "'Paragraph'," in Paragraph, 16(2), (1993):109–110; and in La pensée dérobée. Galilée, Paris (2001), it. transl. by Vergani, M.: Il pensiero sottratto. Bollati Boringhieri,Turin (2003).—see especially pp. 188–190.

and, moreover, as a reinvention of an ever-older 'self' and of the same 'self' as always being more and more 'to come.' [...] It is the self-relationship of a subject who has no myth of himself."[7]

Therefore, the negativity of the prefix *de* does not have to do with a work of annihilation, but rather of dismantling, of dis-placement—as mentioned earlier—of the founding tradition, immemorial of the founding gesture. "Psyché is extended, knows nothing about it!"[8] In this not-knowing and not-knowing-itself lies the possibility of the world to be world, the possibility of Rome to be Rome: always *in* the "to" of the "to-come." In this regard, Nancy explains, "Romulus did not know he was founding Rome; he thought he was founding the new Troy, just like others, in later times, believed they were founding the New Spain, the New England or the New France; the very novelty is a reproduction - while Rome would be, at the same time, the covering, the sealing of the innovation and its incomparable, unprecedented development."[9] Realizing the "to-come" of the "de" of "deconstruction" then means unsealing. It is the opening of the ushering gesture of the founding concept that has been concealed and hidden, indeed buried under the ground, like the foundations on which our houses, our world, then stood and still stand. To unseal is to disclose, to open to ... but not to open toward, into or for any direction, any intentionality, any purpose: this opening is not aimed at anything, but "welcomes the aimless walking, abandoned to the grace of the open."[10] As when, in other words, we are about to walk through a museum gallery, where images-paintings, sculptures, photographs follow one another and open up to our gait. *Opening* or *opening oneself to* is what from time to time, uniquely, accomplishes a proximal sense. Understood in this way, the word "deconstruction" is not meant to be, nor can it be, a process that would simply replace another; it is rather an indication, an approaching to, a subtraction of thought. However, at the same time, it is our chance, the chance of thought; "it is a matter above all else of remaining stripped bare of all received meaning and figures that have already been traced."[11]

Nancy addresses this stripping or undressing in *Being Nude. The Skin of Images* and in *La pensée dérobée*. In these texts, as well as in *The Weight of a Thought*, the approaching, stripping, and undressing represent the peculiarity of the new thinking, which bends to the questioning of writing, language, painting, and photography. Thus, the reader will witness a continuous and prolonged shift of argumentative axis—from the question of voice to that of speech, from that of space and time to that of style, from that of the end of art or the arts to that of the border, from the issue

---

[7] Nancy, J.-L.: Il senso del mondo. Lanfranchi, Milan (1997). quot, pp. 218–219 (my translation).

[8] As well known, the statement "Psyché is extended, knows nothing about it!" is taken from a letter by Freud dated August 22, 1938, written a year before his death, [Freud, S. (1938b). Findings, ideas, problems. Stand. Ed. 23, 299–300]. J. Derrida also insisted on this theme in his work (2005). On touching, Jean-Luc Nancy. Stanford University Press, Stanford, p. 11 and ff.

[9] Nancy, J.-L.: Il senso del mondo, quot, p. 218 (my translation).

[10] Therein, p. 219 (my translation).

[11] Ferrari, F., Nancy, J.-L.: Being nude: the skin of images. Fordham University Press, New York (2014), p. 4.

of the materiality of thought to that of its becoming manifest—within which it will be difficult to find orientation, certainty, answers, and a safe place… Nancy's purpose is to literally stage existence, its body, its outside, its exscription. To stage the skin of every image, of every world, of all worlds, just as painters do, just as when we attend an exhibition. In the painters' or photographers' nudes, dispossession is exposed in the mode of suspension, of proximity or approximation, "on the edge of a sense that is always nascent, always fleeting, on the surface of the skin, and on the surface of the image."[12] Existence is this nakedness, this ever-imminent, ever-resurgent and never-ending exscription; it is the place where everything is touched in a resonant capture of figures and eyes—the irises about which Nancy talks: "Whoever looks and retells his dreams […] without meaningful intent and without trying to fill in the meaning, knows he is letting the dust of the improbable and unprovable run through his fingers. In which case, his pupil is the internal operculum of an hourglass that can be turned over for the desert to escape into intimacy, or intimacy into the desert, measuring out the everyday."[13] In this sense, the everyday proves its disproportionality, experiences it, like existence, love and death; always singular, "so singular that everytime is an exception."[14] Out of the rules. Once again the *ek-*, the sharp point that sticks in the heart of every skin, every body, every figure. Once again the *ek-*, estrangement, imposture, breaking of space-time continuity. The place of the "to" come, of waiting, of the defection of *chronos*. This is why "the place, the weighty, sharp *hic et nunc*, cannot be expelled, displaced, into an ether of 'full sense' (of sensible sense…), but produces sense by remaining a place, a weighty and sharp, pressed and pierced place. Sense always has the sense of the uncompleted, of the unfinished, of the yet-to-come, and, in general, of the 'to'."[15] Defiguration of sense, its fragmentation and uninterrupted exposure, its nakedness.

Just as Bacon's pictorial gesture—to which Nancy refers us—is laid bare, stripped of any narrative, anatomical, classificatory, semantic, symbolic, or sacralizing will, in the search for a figure that is neither "depicted" nor depictable, but simply exposed, deprived of any defining sense; thus, the philosophical gesture to which Nancy aims is that of the enactment of a weighty, thoughtful "resistance" to any will to representation. It is here, after all, that the whole sense of the heaviness of thought, its materiality, its impenetrability, is at stake. Thoughts pressing in one's head against each other, alongside each other, struggling to gain space for themselves; they are consistent and insistent, cannot be avoided or bypassed. They form a common mass, a bulk, a body. Thought cannot be separated from its weight and we constantly experience it; thoughts are always burdensome. Then the co-appropriation between weight and thought would seem to be something that could be taken for granted, but the grasping of that weight by thought, and vice versa,

---

[12] Therein, p. 8.

[13] Nancy, J. L.: Multiple Arts: The Muses II. Stanford University Press. Edited by Simon Sparks, (2006), p. 66.

[14] Therein, p. 67.

[15] Id.: Le iridi, in Id., Il peso di un pensiero, l'approssimarsi. Mimesis, Milan: (2009), p. 69 (my translation).

certainly cannot be taken for granted as well. Indeed, if "the point of the mutual and arch-original appropriation of weighing and thinking is absolutely unquestionable, at the same time, that point marks the absolute place of inappropriateness; we have no access to the weight of sense, any more than we have (consequently) access to the sense of weight.

Yet it is exactly this not having access that makes us both thinking and weighty beings, and grants us this disagreement between weight and thought within ourselves, which makes everything the weight of a thought."[16] Likewise, all the weight of sense, of its ever-possible arising, its coming or, rather, its *to-come*. It is this weight that "arises into presence" and thus beholds every sense and absence of sense, an event that always accompanies it, as a surplus, an outgrowth, an exscription: the weight of the openness to existence. "The being-open is nothing but the being-finite; the 'open,' identical in that to the *closure* of the finite. It is nothing but the *to*, the weightiness of the *to*; the weightiness of the *to* through which sense, to be sense, exceeds and exceeds itself."[17] Excess of ex-isting, of ek-sistence that is realized in its being an *ek-*, outside itself, a subtraction of, an openness to: "the existence of the smallest stone already overflows; however light it may be, it already weighs all the weight of excess."[18]

Therefore, it can be clearly understood that the sense of existence, according to Nancy, is the finite sense of the existence of the world, a sense that "needs a thickness, a density, a mass and therefore an opacity; a darkness through which it provides grip, allows itself to be touched as sense, precisely there where it becomes absent as discourse. Now, this 'there' is a material point, a weighty point: the flesh of a lip, the tip of a pen or stylus, the every writing, as it traces the edge of language and its overflow. It is the point at which all writing is exscribed—abandoning the sense it inscribes—into the things the sense of which is required to form the inscription. Thus, this exscription is the ultimate truth of the inscription. Absent as speech, sense arises into presence in the heart of this absence, as a concretion, a thickening, an ossification, a toughening of sense itself. Like a burden; a sudden, unbalancing weight of thought."[19]

A *dissent* of the sensible, flattened, codified world; a fractal that innervates its fabric, to the point of piercing, fraying, cracking it. In this *dissent*, existence opens up, not as a property attributable to something or someone, not as something determinable and enunciable in the language of meanings, but as the *mineral stupor*[20] that envelops the rocks. Dissent here is not the negation of sense, but its being a sense starting from a non-sense that follows it, that accompanies it, according to the patterns of that very famous Nancyan expression that in French we can find as *d'avec* and as the translation of both *from* and *with* in Italian. That is why "there is

---

[16] Therein, p. 13 (my translation).

[17] Therein, p. 16 (my translation).

[18] Ibid. (my translation).

[19] Therein, pp. 16–17 (my translation).

[20] Id.: The Sense of the World. Univ of Minnesota Press, Minnesota (1997), p. 87.

sense (there is the sense) even in the existence of a child who lives only one day. [...] Since an existence comes into the world, it takes on the whole of sense, the absolute of sense."[21] It takes on, in other words, its *dissent*, its inappropriateness, its finite openness. In Nancy's words, already from the beginning, we are "in the *availability* (understood as the availability of a sense) of the singular, of the non-totalizable, of the unfinished, of the open, or else of the granular, fractal, dispersed totalities";[22] we are "in the need for contingency, in the rigor of wandering, and in the exposure of this being-exposed that is called *existence*."[23] To speak of the finite openness of ek-sistence certainly does not mean to adopt an easy and now too much abused lexicon of *finitude* (the lexicon that, so to speak, serves as a shore for the weak thought—as Nancy points out from the very first pages of "*A Finite Thinking*"). It rather wants to distance itself from it and its common usage in order to point us to that mode of finishing (of fulfillment, of sense) that does not finish, that does not conclude, that does not *in-finitize*, but that justifies the fact that we are "infinitely finite." So, we have come to the end of an epoch—that of the representation of sense. Now "it makes way for the weight of those innumerable figures that are the places, the bodies, the things, the splinters of sense that *we actually are*. We will not say that we have 'finally' found a sense"[24] because once again, "from the beginning,"[25] it is necessary to call into play metaphysics; this is because it has always opened up about the outside of the world, about the beyond/other of the world, because we are singularly, uniquely already placed and exposed in it. What we may find interesting and supporting here is Jacques Derrida's volume entitled *The Work of Mourning*[26], in which the philosopher traces—through the well-known lives of his friends and colleagues—a kind of "sablier du temps,"[27] an hourglass of time. The time of deconstruction, precisely, marked in various ways by authors such as Blanchot, Levinas, Deleuze, Jabès, Lyotard, and Granel, to name just a few of them.

Thus, thanks to a famous line by Paul Celan, "Die Welt ist fort, ich muss dich tragen" [The world is gone. I must carry you],[28] which accompanied the last years of Derrida's life, we are presented, almost symbolically, with the truth of deconstruction, its point of arrival, its overt and unmovable renunciation of the yoke of the world to which we have been bound for more than two millennia, or rather, the accomplished denunciation of the end of the "fabula" of the world. To think

---

[21] Id.: Il peso di un pensiero, l'approssimarsi. Mimesis, Milan: (2009), see p. 17 (my translation).

[22] Therein, p. 15 (my translation).

[23] Ibid. (my translation).

[24] Therein,, p. 20 (my translation).

[25] For this expression we refer to a text entitled Derrida da capo (It. transl. by S. Facioni), sent by Jean-Luc Nancy to the Conference in memory of Jacques Derrida. The conference, organized in Bergamo on Dec. 12–13, 2006, was entitled "Invenzioni dell'altro. A partire da Jacques Derrida."

[26] Derrida, J.: The Work of Mourning. Edited by Pascale-Anne Brault & Michael Naas. University of Chicago Press. Chicago (2001).

[27] Nancy, J. L.: Multiple Arts: The Muses II, quot., see p. 65.

[28] Celan, P., & Joris, P.: Breathturn (First English language edition.). Sun & Moon Press, (1995). p. 28.

metaphysics and its deception all over again in order to weigh its consistency, its presence, to break into its time, to break through its beginning: the lie of transcendence has no more world in this world. No sacrifice, no postponement, no appeal, no resurrection, no *anástasis*.[29] And no origin as well. It is here that the "parallel differences"[30] between Deleuze and Derrida take place: indeed, the one replays the beginning not by an actual start, but by "catching the thought that is always already plunged in its flow,"[31] while the other definitively *distances* itself both from the arch-Husserlian and from the Heideggerian *Ur* to reject the beginning out of itself, thus subjecting it to difference, or rather *différance*, to its delay or deferral from itself. The time of the beginning is in its continuous slipping from itself, occurring only in the present instant, but with the feature that "the present instant still always needs time to present itself."[32]

In other words, "the present needs time to *be* present."[33] Origin precedes and succeeds itself while being can no longer subsistent as such. After Heidegger, Derrida "crosses out," "erases" being. However, as Nancy points out, it is a matter of erasing the sense of being that traces, highlights, bears, or endures its incision (gramma, graphé, graffiti): here is the transition from "archontology" to "grammatology" and thus to "archi-writing." Being which "exists" withdraws from all subsistence, is no longer foundational, no longer sinks into the ground like the roots of a tree; rather, it leaves a mark, a sign that is not a sense, because the mark is erased and the sense is lost: the end of sense, the absence of fulfillment, the aporia. "But aporia is not an impasse. It should be also said that it is the finitude of the beginning itself. And immediately after that, it should be added that this is what we are responsible for. We are just that, and philosophy is nothing but the utterance of this responsibility and the commitment to it. For a given sense, indeed, we could not be responsible: who and what provided it and to which it returns has already answered for it.

---

[29] On this point, see Nancy, J.-L.: Noli Me Tangere: On the Raising of the Body. Fordham University Press, New York (2009).

[30] Here we are referring to one of Jean-Luc Nancy's latest texts dated 2005, entitled Les différences parallèles, Deleuze et Derrida, in Gilles Deleuze, André Bernold & Richard Pinhas (eds.). In this volume, Nancy makes explicit not only his derivation and thus the legacy of thought left to him by Deleuze and Derrida, but also their "parallel" sharing and belonging to a single need: the thought of difference. If thinking about Deleuze and Derrida jointly turns out to be a priority task of Nancy's reflection, this is because—as the two editors well acknowledge—"thinking of singularity, of difference, is the philosophical task of our time" (p. 98, my translation). On the topic of difference, deconstruction, and post-structuralism in France, see the important works by: Descombes, V.: *Le Même et l'autre: quarante-cinq ans de philosophie française* (1933–1978). Éditions de Minuit, Paris: (1979).; Lyotard, J.-F.: La Condition Postmoderne: Rapport Sur Le Savoir. Les Éditions de Minuit, Paris (1979); Laruelle, F.: *Les* Philosophes de la différence. Presses Universitaires de France, Paris (1986); Roman, J.: *Chronique des idées contemporaines*. Rosny: Bréal; Descamps, C. (2003). *Quarante ans de philosophie en France. La pensée singulaire de Sartre à Deleuze*. Bordas, Paris (2000).; Tarizzo, D.: Il pensiero libero: la filosofia francese dopo lo strutturalismo. Cortina, Milan (2003).

[31] See, in this regard, Nancy, J-L.: Derrida da capo, quot. (my translation).

[32] Therein (my translation).

[33] Therein (my translation).

However, for the sense that is not given and which, for that very reason, eludes sense—to the sensible sense of sense, of the dissemination that encompasses every possibility of sense in its very transmission and as transmission - there is necessarily responsibility."[34]

There is responsibility for the ungiven sense, for the *to-come* of sense breaking with the progressive movement of history: what—to be clear—from Hegel onward has been conceived as a process, as the becoming of the sense of the world. However, and this is precisely the point highlighted by Nancy, there is no longer any "Spirit of the world,"[35] nor a history of it anymore. In other words, there is no longer any sense of the world because no sense is originally given. Therefore, to adopt the word deconstruction or to embrace it means to assume that "each time unique" is "the end of the world." It means "I must carry you"—as Celan writes. It means putting an end to the consolatory tone and carrying the burden of "the weight of thought" to launch a truly "new" re-start.

All this explains why his latest works are marked by a continuous, unrelenting concern for the urgencies of the present, as evidenced by his two recent volumes entitled *An All-Too-Human Virus*[36] and *The Fragile Skin of the World*[37] (the original version of the latter was written with Jean-Christophe Bailly and Juan-Manuel Garrido), edited in 2020, led by that attention to contemporaneity that has always been, for the French philosopher, the driving force behind his thinking. The attraction to the present, as he himself affirmed, "was born out of the desire to join to our worries for tomorrow a welcome for the present, by way of which we move towards tomorrow. Without this welcome, anxiety and frenzy devastate us. Yet we would remain stupid if we didn't worry. This is the starting point for a proximity or a companionship of texts from diverse regimes and registers, all oriented towards the same concern about what is currently happening to us—we, late humanoids. What happens to us when we ourselves arrive at an extremity of our history, whether this extremity should turn out to be a stage, a rupture or, quite simply, a last breath."[38] "Concern" and "worry" are the terms that resonate here, arousing an "attraction" that involves us all, like a magnet, a mineral which life seems so distant, so far away from us. Indeed, however, Nancy speaks of the mineral listening and awe of rocks—not by accident. He reminds us that we must take care of this world, be worried about it, otherwise "we would remain stupid," or better inert, motionless. Instead, caring is action toward/for something or someone. It is—if we look closely and lend an ear—the original movement of existence: its being in motion that continually produces birth and creation. Thus, we cannot but speak of this "care" today, because it is at the heart of all existence, whether human, vegetal, animal, or mineral.

---

[34] Therein (my translation).

[35] See Nancy, J.-L.: The Sense of the World, quot., p. 4.

[36] Id., Un trop humain virus, Bayard, Paris (2020).

[37] Nancy, J.-L., Bailly, J-C., Garrido, J.M.: La peau fragile du monde. Gallimard, Paris (2020).

[38] Id., The Fragile Skin of the World, transl. by Corey Stockwell. Polity, Cambridge (2021), p. 6.

The themes of the living, of borders, of the decline/declination of the identity subject, are thus the cores of a philosophical reflection that has always "touched" the contemporary, questioning all truthful concretions devoid of this ability to disenclose.

Here is Nancy's real philosophical legacy: a task, a "marker," for all of us today, as inescapable as it is imperative.

From *Ego sum* to *The Inoperative Community*, from *Hegel. The Restlessness of the Negative* to *The Sense of the World*, from *A Finite Thinking* to *Dis-Enclosure: The Deconstruction of Christianity*, up to his previously mentioned most recent volume, *The Fragile Skin of the World*, the theoretical tension of his thought unveils the future of today's philosophical reflection, so haunted by insurgent racial hatreds, the blows to the meaning of democracy, the oblivion of "singular/plural freedoms." This is because philosophy is expressed there, where every existence becomes an index of a place, of a space, of a lived topography that is open to its "excription," to its inescapable outside. It is precisely in this very "expression" that Nancy's philosophy becomes a political instance and replays "the risk of extremes," that is, the one that makes us prone and available to "listen to the stone," to "preserve the wide spaces" of the open air, to penetrate into the "sound of the night"—to quote Rilke's verses[39] which were so dear to him and that seem to point toward that night from which, by now, Jean-Luc will keep speaking to us.[40]

Fisciano, Salerno, Italy   Daniela Calabrò

---

[39] Cf. Rilke R. M.: The Book of Hours, Riverhead Books, (1997).

[40] The legacy of Jean-Luc Nancy's thought has been the focus of some recent publications in his honor; I mention only a few of them here: Cohen-Levinas, D.: *Être en vie*, in Shift. International Journal of Philosophical Studies, 2/21–1/22, (2022): 49–56; Cohen-Levinas, D.: Sans salut. Être partout où est la vie, in Post-filosofie, 15, (2022): 15–22; Cohen-Levinas, D.: Être en vie, in Jean-Luc Nancy. Anastasis de la pensée, (D. Dwivedi, J. Lebre, M. Montevil et F. Warin eds.). Hermann, Paris, (2023): 47–54; Doppelt, S.: Still Life, in Jean-Luc Nancy. Anastasis de la pensée, quot., (2023): 175–182; Dwivedi, D.: El comienzo de Jean-luc Nancy, in Shift. International Journal of Philosophical Studies, 2/21–1/22 (2022): 57–64; Dwivedi, D.: L'inizio di Jean-Luc Nancy, in Post-filosofie, 15, (2022): 35–46; Dwivedi, D.: Jean-Luc Nancy: Identification et indestinance, in Jean-Luc Nancy. Anastasis de la pensée, quot., (2023): 33–43; Goetz, B.: Un Maître particulièrement amical (et « exubérant »), in Jean-Luc Nancy. Anastasis de la pensée, quot., (2023):195–198; Haller, G.: Aime qu'il passe, in Shift. International Journal of Philosophical Studies, (2022):199–209; Jandin, P.-P.: Une lumière crépusculaire, in Jean-Luc Nancy. Anastasis de la pensée, quot. (2023):183–190; Joseph, L.: L'appel de l'intime: Jean-Luc Nancy, in Jean-Luc Nancy. Anastasis de la pensée, quot., (2023): 101–108; Lèbre, J.: Part'âges, in Jean-Luc Nancy. Anastasis de la pensée, quot., (2023): 19–26; Recchia Luciani, F.R.: Jean-Luc Nancy: a Philosophy of « Being-toward-life », in Shift. International Journal of Philosophical Studies, (2022): 137–146.

Contents

1	**Deposition. Starting from Descartes**	1
	1 The End of the World and the End of Thought	1
	2 The Deposition of Cogito.	9
2	**Exposition. Starting from Hegel**	25
	Appendix.	35
	"The Thought Awaits Us All"... After and Beyond Hegel	35
3	**Ontological Partition**	43
	1 The Unfolding of the Body	43
	2 Ex-peau-Sition: The Expropriation of/from the Body	51
	Appendix.	63
	The Skin of the World: Finitude and Existence	63
4	**Compearance**.	73
	1 Philosophy of Touch	73
	2 "Being-With and Being-There"	79
	Appendix.	89
	On Bodies: Perspectives of a Dialogue Between Jean-Luc Nancy and Roberto Esposito	89
5	**"What Is Missing: The Poem of Our Being-Together"**	103
	1 After Communism, to Think the Community	103
	2 The Question of Sacrifice in the Contemporary Thought	112
6	**The Restlessness of the World**	125
	1 Folds of the World: Community	126
	2 Politics to Come.	133
	3 The Freedom in Question.	135
Bibliography of Jean-Luc Nancy		147

Chapter 1
Deposition. Starting from Descartes

1 The End of the World and the End of Thought

There is no longer any world: no longer a mundus, a cosmos, a composed and complete· order (from) within which one might find a place, a dwelling, and the elements of an orientation. Or, again, there is no longer the "down here" of a world one could pass through toward a beyond or outside of this world. There is no longer any Spirit of the world, nor is there any history before whose tribunal one could stand. In other words, there is no longer any sense of the world. We know, indeed, that it is the end of the world, and there is nothing illusory (nor "fin de siècle" nor "millenarian") about this knowledge. Those who scrive to denounce the supposed illusion of the thought of an "end" are correct, as opposed to those who present the "end" as a cataclysm or as the apocalypse of an annihilation. Such thought is still entirely caught up in the regime of a signifying sense, whether it proposes itself in the final analysis as "nonsense" or as "revelation." But the same adversaries of the thought of the "end" are incorrect in that they do not see that the words with which one designates that which is coming to an end (history, philosophy, politics, art, world …) are nor the names of subsistent realities in themselves, but the names of concepts or ideas, entirely determined within a regime of sense that is coming full circle and completing itself before our (thereby blinded) eyes.[1]

[…] Consequently, when I say that the end of the world is the end of the mundus, this cannot mean that we are confronted merely with the end of a certain "conception" of the world, and that we would have to go off in search of another one or to restore another one (or the same). It means, rather, that there is no longer any assignable signification of "world," or that the "world" is subtracting itself, bit by bit, from the entire regime of signification available to us - except its "cosmic" signification as universe, a term that for us, precisely, no longer has (or does not yet have) any assured signification, save that of a pure infinite expansion.[2]

[…] We must therefore think this: it is the "end of the world", but we do not know in what sense. It is not merely the end of an epoch of the world or the end of an epoch of sense because it is the end of an epoch - an epoch as long as the "Occident" and as long as "history" itself - that has entirely determined both "world" and "sense," and that has extended

---

[1] Nancy J.-L.: The Sense of the World, quot., p. 4.
[2] Therein, p. 5.

© The Author(s), under exclusive license to Springer Nature Switzerland AG 2024
D. Calabrò, *The Thought Awaits Us All*,
https://doi.org/10.1007/978-3-031-75401-2_1

this determination over the entire world. Indeed, we cannot even think of what is happening to us as a modulation of the same world or sense.³

These three intense passages, which constitute the opening of one of the most important works by Jean-Luc Nancy, titled "The Sense of the World," reveal the fundamental point on which his reflection is centered: the expression "sense of the world" has lost its founding meaning. It is with this loss that we are confronted today. If the search for a sovereign truth, bearing the character of absolute certainty, inaugurates all modern philosophy from Descartes until the early 1900s, and if in such an order of truth the subject becomes the place where this sovereignty is given—the end of metaphysics is now accomplished. Along with it, the end of philosophy. This fulfillment is the very space of our present. Moreover, this is—as well known—*the* question around which, or rather perhaps it would be better to say *from which*, the whole of twentieth-century reflection originates. *This* is where Nancy starts from again. He examines this question in the precise awareness that on, it in a certain sense, depends not only and not so much the fate of philosophy, but—as we shall try to see along the analysis below—the very fate of what we have so far called the West. Not surprisingly, this Nancy is a keen and acute reader of Nietzsche and Heidegger, that is, of those who first and most radically addressed and contemplated the end of philosophy.

In fact—just to repeat the well-known "antecedents"—the emptying to which the Hegelian speculative setup is gradually subjected, due to the progressive loss of the sense of the whole and the "shattering of ancient identities, the radical experience of the negative and the impracticability of any synthesis, whether dialectical or scientific"⁴ and thus the philosophical void created after Hegel, prompted Nietzsche first to question, in the "deepest, most rigorous, hardest, meanest"⁵ the great metaphysical ideals of God, Truth, and Good. It is precisely in this situation that—as aptly defined—the "nihilistic fullness"⁶ by which the entire past century is profoundly marked occurs. An epochal shattering the searing figure of which can be summarized by Nietzsche's words, which constitute the incipit of *Ecce homo*:

> I know my destiny. There will come a day when my name will recall the memory of something formidable - a crisis the like of which has never been known on earth, the memory of the most profound clash of consciences, and the passing of a sentence upon all that which theretofore had been believed, exacted, and hallowed… I contradict as no one has contradicted hitherto… For when Truth enters the lists against the falsehood of ages, shocks are

---

³Therein, p. 6.

⁴Volpi, F.: "Afterword" to M. Heidegger, Nietzsche. It. transl. by F. Volpi. Adelphi, Milan (1994). p. 944 (my translation).

⁵Nietzsche, F.: La gaia scienza. It. transl. by F. Masini. Adelphi, Milan: (1977), p. 18 (my translation)

⁶In this regard and for the following remarks, see Volpi, F.: Il Nichilismo. Laterza, Rome-Bari: (1996), pp. 53 and ff.

1 The End of the World and the End of Thought

bound to ensue, and a spell of earthquakes, followed by the transposition of hills and valleys, such as the world has never yet imagined even in its dreams.[7]

The state of the crisis of thought, announced with an almost apocalyptic tone in these words, and the consequent end of metaphysics as the last act of the West's claimed logic-rational power, tragically run through the entire twentieth century. However, if, on the one hand, Nietzsche can be read as the thinker who announced the end of philosophy, on the other hand, Heidegger can be seen as the one who definitively carried the weight of that announcement in order to think thoroughly about "the negativity inherent in Being."[8] This is precisely thanks to and through a close, long, troubled confrontation with Nietzsche—of which there is extensive evidence in the majestic volume dedicated to him, in which Heidegger starts his decisive confrontation with European "nihilism." This is where he brings up again the question of metaphysics and its end, uttering the words that could serve as a prologue to Nancy's own reflection:

> ... our talk of the end of metaphysics does not mean to suggest that in the future men will no longer "live" who think metaphysically and undertake "systems of metaphysics." Even less do we intend to say that in the future mankind will no longer "live" on the basis of metaphysics. The end of metaphysics that is to be thought here is but the beginning of metaphysics' "resurrection" in altered forms; these forms leave to the proper, exhausted history of fundamental metaphysical positions the purely economic role of providing raw materials with which-once they are correspondingly transformed-the world of "knowledge" is built "anew." But then what does it mean, "the end of metaphysics"? It means the historical moment in which the essential possibilities of metaphysics are exhausted. The last of these possibilities must be that form of metaphysics in which its essence is reversed.[9]

As we said—*this* is where Nancy starts again: from the "end of philosophy."[10] But then, at this point, the crucial question is: what is meant by this expression? All this provided that, as the fundamental Heideggerian lesson itself teaches, we do not want to reduce it to an effective abandonment of a practice of thought constitutive of our culture; but neither to an epigonal and nostalgic archival game, limited to dusting off or throwing together worn-out assumptions, or to a surrendering to practices borrowed from poetry and arts in general, apparently very seductive but totally misleading. In this sense, however, we believe that Nancy's response is exemplary. Indeed, if we look at the pages of one of the writings that more closely "work" on this question, *A Finite Thinking*, we can read that:

---

[7] Nietzsche, F.: "Why I am a Fatality," in Ecce homo. Trans. Anthony Ludovici and Paul Cohn. Edinburgh: T.N. Foulis, (1911).

[8] Volpi, F. "Afterword" to M. Heidegger, Nietzsche, quot, p. 944 (my translation).

[9] Heidegger, M., Nietzsche. Vol. 3, The will to power as knowledge and as metaphysics. Vol. 4, Nihilism. Farrell Krell, D., Stambaugh, J., & Capuzzi, F. A. eds. Harper, San Francisco (1991) p. 149.

[10] It is no coincidence that he pivots his own reasoned reconnaissance of the French philosophy of recent decades (also in its interweaving with some vectors of the Italian one) around and starting from that question.—Tarizzo, D.: Il pensiero libero, quot.. Also very useful is D'Agostini, F.: Analitici e continentali. Raffaello Cortina Editore, Milan (1997) and Roman, J.: Chronique des idées contemporaines. Editions Bréal, Paris (2000).

The title "a finite thinking" puts three very simple things into play: on the one hand, it denotes that there is, for us, a thinking that's finished, a mode of thinking that has been lost with the destruction of sense, that is, with the completion and buckling of the West's resources of signification and meaning (God, History, Man, Subject, Sense itself...). And yet, in its accomplishment and withdrawal, like a crashing wave whose ebb leaves behind the lines of a new high-tide mark, this thinking leaves us with a new configuration (its own, then its own undoing of itself at its own limit). Equally, it suggests that a thinking equal to the significance of the end has come our way, if I can put it in this way, a thinking that has first of all to measure itself against the fact that "sense" *could* have ended and that it *could be* a question of sense's essential finitude-something that would, in turn, demand an essential finitude of thinking.[11]

Therefore, the only task for thought today is not to deconstruct its own sense in search of a solution, but rather to understand how the thought of the absence of solution is the very locus of sense. For this very reason, then:

...it doesn't really matter whether we call ourselves "moderns" or "post moderns." We're neither before nor after a Sense that would have been non finite. Rather, we find ourselves at the inflection of an end whose very finitude is the opening, the possible - the only - welcome extended to another future, to another demand for sense, one that not even the thinking of "finite sense" will be able to think through, even after having delivered it.[12]

What history has provided us with is a meaning now destined to its extreme finitude. To think of such finitude without bridging or pacifying it, without following any negative theology or ontology, means to simultaneously set ourselves in a space that is made and unmade without mediation. "A finite thinking is one that rests on this im-mediation"[13] Somewhere, somehow, a horizon has been lost and the comfort of a limit drastically dissolved. What remains is the affirmation of finitude or definitude, so to speak, the absolute "débordement" of which—to use a word dear to Nancy—leaves us all exposed on the limit, almost as liminal figures of Being. The loss of stabilizing and established—i.e., foundational—outlines is both being on the limit and the limit of Being itself. These assertions, far from sounding like mere or redundant mince words, are actually the authentic stakes of thinking; indeed, more precisely, they are the true condition and urgency of new thinking. The loss of the horizon itself would thus seem to be the horizon of philosophy. Therefore, Nancy's position seems clear from these very first lines: if, on the one hand, the end of metaphysics has cut all ties with traditional philosophy and if, on the other hand, the deconstructive process has ushered in the upcoming space of the end of meaning as

---

[11] Nancy, J.-L.: A finite thinking. Stanford University Press, Stanford (2003), p. 4. On the concepts of the finitude of existence and thought, see the following texts: Baptist G.: La fedeltà all'apertura del finito. A partire dalle Piccole conferenze, in B@belonline/print, 10–11, (2011): 33–40; Cavalcante Schuback, M., Exister: transitivement, in Jean-Luc Nancy. Anastasis de la pensée, quot., pp. 65–72; Fynsk C.: Experiences of Finitude, in J.-L. Nancy, The Inoperative Community, University of Minnesota Press, Minneapolis and Oxford, (1991) pp. VII-XXXV; James I.: The fragmentary Demand. An Introduction to the Philosophy of Jean-Luc Nancy, Stanford University Press, Stanford (2006)

[12] Therein, p. 15.

[13] Therein, p. 14.

death or as "awaiting the limits of truth,"[14] the place of "immediation" of meaning cannot be given once again in an archetypal or archaeological way. Thus, no return to an origin, but rather exposition of/exposure to a necessarily finite sense in which "the very absolute of existence" resides.[15] More precisely:

> in our own time, it's pointless to seek to appropriate our origins: we are neither Greek, nor Jewish, nor Roman, nor Christian, nor a settled combination of any of these-words whose sense, in any case, is never simply given. We are neither the "accomplishment" nor the "overcoming" of "metaphysics," neither process nor errancy. But we do exist and we "understand" that this existence (ourselves) is not the senselessness of a reabsorbed and annulled signification. In distress and necessity, we "understand" that this "we," here, now, is still and once more responsible for a singular sense.[16]

Here, in this new formulation that excludes any recovery of a possible infinity and equally indicates farewell to any universality, lies the figure of Nancy's thought and the real novelty—the real challenge—he introduced into contemporary reflection and debate. In fact, it is precisely here that the space is opened, now, to speak of an "us" or plurality, without turning this "us" into a substantial and exclusive identity and thus falling back into a renewed self-position of the cogito. In other words, there are the conditions to speak of an "us" that is commensurate with contemporary times. This is what we have left to think about—after modernity.[17]

In this context, therefore, Nancy triggers his characteristic movement the only possible movement allowed for what might still be called "philosophy": far from considering this general escape from meaning a catastrophe or a loss, as the philosopher writes, "I want to think of it as the event of sense in our time, for our time. It is a question of thinking sense in the absence of sense. […] It is a question of thinking what 'sense' can be when we one has come to the end of sense."[18] Philosophy can no longer be, as it once was, its ultimate provider, nor can it continue to be, according to Kant's *lectio*, "the philosophy that does not want to give sense but to analyze the conditions for delivering a coherent sense.'"[19] Then, again, the question we posed at the beginning comes back and must be posed to Nancy: if philosophy today

---

[14] Derrida, J.: Aporias: dying—awaiting (one another at) the "limits of truth" (mourir—s'attendre aux "limites de la vérité"). Stanford University Press, Stanford (1993).

[15] Nancy, J.L.: A finite thinking, quot., p. 11.

[16] Therein, p. 15.

[17] In this regard, we consider it useful to emphasize—in total contrast to Heidegger's and Nancy's positions—the work by Giddens, A.: The consequences of modernity. Polity Press, Minnesota (1991). Here, the author not only distances himself from those who label our epoch with the term "post-modern," but also resolutely affirms that the "post-modern condition" is nothing more than the extreme radicalization of modernity; however, this is not in the sense of a historical evolution, but rather in the direction of a kind of discontinuity that structurally changes its constitution. For Giddens, therefore, we have not yet emerged from modernity and it is rather a matter of exploring unexperienced possibilities within it. Of a similar nature is also the work by Touraine, A.: Critique de la modernité (Critique of Modernity). Fayard. Paris (1992)

[18] Nancy, J.-L.: (1993) 'You ask me what it means today…' An epigraph for Paragraph, in Paragraph, 16 (2): 109.

[19] Ibid.

can no longer provide meaning nor the explanation/construction of the conditions to make it possible, what can it do? The answer the philosopher offers is of both dazzling simplicity and daunting complexity. In fact, by echoing Nietzsche's response to the end of sense, he asserts that the latter "is revolution itself: the destitution of the authority of sense or of sense as authority"[20] and consequently, is literally *"the entry into the unheard-of."*[21] In this sense, as Nancy himself points out, it is really the purest assumption and continuation of what authors and artists—such as Rimbaud[22]—had already understood in the point of articulation and transition from one epoch to another. This is precisely because "in saying sense is absent, in saying that *this absence is what we are exposed to*, and that this exposition constitutes what I will call not only our present history but, along with Rimbaud, our *refound eternity.*"[23]

The "unheard-of"—what has never yet been heard and towards which, by echoing Rimbaud, Nancy makes a sign—here finds its explanation and its "simple, hard and difficult"[24] meaning. It is a matter of leading philosophy now towards a different *practice*,[25] which consists in a way of "describing from the outside." A "describing from the outside" that is thus the reverse movement of a double philosophical practice, for on the one hand it results in the concrete action of speaking about the end of philosophical thought as the inner limit to its very sense. But on the other hand—in precisely doing away with the "description" of universal senses and presuppositions already given from within philosophy—it involves exposing philosophy itself to its "outside," or to the "inscription" on its "skin," so to speak, of the events of the world in their no longer universalizable singularity. However, it comes with one caveat, namely, that such an exercise of "excription" (description "of the outside/from the outside") does not simply define a new horizon of philosophy; it is not a simple dialectical change designed to renew the possibility of philosophy. Finiteness is not a negativity that is taken away and reconciled. Instead, an event fixes attention "within" and "on" its own boundary. The lost horizon of sense thus becomes the space in which its very absence is exposed. Then, returning to the core question from which we started, how can we do philosophy in the absence of a horizon of sense? How can we make our ears "ready" for the unheard-of, or rather for that which has not yet been heard? The name Nancy assigns to such a task is that of *poiéin*, to be understood as a *way* for thought to be exposed to its limit, without any

---

[20] Ibid.

[21] Ibid.

[22] Rimbaud is one of the significantly recurring "places" in Nancy's discourse. See, for example, Nancy, J.L.: A finite thinking, quot.; and Id.: Il pensiero sottratto, it. transl. by Vergani, M. Bollati Boringhieri, Turin (2003). (see, in particular, pp. 188–190).

[23] Nancy, J.-L. (1993). "You ask me what it means today…" An epigraph for Paragraph, in Paragraph, 16 (2): 109.

[24] Nancy, J.-L.:. A finite thinking, quot., p. 8.

[25] On the concept of "practice" as a mode of thought, Carlo Sini has focused his philosophical reflection. See, in particular his work entitled Gli abiti, le pratiche, i saperi, Jaca Book, Milan (1996) and part two of his volume Etica della scrittura, Il Saggiatore, Milan (1992).

comforting horizon, in which only the eternal excription of meaning on retreat prevails, to such an extent as to grasp now the finite—"at the heart of all philosophy, however 'metaphysical' it may be."[26]

This is why the task of a "finite thinking," configured in this way, cannot be translated according to the philosophical need to re-propose a new immanence. This is where Nancy's distance from Deleuze is explained, clarified by Nancy himself in a short divergence text within which their different philosophical paths are framed: "Everything is played out in connection with Hegel: either one begins *at a distance* from him, or one distances him from within, one smashes him down."[27] Deleuze opts decisively for an unprecedent shift of thought: "folded thought: thought which no longer consists in unravelling, in connection, in representative subsumption, in the determination or convocation of ends."[28] However, this philosophical option, which consists in the banishment of every possible representational-causal relation and which thus goes against every historical-processual institution (see Hegel, specifically), leads to a conception of Being without Being and without process; moreover, it is the immanentization of the "point of the world" in which the whole world abides, the fold within which the world bends (that is, within which the world becomes) is immanent to itself. Such a conception, moreover, cannot find any harmony with the Heideggerian *Dasein*, because, "Deleuze's thought is not played out in *Being-in-the-world*, but in the effectuation of a universe, or of several."[29] As Nancy insightfully observes, he does not mind competing with any philosophy, but rather:

> One might say that Deleuze wants to take things after the fold of being. He wants nothing before this fold. He is not interested in anything that comes before this fold. And in fact, there is nothing before. In a sense, the fold is being itself […]. Without a doubt the incision of the fold, the folding itself in so far as it divides between the two veins of philosophy, is related to negativity: either the negative has the simple plenitude of chaos, or it hollows out being's lack of itself. For my part, I cannot understand how to avoid this hollowing out (death, time, genesis, and end). This does not necessarily imply anguish or tragedy, with their silent temptation to appropriate the negative as such, still, to dialecticize and overcome it. But it signifies that behind chaos itself, or rather, in the *hollow* of chaos, and thus also in the hollow of the passage, there is being: not a substance, but the transitivity which bears me. I ca neither overcome nor dismiss this incomprehension. It appears inescapably as if there are two massifs, two continents, two tectonic plates of philosophy. Being or chaos, genesis or distribution, death or the passage across. The one slides over the other or against it, the one folds on the other - without passage from one to the other, without a synthesis of the two.[30]

Therefore, in this confrontation with Deleuze, while acknowledging to some extent the proximity of thought with the latter, Nancy cannot help but "take a fold

---

[26] Nancy, J.-L.: A finite thinking, quot., p. 11.

[27] Id.: The Deleuzian Fold in Thought, in Deleuze: A Critical Reader, ed. Paul Fatten. Oxford: Blackwell, (1996) p. 113.

[28] Therein, pp. 109–110.

[29] Therein, p. 111.

[30] Therein, pp. 112–113.

from his thought."³¹ As if to say, to take a distance that is nonetheless inscribed in the "proximity which remains within the order of the fold, first of all in the sense of an inclination, a bent or tendency, but also in the sense of the folded form itself, the mark of a delicate articulation, a pleat if you like, a crease or a shifting of thought."³² Therefore, a proximity of thought that Nancy recognizes in Deleuze and which arrests, since Deleuze's philosophy remains "philosophy folded in two, at right angles to itself."³³ It would be a fold that turns to its own closure, or rather, that is closure itself; a genesis that bends in place, as when one leaps in place: reduction to immanence, flattening of chronological time, eternity of becoming. Instead, the point Nancy is making is to think of finiteness not as that which implodes into a surface of immanence, nor even as that which preserves transcendence for us, but rather as the continuous finitization of all senses. However, precisely by thinking finiteness as such, finite thought must account for these other interpretations that have never grasped it without opposing it to a transcendence, without subjecting it to a dialectic, or without turning it into a "will to absolute immanence.'"³⁴ For this reason, if we have to speak of "immanence''when referring to finite thinking, what the latter seeks to grasp is written in the plural, in the constant leaning beyond itself and in the partitioning from the existent as such. As Nancy explains, "Finitude designates the 'essential' multiplicity and the 'essential' non reabsorption of sense or of being."³⁵ In other words, it is "the *without-essence* of existing."³⁶ More rigorously, "being isn't Being; it's neither substantive nor substance. 'Being' is only being, the verb."³⁷ Therefore, finite existence can only be an existence devoid of immanence and transcendence, the sense of which is given in the openness to plural finite senses. "…in finitude, there is no question of an 'end', whether as a goal or as an accomplishment, and that it's merely a question of the suspension of sense, infinite, each time replayed, reopened, exposed with a novelty so radical that it immediately fails."³⁸ In this continuous failing, in this endless subtracting, which is finitude as such, is inscribed the movement of existence: "Birth has already turned us toward it. But how can we simply open our eyes? Death has already closed them."³⁹ Therefore, to think the finite movement of existence no longer according to an immanence of sense in the face of an infinite transcendence opposed to it, but rather as a simple finite that does not make immanence precisely because it

---

[31] Therein, p. 107. See, in this regard the excellent essay by: Vaccaro S.: Deleuze e Nancy: pieghe di prossimità, in A. Potestà, R. Terzi (a cura di), Annuario 2000–2001. Incontro con Jean-Luc Nancy, Cortina, Milano (2003), pp. 169–179.

[32] Ibid.

[33] Therein, p. 109.

[34] Id.: The Inoperative Community, ed. by Peter Connor, transl. by Peter Connor et al. University of Minnesota Press, Minnesota (1991), p. 12.

[35] Id.: A finite thinking, quot., p. 9.

[36] Ibid.

[37] Ibid.

[38] Therein, p. 10.

[39] Therein, p. 11.

dislocates, displaces, causes all instituted immanence to lose any sense. Thus, this is the task of finite philosophy: to think that "There's not an 'ounce' of sense that could be either received or transmitted: the finitude of thinking is indissociable from the singularity of 'understanding' what is, each time, a singular existence."[40] Here are to be found the spacings of every birth and every death. However, "here" is an inappropriate place, like the finite sense of every existence that does not return to itself. To conclude, Nancy writes that the task of a finite thinking is to "expose itself to what is finite about sense":[41]

> Not a thinking of relativity, which implies the Absolute, but a thinking of absolute finitude, absolutely detached from all infinite and senseless completion or achievement. Not a thinking of limitation, which implies the unlimitedness of a beyond, but a thinking of the limit as that on which, infinitely finite, existence arises, and to which it is exposed. Not a thinking of the abyss and of nothingness, but a thinking of the un-grounding of being: of this "being," the only one, whose existence exhausts all its substance and all its possibility. A thinking of the absence of sense as the only token of the presence of the existent. This presence is nor essence, but - *epekeina tes ousias* - birth to presence: birth and death to the infinite presentation of the fact that there is no ultimate sense, only a finite sense, finite senses, a multiplication of singular bursts of sense resting on no unity or substance. And the fact, too, that there is no established sense, no establishment, institution or foundation of sense, only a coming, and comings-to-be of sense.
>
> This thinking demands a new "transcendental aesthetic": that of space-time in the finite here and now, which is never present, without, however, being time pressed up against its continuum or its ecstasy. Finitude: the "a priori" irreducibility of spacing. Equally, though, this thinking demands the material transcendental aesthetic of the disparity and dislocation of our senses, our five senses, whose organic and rational unity cannot be deduced or grounded. The division of the five senses, which one could say is emblematic of finitude, inscribes or ex-scribes the division of finite sense.[42]

Jean-Luc Nancy's name inscribes itself in the future of this finite horizon of thinking; a future that, by exposing itself to "exposure itself,"[43] delivers a new path to philosophy.

2 The Deposition of Cogito

> So after considering everything very thoroughly, I must finally conclude that this proposition, I am, I exist, is necessarily true whenever it is put forward by me or conceived in my mind[44]

---

[40] Ibid.
[41] Therein, p. 30.
[42] Therein, p. 27.
[43] Id.: Le poids d'une pensée. Le Griffon d'argile, Québec (1991), p. 15 (my translation).
[44] Cottingham, J. (ed.) Descartes: Meditations on First Philosophy: With Selections from the Objections and Replies. Cambridge University Press, New York (1996), p. 17.

This sentence, taken from Descartes' Meditations, forms the exergue of one of Nancy's most important works, entitled *Ego sum*.[45] Therefore, why Descartes? Moreover, why today—as Nancy well makes clear[46]—in an age of crisis of the subject, there is an urgent need to rethink the meaning of the transformation of the *sum* into the veritable object of the *cogito*? Why does the sinking into which the subject has plunged powerfully marks the epoch of the "end of philosophy"? Again: is there something else taking shape within Cartesian philosophical speculation? As if to say: is there something "unthought" that was like a nagging thought in Descartes' mind and brought him right to the threshold where the theoretical operation of the self-positioning of the cogito experienced the vertigo or excess of existence—of the sum—and from which it hastily retracted?[47] What about that vertigo or excess? Is it something we need to take up and rethink? Such are the questions posed by Nancy. It is no coincidence that the title of his volume on Descartes—*Ego sum*—in order to deconstruct and reinvent it, reiterates one of the best-known philosophical formulas, the one that pioneered modern thought. Already in the title, the French philosopher wants to be *provocative*: a provocation in the literal sense of the term, in that he wants, in other words, to *call to himself* the two terms—*ego and sum*—which together have represented the viaticum of Western thought from the seventeenth century onward, so as to subtract them from that very Western framework, which first filled them with sense and then emptied them.

Therefore, all this with Descartes—starting with the subject, for the latter takes center stage again in contemporary philosophy[48] according to a duality of modes that Nancy succinctly defines as follows:

---

[45] Nancy, J.-L.: Ego sum: Jean-Luc Nancy. Aubier-Flammarion, Paris (1979).

[46] In this need to deal with Descartes once again, in order to come to terms with our modernity and its "destiny," Nancy "repeats" a gesture that, not coincidentally, constitutes a sort of indispensable starting point for almost all philosophers or thinkers in the twentieth century who have wished to measure themselves against this destiny. Besides the fundamental Freudian critique of the Cartesian principle of "consciousness," which ushers a real new Weltanschauung, I shall only mention here E. Husserl's famous (but always highly topical) analyses, both in the Descartes' Meditations ... (Cottingham, J. ed., 1996. Descartes: Meditations on First Philosophy: With Selections from the Objections and Replies, quot.), as well as in the work dated 1970, The crisis of European sciences and transcendental phenomenology (Northwestern University Press, Evanston: – in particular, see Part II, pp. 2–49), and in M. Heidegger's analyses, especially in the essay I have particularly taken note of here dated 1968, Sentieri interrotti. La Nuova Italia, Firenze, pp. 71–101.

[47] Probably the first to point the finger at this Cartesian reflection was M. Merleau-Ponty in the well-known critiques of Descartes' thought contained both in (1945) The Phenomenology of Perception. Edited by Donald A. Landes, Routledge, New York, pp. 107 ff. and passim), in the last course he gave at the Collège de France, "Cartesian Ontology and Ontology Today" published in his work dated 2022, The possibility of philosophy: course notes from the Collège de France, 1959–1961. Edited by Stéphanie Ménasé, Keith Whitmoyer & Claude Lefort), Northwestern University Press, Evanston, Illinois and in (1964) Eye and Mind. In The Primacy of Perception. Northwestern University Press, Evanston, Illinois, pp. 159–192). On this aspect has rightly insisted Lisciani Petrini, E. in La passione del mondo. Saggio su Merleau-Ponty. ESI, Naples, (2002) pp. 49–68.

[48] A concise but accurate reconstruction of the concept of "subject/subjectivity" has been outlined by Bonito Oliva, R. in Soggettività. Guida Editor, Naples (2003).

our current situation consists, and insists, in the prolix expansion of the anthropological subject—a necessary consequence, and indeed more than a consequence: it is the effectuation of a metaphysics of the Subject, but at the same time, the forgetting of the metaphysical origin [*provenance*] and nature of this subject, a forgetting, ignorance, or denegation of metaphysics (or ontotheology) that is perpetuated by this subject. In this respect, the most pressing task [*actuelle*] can only be the most philosophical: it consists in showing this effectuation as such, and correlatively - in the mode of a paradox that will only surprise those whose ability to forget has definitely engulfed everything - this task consists in showing the ineffectivity of this effectuation. In other words, the task is to show how the anthropological profusion of the subject covers over and muffles the question—that is, as we will see in what follows, the voice - of someone: this someone, neither a subject nor the Subject, will not be named, but this book would like to let it call itself: *ego*.[49]

In this way Nancy identifies the setting—or rather the question, *die Sache*—that, in a different modulation, sometimes hidden, sometimes in full evidence, pervades modern age, until marking the first "cracks" with the reflection of the late nineteenth and early twentieth centuries. Then, the torment of the subject or the "ordeal of consciousness" takes on the characteristics of a unique drama in which the Cartesian lectio offers itself as the incipit of a "thought of the modern" that has not ceased to reckon with itself. Thought of the modern or of modernity that faces contemporaneity in the guise of a "fulfillment of subjectivity," or to put it better, of a "deposition" or "dissolution" of the Subject, wholly grounded on the "principle of reason"[50] and on the alleged unwaveringness of the *logos*.[51] Prelude to the end of onto-theology. All of this explains why Nancy's philosophical reflection cannot but start from the modern, from its most representative exponent, or rather from the one who—as mentioned in the opening—accomplished the alchemical, most radical operation: turning the *sum* into the verifiable "object" of the *cogito*. Moreover, it is understandable, then, the reason for which the above sentence constitutes the exergue of Nancy's volume on Descartes. Indeed, the sum of existence, in Cartesian reflection, is deposed, engulfed remorselessly, by all-encompassing reason; it becomes the "object" of thought: "bodies themselves are perceived not, strictly speaking, by the senses or by the imaginative faculty, but by the intellect alone, and that they are not perceived because they are touched or seen, but only because they are understood."[52] This is the operation by virtue of which, as Heidegger writes, "for the first time, the being is defined as the objectness of representation, and truth as the certainty of representation."[53] Therefore, from this moment on, not only does the entire domain

---

[49] Nancy, J.-L.: Ego sum: corpus, anima, fabula. Edited by Marie-Eve Morin, Fordham University Press, New York (2016). p. 3.

[50] As we know, precisely to the radical analysis of this question—the principle of Reason of Modernity—is dedicated the M. Heidegger's work published in 1991, The Principle of Reason. Indiana University Press, Indiana.

[51] To understand the problematic breadth of the "deposition of the logos" as an "overall figure of contemporary thought" and its consequences at a logical (and ethical) level, see Tarca, L.: Elenchos: ragione e paradosso nella filosofia contemporanea. Marietti, Genova (1993).

[52] Cottingham, J. (ed.) Descartes: Meditations on First Philosophy: With Selections from the Objections and Replies. Quot., p. 24.

[53] Heidegger, M.: The Age of the World Picture, in Off the Beaten Track. Edited by Julian Young & Kenneth Haynes, Cambridge University Press. New York, (2002). p. 66.

of being become a positum of the subject and constantly at the subject's disposal, but precisely because of this it is turned into an "object of calculation" (and thus "controlled in advance") and "the very essence of man" undergoes a parallel transformation: "This objectification of beings is accomplished in a setting-before, a representing [vor-stellen], aimed at bringing each being before it in such a way that the man who calculates can be sure - and that means certain - of the being." In short, the world receives "sense" from the cogitations of the Ego, in a transcendence that fixes it, grounds it, establishes its measures, through, as Galimberti writes, summarizing an entire complex of demystifying analyses crossing the whole of the past century—"that idealizing operation that puts us in touch not with things, but with their mathematical forms; thus, it is no longer the body or the world that tells about itself, but it is the anticipatory functions of the Ego that reveals what the body is and what the world is."[54] In this lies something tacit, something not very visible: the abstraction from which the Ego cogito originates turns into that which is real, corporeal, extended, and material. The experience of the world, the pure and simple observation of nature is flattened—in the geometric sense of the term—on the axial coordinates of the Cartesian diagram.[55] Yet—and here is the focal point that Nancy aims to highlight—it is precisely within such a setting that the very dissolution of modern subjectivity is already concealed, for it is within the very evidence of the Ego, or even within—to put it in the now well-known Nietzschean terms—the Apollonian vision of the real, that the abyss of the Dionysian opens. All this was very clear to Nietzsche: from *The Birth of Tragedy* to *Untimely Meditations*, from *Human, All-Too-Human* to *On The Genealogy of Morality* and *The Gay Science*, the German philosopher denounces the real critical point: the concealment of the crisis of subjectivity behind the increasingly "overflowing" egoic totality. As to say: the subject, in its classical metaphysical definition, has, or rather, "believes" to have the unassailable sense of originality and ultimacy. However, all this is not only the result of a precise operation that connects a set of representations deemed "true" in an apparently necessary and universal way, but above all, within itself it faces the condition of something "unseen" and therefore an even more constraining subjectivation,[56] to which it is formally delivered, by what Nietzsche calls "the ghost of the ego." Therefore, there is certainly a reason, if—as has already been

---

[54] Galimberti, U.: Il corpo: antropologia, psicoanalisi, fenomenologia. Feltrinelli, Milan (1983), p. 69 (my translation).

[55] Hence, Galimberti continues, "mathematical-ideal evidence, produced by the Ego through a process of abstraction from sensible experience, is resolved in the indifference of all differences in the latter, to which the ancient Platonic criterion of participation is applied as a criterion of truth. This means that real experience is true if it partakes in the mathematical model of ideal experience; a model that is absolutely identical with itself, indifferent to all differences." See Galimberti, U. (cited above), p. 71 (my translation).

[56] In this regard, it is useful to focus our attention on the lecture by M. Foucault at the Collège de France in 1981–82 (The hermeneutics of the subject: lectures at the Collège de France, 1981–1982. Edited by Frédéric Gros, François Ewald & Alessandro Fontana. Palgrave-Macmillan. New York, 2005), where the philosopher makes explicit and questions a sort of dividing line with regards to the relationship between subject and truth, thus of the subjectivation of the cogito.

mentioned—Nietzsche represents, in the complex and intricate ramification of Nancy's reflection, a decisive place of reference and connection. For this reason, in the 1968 essay devoted precisely to Nietzsche, he writes: "Although resuscitated by our arbiters of style -more than that—Nietzsche seems encountered on our way, unexpectedly, but as a necessity, on the detours of the paths that thought—whether it calls itself 'science', 'philosophy', or does not name itself—paves to think the depth of our world."[57] As if to say, also thanks to Nietzsche, the very statute of any pro-Sophistic discourse can no longer be thought of as a place of truth, as the transparent restitution of an origin. This is why, then, "the depth of our world," to borrow Nancy's words again, does not find a "home" in the apodictic certainty of the ego cogito, but rather, in its retracting itself. In this way—according to the French philosopher—the famous, but also very misunderstood, Nietzschean phrase: *"mundus est fabula"*[58] should be read. Such words in *Ego sum* are echoed again by those in the essay on Nietzsche: "The truth told as fable is the discourse laid bare in its structure, the origin torn from its sealing—or its evasion—in the logos: logic, prophecy, poetry are equally deposed."[59] Thus, reflecting on Nietzsche leads Nancy to confront Descartes once again and even more radically. Indeed, *Ego sum* represents to some extent a kind of *détour* from his initial line of thought. Nevertheless, it is a *détour* that, far from distancing Nancy from the question of philosophy, brings him ever more pressingly closer to it: the thought *within* the subject establishes itself at the limit of its own enunciation. What is at issue here, then, is to show how the Cartesian subject "is posited and is not posited as intellectual intuition, and hence how it is and is not offered in the visual speculation of itself, in the theory of its being-Self: sight devoid of transparency, face deprived of eyes as well as of mirror."[60] In this sense, it is possible to say that, thanks to Descartes, the space opens up *together with* and simultaneously to the establishment of the Subject and of its own crisis. Therefore, Nancy's *provocation*—or his invocation—of the terms *ego and sum* is aimed at "provoking" or showing a real "collision" taking place between them, such as to deepen and bring a decisive contribution to the "dissolution" of the subject itself. In this sense, Nancy embraces—from his earliest works—the deconstructive process of the subject ushered in by post-Heideggerian twentieth-century

---

[57] Nancy, J.L. & Lewis, Th.: Nietzsche: "Yet Where Are the Eyes to See It?". Symposium 23 (1) (2019):189–211, p. 190.

[58] Id.: Ego sum: corpus, anima, fabula. Quot.. see, in particular, pp. 65–87.

[59] Id. & Lewis, Th.: *Nietzsche: "Yet Where Are the Eyes to See It?"*. *Symposium* 23 (1):189–211, quot. p. 204. On this topic, see also, again by Nancy Il ventriloquo, it. transl. by F. F. Palese, Besa, Lecce (2003), a text in which, by rereading the Sophist, the philosopher deals with the delicate question of mimesis; and Nancy, J.-L.: The Discourse of the Syncope: Logodaedalus. Stanford University Press, Stanford, (2008), in which Kantian criticism is presented not as a discourse of truth, but as a syncopated figure of the "style".

[60] Id.: Ego sum: corpus, anima, fabula, quot.

philosophy, proposing to come to "deny every hypothesis of substantial subjectivity and individual essentiality."[61]

However, in order to fully understand and evaluate Nancy's contribution to this line of thought in all its breadth, we need to make a brief détour, to outline a quick overview limited to a few authors of contemporary French thought, and to consider, with a quick glance and in relation to the ego/sum question, the different positions or points of view by Foucault, Blanchot, and Derrida. All authors to whom, in various ways, Nancy's reflection refers—either because it is directly connected to them, or, as in the case of Foucault, because it intentionally diverges from them. All these authors, in fact, have focused attention on the antinomian thought/existence axis and have come to outline, each in its own way (but not without mutual influences), a decisive explication of the contemporary condition, deprived of the subject as a certain foundation.[62]

In posing the question of the subject, Foucault certainly does not fail to recognize Marx, Freud, and Nietzsche as the fathers of the decentralization of subjectivity and the traditional sovereignty[63] of self-consciousness. However, Foucault's references also move in the direction of structuralism, which, in the second half of the twentieth century, made a decisive contribution to the question of the crisis of the subject. Indeed, it is no coincidence that in a 1966 interview, referring to the work by Lacan, Foucault noted how, in the study of neurosis, the subject is increasingly replaced by structures and systems. In this way, it is no longer the subject to be the subject of the neurosis and to speak of it as its unquestionable origin, but rather it is the neurosis that speaks through the subject; as if to say that the subject speaks of itself, exposes itself through it. All that the subject says is nothing but a kind of "surface effect, a shimmer, a foam." What the subject displays as the foundation, the cause, and reason for its conduct is a symptom, a "surface effect" of something deeper that must be traced back to a system, to a structure. This structure is of a linguistic nature, in the sense it draws from language, from its structural duplicity of signifier and signified, the real raison d'être of every subjective word and every individual egoic existence. It is this structuring, typical of language, the real subject.[64]

As Foucault argues, "At the beginning of this century, psychoanalytic, linguistic and then ethnological researches deprived the subject of the laws of his pleasure, the forms of his language, the rules of his action, the systems of his mythical

---

[61] Moreover, along these lines goes the important work by Damasio, A.R.: Descartes' Error: Emotion, Reason, and the Human Brain. Putnam, (1994). The expression quoted in the text is from Piazza, V. Jean-Luc Nancy e il pensiero dell'esposizione, in Vv. Aa. Incontro con Jean-Luc Nancy, "Annuario" 2000–2001, Cortina, Milan (2003), p. 115 (my translation).

[62] On the contemporary condition of the subject and its status we find it useful to refer to the third chapter (entitled The Institution and the Imaginary: A First Approach) of the work by Castoriadis, C.: The Imaginary Institution of Society, transl. by Blamey, K. MIT Press, (1987), pp. 115–164.

[63] On the term "sovereignty"- central to understanding Bataille's philosophical reflection at the point of tangency with Nancy's political reflection—we will later come back.

[64] See Foucault's Interview with Chapsal, M. in "La quinzaine littéraire,"5, (1966) p. 15. However, these themes are extensively developed especially in Id., 1926–1984 The archaeology of knowledge. Harper & Row, New York (1976).

discourses."[65] Here references are made not only to Lacan, but also to Levi-Strauss and De Saussure, with whom Foucault interacts on several occasions. Suffice it to recall Focault's original words in *The Archaeology of Knowledge*: "Lastly, more recently, when the researches of psychoanalysis, linguistics, and ethnology have decentred the subject in relation to the laws of his desire, the forms of his language, the rules of his action, or the games of his mythical or fabulous discourse."[66]

Nevertheless, it is from a sentence in *Les mot et les choses* that Foucault translates the discourse carried on in the two aforementioned works into a unicum, precisely where his reading of Nietzsche penetrates at philological level between language and interpretation: "Philology as the analysis of what is said in the depths of discourse has become the modern form of truth." Thus, the sovereignty of the subject is shaken from the depths and even—to use a Freudian term—removed. Man himself becomes a "fold" of knowledge and language.

However, what emerges in the empty place unoccupied by the subject? What is thought or what is it possible to think in the place and in the space of the subject? According to Foucault—and in some ways according to Nancy himself, albeit with different modes and purposes of thinking—there are no subjects, but rather enunciative functions. This means that the subject is no longer the foundation of this and that, but the result or effect of such multiple enunciative functions. Therefore, the subject does not pre-exist the latter as their supposed foundation, but lies within the linguistic function to which it is partly subject. This is why the use of the third person, rather than the first person, as the subject of one's action, is quite normal among children.

> The Freudian child (I will not say subject) is not initiated into an "oral stage." He first opens himself as a mouth, the open mouth of the cry, but also the mouth closed upon the breast to which the child is attached in an identification more ancient than any identification with a figure, as well as the slightly open mouth, detaching itself from the breast, in a first smile or a first facial expression, the future of which is thinking. The mouth is the opening of Ego, Ego is the opening of the mouth. What comes to pass there is that ego spaces itself out there. «Clearing-away [Räumen, espacer, spacing] brings forth what is free, the open for human's settling and dwelling.» But the human being is that which spaces itself out, and which perhaps only ever dwells in this spacing, in the *areality* of his mouth. «The buccal space. One of the oddest inventions of the organism. Dwelling of the tongue. Seat of reflexes, of various degrees of persistence. The areas that taste are discontinuous. Multipurpose machinery.»[67]

Back to Foucault, the subject thus becomes deposed; what remains is an archaeological and archival knowledge that finds its place of emergence in the enunciation.

---

[65] Id., Due risposte sull'epistemologia. Archeologia delle scienze e critica della ragione storica, ed. by De Stefanis, Lampugnani Nigri,, Milan (1971). p. 20 (my translation).

[66] Id., 1926–1984. The archaeology of knowledge, quot., p. 13.

[67] Nancy J.-L.:.: Ego sum: corpus, anima, fabula, quot., pp. 111–112. Important to note Nancy's double reference—within the quotation highlighted here—to Heidegger (2002. "L'Art et l'espace", in Questions III et IV, Gallimard, Paris) and Valery, P., & Corke, H. Collected Works of Paul Valery, *Volume 2: Poems in the Rough*. Princeton University Press, Princeton (1969). p. 50. This discourse will also be taken up by Derrida in his writing dedicated precisely to Nancy. See Derrida, J.: Le toucher, Jean-Luc Nancy. Editions Galilée, Paris (2000), pp. 43 and following.

This archaeological condition remains invisible to individuals; so does the archive of defined fields of enunciations and their variable conditions of possibility. Foucault's gaze is aimed at the prehuman silence behind the voice of philosophy, at the realm of unspoken words and anonymous practices lying behind all *cogitatio*. However, the question is: in what sense can the speaking voice in Foucault's works still talk about "conditions of possibility" and aspire to "knowledge"? What type of "knowledge" is the one that Foucault builds? In what sense would the archive be truer than ideology? For what point of view? For what subject? Faced with these and other similar questions, he has always backed away, taking refuge in the simple expedient of declaring himself a "historian of ideas" and not a "philosopher."

Foucault's work is unfinished in every sense: not only because it is interrupted by the premature death of its author, but also because it is intimately open to a horizon of problems and insights that it itself fails to master, or at least to frame in a suitable way for its undoubted propulsive force. On such a horizon stands Maurice Blanchot's philosophical reflection.

The crisis of the subject, as surfaced in Foucauldian thought, is actually rooted in Blanchot within the crisis of all questioning and answering of the word. This happens because of the unsettling and enigmatic discovery that there is always an infinite, unfillable and unfilled distance, both between the word and all other things and among speakers, insofar as they relate to one another in communication. Between word and thing, between locutor and hearer, an invincible distance arises and spreads, an inalienable part of their situation (what Blanchot calls the "dissymmetry of the relations of communications") and which, however, is the cause of the original alienation of the subject. We cannot take it away without also taking away the subjects, but on the other hand, insofar as it is already always present, the subjects then already find themselves forever decentered in an outside and in an *other* that they do not master and do not know. The subject, the very subject of knowledge, is made of some ignorance that no Socratic questioning would be able to overcome or understand. Ignorance that stands on another level than any questioning and answering, that is, in another place than that in which the self-aware subject lies (which, moreover, is established precisely by virtue of this void). Blanchot's acumen lies in posing the question of the subject in relation to knowledge and truth, following a line of thought that, once again, is led by Nietzsche and from which Foucault himself, as we have seen, has been largely inspired.

Paradigmatically, in one of his most important works, Blanchot refers to the figure of the "master" and his word:

> The master represents a region of space and time that is absolutely other. This means that, by his presence, there is a dissymmetry in the relations of communication [...] The presence of the master reveals a singular structure of interrelational space, making it so that the distance from student to master is not the same as the distance from master to student—and even more, making it so that there is a separation, a kind of abyss between the point occupied by the master, point A, and the point occupied by the disciple, point B: a separation that will hereafter be the measure of every other distance and every other time. Let us say more precisely that the presence of A introduces for B, but consequently also for A, a *relation of infinity* between all things, and above all in the very speech that assumes this relation. The master is destined, then, not to smooth out the field of relations but to upset it, not to

facilitate the paths of knowledge, but above all to render them not only more difficult, but truly impracticable - something that the Oriental tradition of the master shows rather well. The master offers nothing to be known that does not remain determined by the indeterminable "unknown" he represents, an unknown that affirms itself not through the mystery, the prestige, or the erudition of the teacher, but through the *infinite distance* between A and B. [...] The relation of master to disciple is the very relation of speech when the incommensurable becomes measure therein, and irrelation, relation.[68]

However, to what does the infinite distance announced in the word allude, "in the unknown" of its "knowledge"? The mark of this unknown is precisely in the question (in the very structure of the word as a questioning); "The question, if it is incomplete speech, rests upon incompleteness. It is not incomplete as a question: on the contrary, it is speech that is accomplished by having declared itself incomplete. The question places the full affirmation back into the void, and enriches it with this initial void. Through the question, we give ourselves the thing and we give ourselves the void that permits us not to have it yet, or to have it as desire. The question is the desire of thought."[69] Yet desire is precisely this void that runs through the question itself, its *neutral* origin. In Blanchot, the neutral is the question of origin, of an origin that is neither subject nor object, neither being nor world, neither word nor thing. It is because of its positioning, disposing and emerging *in* and *from* the dimension of the neutral that every question waits in vain for an answer. "The question," Blanchot continues, "awaits an answer, but the answer does not appease the question, and even if it puts an end to the question, it does not put an end to the waiting that is the question of the question."[70] A question of the origin that all questions conceal and that marks with itself that anguish of being before every being, that anguish of not being able either to begin or to end that lies at the bottom of being a subject: I—and no one else, can neither begin nor end; in every instant my being is already there, unable by essence to be aware of and to experience birth and death, the *incipit* and the *exitus* of its path, the alpha and the omega of its "sense." Therefore, Blanchot's position gains an absolute radicality: the profound question "questioning the world by way of a non-world," "places us in relation with what has no end" (the neutral). So that "the question that escapes is not to be confused with the problematic of being"—has quite another scope. This means that the question and crisis of the subject is not the ultimate question either. The problem of the Foucauldian "archaeological" displacement of the subject in its anonymous enunciative practices is only a superficial symptom of a deeper upheaval. It can be highlighted with the problem of "distance," to which Blanchot effectively introduces us. In the distance of the word, it is not only the subject as a foundation that fails, but also and perhaps even before that, *every* possibility of foundation, or better, the foundation itself as a word and as a concept; together with it, every questioning and thinking of the foundation. The mark of the metaphysics of all time

---

[68] Blanchot, M.: The infinite conversation. University of Minnesota Press, Minnesota (1993), pp. 5–6.
[69] Therein, p. 12.
[70] Therein, p. 14.

(subject-foundation-truth) thus really turns out to be utterly illusory: nothing more than a question destined actually to blinding and self-blinding. Thinking of and questioning the profound seem to be incompatible expressions, for to think the profound means to reduce and erase the profound within the whole question, to translate the dark into the bright and illusory transparency of the spirit (of the spiritual subject). Human being is deprived of all truth, since "man" is exactly what hides within himself the "non-human" truth of man. The very being of man as human (as "human man," according to Heidegger in his Letter on Humanism[71]) is his non-truth, his condemnation to error and wandering, to the never-definitive answer, and indeed to the never-ending question that already carries within itself the error of distance, of its unbridgeableness and irreducible extraneousness. Thus, if knowledge is human, non-human is the (impossible) truth of knowledge, which, being knowledge, is already in another place than its object.

In short, in the world of speech, of questioning, we are already hopelessly caught up in the logic of the Other, deferred to a nothingness of meaning that is the very bottom of the apparent meaningfulness of speaking. Then, it is on the thread of voice that we must retrace the institutive paths of truth: we must carry out the deconstruction of the plots that voice has woven, making them the property of the subject that speaks and therefore "is," the *primum mobile* that does not want to be removed.

This is precisely what Derrida's operation is about.[72]

To follow what the philosopher writes about this in work entitled *Speech and Phenomena*:

> In order to really understand where the power of the voice lies, and how metaphysics, philosophy, and the determination of being as presence constitute the epoch of speech as technical mastery of objective being, to properly understand the unity of *tēchnē* and *phōnē*, we must think through the objectivity of the object. The ideal object is the most objective of objects; independent of the here-and-now acts and events of the empirical subjectivity which intends it, it can be repeated infinitely while remaining the same. […] The ideality of the object, which is only its being-for a nonempirical consciousness, can only be expressed in an element whose phenomenality does not have worldly form. *The name of this element is the voice. The voice is heard.* […] The "apparent transcendence" of the voice thus results from the fact that the signified, which is always ideal by essence, the "expressed" *Bedeutung*, is immediately present in the act of expression. This immediate presence results from the fact that the phenomenological "body" of the signifier seems to fade away at the very moment it is produced; it seems already to belong to the element of ideality. It phenomenologically reduces itself, transforming the worldly opacity of its body into pure diaphaneity. This effacement of the sensible body and its exteriority is for consciousness the very form of the immediate presence of the signified. […] When I speak, it belongs to the phenomenological essence of this operation that J hear myself [*je m'entende*] at the same time that I speak. The signifier, animated by my breath and by the meaning-intention (in Husserl's language, the expression animated by the *Bedeutungsintention*), is in absolute proximity to me. The living act, the life-giving act, the *Lebendigkeit,* which animates the body of the

---

[71] Heidegger, M.: Letter on "Humanism". In W. McNeill (Ed.) Pathmarks. Cambridge: Cambridge University Press, (1998). pp. 191–242

[72] Considerably significant, and worthy of remark, is Derrida's 1970s dialogue with Blanchot carried out in the work Parages. Edited by John P. Leavey & Tom Conley. Stanford University Press. Stanford, (2011).

signifier and transforms it into a meaningful expression, the soul of language, seems not to separate itself from itself, from its own self-presence. It docs not risk death in the body of a signifier that is given over to the world and the visibility of space. It can show the ideal object or ideal *Bedeutung* connected to it without venturing outside ideality, outside the interiority of self-present life. [...] It is implied in the very structure of speech that the speaker hears himself: both that he perceives the sensible form of the phonemes and that he understands his own expressive intention.[73]

Therefore, the power of voice is the very power of subjectivity. Nevertheless, as Derrida has pointed out, it is an illusory power. The pure self-affection of the subject through voice *seems* to face no obstacle. In fact, consciousness and its voice (since consciousness "is the voice") are already always threatened by the extraneousness of the sign, of the "writing."[74] Hence, there is no truly foundational self-positioning: "Hearing oneself speak is not the inwardness of an inside that is closed in upon itself; it is *the irreducible openness in the inside*; it is the eye and the world within speech."[75] It is necessary to deconstruct the notions of "concept," "word," and "signifier" and attack "the very order of the concept [...] to effract what metaphysics would call the "real" but that we can no longer refer to as such, simply because there is no longer any homogeneity."[76] As Derrida explains in this interview, it is necessary to "work sharply"[77] and attack "the very order of the concept,"[78] leaving "its movable tips and gimlets embedded in the material thickness of the semantic."[79] However, such a perforation "which reinscribes and displaces within itself the very order of the theorist, cannot be summarized in philosophical theses."[80] This is why the philosopher warns that it is good to give it up now. As if to say, "by cracking the wall toward the other from the concept, one attempts a blow or a cut"[81] that already takes us beyond "all sorts of secular chains, which have found their strongest representation, form and power in Hegelian thought."[82] It is therefore not a matter of a

---

[73] Id.: Speech and phenomena, and other essays on Husserl's theory of signs. Northwestern University Press, Evanston (1973), pp-75-78. About these issues, in particular we refer to the careful analyses by Resta, C. in Ead., Pensare al limite. Tracciati di Derrida, Guerini, Milan (1990). For a general study of Derrida's thought, indispensable is the work by Ferraris, M. Postille a Derrida, Rosenberg & Sellier Turin (1990). Also very useful are the essays contained in the issues of "aut", 248–249/1992; 260–261/1994; 267–268/1995; 271–272/1996; 273–274/1996 and 327/2005; the latter, in particular, was entirely devoted to the philosopher of deconstruction.

[74] On the issue of voice and writing, as opposed to Derrida's view, C. Sini has carried out accurate analyses in his work entitled *Etica della scrittura*, quot., to which we refer.

[75] Id.: Speech and phenomena, and other essays on Husserl's theory of signs. Quot., p. 86.

[76] Id.: Posizioni: scene, atti, figure della disseminazione, it. transl. by Chiappini, M. & Sertoli, G., Bertani, Verona (1975), p. 132 (my translation).

[77] Ibid. (my translation).

[78] Ibid. (my translation).

[79] Ibid. (my translation).

[80] Ibid. (my translation).

[81] Therein, p. 131 (my translation).

[82] Ibid. (my translation).

simple overturning, but rather, to use Derrida's words again, of an "*effraction*."[83] Thus, such a movement does not—and could never—end in discursive critique; the effraction Derrida urges thought to undertake is a movement that is:

> generative, affirmative, seminal, operating by grafts, hybridizations, expropriations, removals, devoid of regional limit, moving outside the code, to the heterogeneous, precisely because it makes the reference jump - or dance. The disseminal, the seminal difference [...] is reduced neither to archaeological originality, which is always blocked, divided, rough-hewn, nor to spontaneous productivity (theological creation or parousiastic manifestation, upgraded or formalized).[84]

The effraction of thought is what remains after "the mad protrusion of the cogito into the hyperbolicity of doubt";[85] it is that *aporia* on which Derrida invites us to rest. The resulting philosophical quest is thus devoid of a predetermined itinerary, of an orderly proceeding, but is made rather of a dwelling on the edges—of a way of thinking which is not based on univocity and definition. That said, moreover, it must not dialectically result in a reabsorption of the other, in the annihilation of the border. Indeed, the boundaries where aporia holds us concern cultures, disciplines, but also, and perhaps first and foremost, demarcations between concepts; instead of a straight line, there appear interweavings, contaminations, grafts, and nuances. In other words, "the boundaries of 'one's own,' of one's life, or of one's identity, are not given as sharply traced to the representation of a subject: to be with oneself means to await oneself, namely, to lean oneself toward a boundary that cannot be determined, that one's steps cannot overcome, but through which something passes, almost like smuggling: something that cannot be controlled, that cannot be filtered, but in which something of ourselves "is at stake."[86] All this does not imply an "absence of boundaries," of "identity," and thus some "indistinction." On the contrary, precisely because the identity boundary does not allow itself to be defined, that boundary remains secret, inappropriable: "the secret inhabiting our own preserves us before we preserve it. We are bound to it, and therefore finite, precisely because, in its indeterminacy, we cannot overcome it."[87] In Derrida's words:

> Let us figuratively call Marrano anyone who remains faithful to a secret that he has not chosen, in the very place where he lives, in the home of the inhabitant or of the occupant, in the home of the first or of the second *arrivant,* in the very place where he stays without saying no but without identifying himself as belonging to. In the unchallenged night where the radical absence of any historical witness keeps him or her, in the dominant culture that by definition has calendars, this secret keeps the Marrano even before the Marrano keeps it. [...] Thanks to this anachronism, Marranos that we are, Marranos in any case, whether we want to be or not, whether we know it or not, Marranos having an incalculable number of ages, hours, and years, of untimely histories, each both larger and smaller than the other,

---

[83] Therein, p. 132 (my translation).

[84] Therein, p. 133 (my translation).

[85] See, in this regard, Derrida, J.: Writing and Difference. Routledge, Chicago (1978); in particular, see the chapter entitled "Cogito and the History of Madness."

[86] Berto, G.: Pensare "secondo l'aporia'"in Derrida, J.: Aporie. Morire—attendersi ai "limiti della verità", Bompiani, Milan (1999) p. XIII (my translation).

[87] Therein, p. XIV (my translation).

2 The Deposition of Cogito

each still waiting for the other, we may incessantly be younger and older, in a last word, infinitely finished.[88]

Infinitely finished. With these words, Derrida closes the volume devoted to aporia, the passage of death. Such a passage is expected at the borders, crossed by a radical otherness: "everyone's death is each time unique, the end of world. Which means that *the* world is present entirely in each one, as each one. Each and every time it rises and falls, subtracted from permanence and identity, redelivered to eclipse and otherness."[89]

It is from such questions that, so to speak, Nancy "starts over," walking along the deconstructive path traced by Derrida. Then, his perspective is to come to terms with the Cartesian subject, giving the latter and that question a specific turn that will remain characteristic and recurrent in the philosopher's reflection. In the "irreducible opening" of the subject, i.e., of the self, already sharply identified by Foucault, Blanchot and Derrida, Nancy sees in turn an "empty opening - eye and mouth [...] seeing mouth, speaking eye, muted eye, blind mouth" in which "the Subject is *depos(it)ed*, in all senses of the word. The Subject lays down (dépose) its certainty on the edge of this open gap.".[90] However, such a 'crisis' of the Subject—and this is the point that Nancy wishes to highlight—is to be found entirely within Cartesian reflection: in the philosopher's view, the ab-solute subjectivity of substance is indeed the subject's actually "*abyssal*" experience of itself:

> Theory – that is, the subject - has always consisted in posing itself as the thought of the open abyss between the act of thinking and the discourse of thinking. [...] The theoretical operation has always properly consisted in the self-position, not of an immediate and naïve (or native) 'knowledge', as a simplistic schematization of metaphysics might lead us to believe, but of the abyss between the thing and knowledge; this operation has even consisted, since Descartes at least, in the self-position and the self-foundation of the abyss between the thing of knowledge and the knowledge of that thing. This self-foundation of the abyss, this manner of exacerbating the abyss while at the same filling it, is the Subject's operation par excellence.[91]

In short, the Cartesian concept of "self-positioning"—to which the French philosopher will critically return on several occasions also in the subsequent works—is the most tangible expression of a "reflected foundation" that implies two mutually validating consequences; the subject is that which, by self-founding, founds a unity, and secondly, by being the support and basis of this unity, appropriates itself.[92] But

---

[88] Derrida, J.: *Aporias: dying—awaiting (one another at) the "limits of truth" (mourir—s'attendre aux "limites de la vérité")*. Stanford University Press, Stanford (1993)p. 81.

[89] Nancy, J.-L.: Resta, vieni, it. transl. by Berto, G. in "aut," 324, 2004, p. 13 (my translation). This small excerpt was taken from the letter Nancy wrote in memory of Jacques Derrida, a few days after his death. Moreover, it is precisely in this direction that moves Derrida's volume The Work of Mourning. Edited by Pascale-Anne Brault & Michael Naas. University of Chicago Press, Chicago (2001).

[90] Nancy J.-L.: Ego sum: corpus, anima, fabula, quot., p. 18.

[91] Therein, p. 8.

[92] See, in this regard, Ibid.

in this double "operation of the Subject"—self-founding and self-appropriating—actually conceals the abyss between "the thing of knowledge and the knowledge of the thing": as if to say, between being and cogito, between *sum* and *Ego*.[93] Ego sum thus becomes the "place" where the irreconcilable split between the two terms that Descartes and the whole tradition following him wished to hold together—to "reconcile"—is brought to light, as well as the occurrence (the event) of the Subject, which, far from establishing an all-encompassing totality of being, is always—on the contrary—the occurrence of the limit of the subject: "edgeless opening that delimits the Subject and where the Subject overflows itself—or within which its identity withdraws and distinguishes itself [...] This is why *ego sum* exhausts, in being uttered and because it is uttered, in the instant of its uttering, any essence of subject."[94] In Nancy, "existence is not a mode of being, but a self-positioning that intends to escape both the immanent presence of being as the original horizon of origin, and the vertical projection onto an axis of transcendence from which to receive the light of its own unleashing."[95] Thus, in this sense, self-positioning (which is existence itself) cuts all "archaeological" links with the essence of the *cogito* and progresses between the folds of the *sum*:

> This free dissemination (whose formula might well be only a tautology) is not the diffraction of a principle, nor the multiple effect of a cause, but is the an-archy – the origin removed from every logic of origin, from every archaeology – of a singular emergence, and therefore always plural, of which being as being is not the foundation, nor the element, nor the reason, but the truth, namely: freedom.[96]

In this way, Nancy carries out a real deconstruction of the original—"archaeological"—foundation of the Cartesian positum and moves toward the desubstantialization of being. In other words, from *Ego sum* on, Nancy makes explicit the project of erosion of the subject.[97] To quote his words:

> The subject ruins itself and collapses into this abyss. But ego utters itself there. It externalizes itself there, which does not mean that it carries to the outside the visible face of an invisible interiority. It means, literally, that ego makes or makes itself into *exteriority*, spacing of places, distancing and strangeness, that make up a place, and hence space itself, primordial spatiality of a true *outline* in which, and only in which, *ego* may come forth, trace itself out, and think itself.
> This is thought – *ego, unum quid* – that can alone find out that it does not give rise to any recognition of its subject, of the human being. This thought is always in advance withdrawn from the possibility of recognizing itself, and hence from the possibility of thinking. *Ego*

---

[93] On the inescapable split between the sum of the Ego and the cogito—taking it to its most rigorous and radical consequences—also insisted Vitiello, V. in Topologia del Moderno. Marietti, Genova (1992).

[94] Nancy, J.-L.: Ego sum: corpus, anima, fabula, quot., p. 18.

[95] Vaccaro, S. Deleuze e Nancy: pieghe di prossimità, in V.v. A.a., Incontro con Jean-Luc Nancy, quot. p. 170 (my translation).

[96] Nancy, J.-L.: The experience of freedom. Stanford University Press, Stanford, (1993) p. 13.

[97] See, in this regard, Nancy, J.-L.: *Un sujet?* in V.v. A.a., Homme et sujet, edited by Weil, D. L'Harmattan. Paris, (1992), pp. 47–114; and Id. Qui vient après le sujet? in "Cahiers Confrontation", 20, 1989.

contracts thought to the point where it is wrenched away from itself. It is not a violent act—or it is one to the extent that, from Descartes onward, thought has refused to confront its own convulsion: violence is begotten in what one refuses to confront. But the convulsion of *ego* is not in itself violent—it is neither disorder, nor illness, even though, without doubt, a chaos stirs within it. It is rather the injunction of an ordeal and a task in which could well consist the least improper future of the human being.[98]

The subject has imploded. The identity madness of the cogito hides—as we have seen so far following Nancy's reasoning—a cache, a constitutive secret that is the presence of others in us. Well, it is precisely in this "alteration" of the ego that the French philosopher retraces the experience of Hegelian consciousness, which finds itself annihilated in its understanding of itself as "other than itself." It is from such an experience that the "exposition" 'takes place: a term that, in Nancy's reading, translates the very being of the subject—starting from Hegel.

---

[98] Id.: Ego sum: corpus, anima, fabula, quot., p. 112.

Chapter 2
Exposition. Starting from Hegel

Everything is played out in connection with Hegel: either one begins at a distance from him, or one distances him from within, one smashes him down.[1]

It is in a collected volume devoted to Deleuze that we find this particularly significant and peremptory statement. A statement that we must keep well in mind, because herein lies Nancy's whole programmatic purpose: not to distance himself from Hegel, but rather to distance him from within, to un-ground him.

However, let us take a step back.

We are at the first lines of *Phenomenology of Spirit*:

Besides, it is not difficult to see that ours is a birth-time and a period of transition to a new era. Spirit has broken with the world it has hitherto inhabited and imagined, and is of a mind to submerge it in the past, and in the labour of its own transformation. Spirit is indeed never at rest but always engaged in moving forward. But just as the first breath drawn by a child after its long, quiet nourishment breaks the gradualness of merely quantitative growth-there is a qualitative leap, and the child is born-so likewise the Spirit in its formation matures slowly and quietly into its new shape, dissolving bit by bit the structure of its previous world, whose tottering state is only hinted at by isolated symptoms. The frivolity and boredom which unsettle the established order, the vague foreboding of something unknown, these are the heralds of approaching change.[2]

This is what Hegel states in the first pages of the Phenomenology of Spirit. As if to say, *simul*, the dissolution of the post-revolutionary world and the structure of the new world. In this opening, with confident determination, Hegel confronts the irruption of the negative into history: "The gradual crumbling (…) of the whole" is the clearest proof of this. Indeed, there is a movement of the spirit that—to borrow the philosopher's words again – "has broken with the world it has hitherto inhabited and imagined." Here is the nodal point of this twentieth-century reflection on Hegel, the one for which, in fact, there would be an "unthought" to be rediscovered in the philosopher from Stuttgart. That unthought would consist in the philosopher's belief—especially found in his work dated 1807- that the metaphysics of Being has ended. The end of metaphysics would coincide with the irruption of the negative into

---
[1] Nancy, J.-L.: "The Deleuzian Fold in Thought" in Deleuze: A Critical Reader, ed. Paul Fatten. Blackwell, Oxford (1996), p. 113.
[2] Hegel, G. W. F. : Phenomenology of spirit. Edited by Arnold V. Miller & J. N. Findlay, Clarendon Press, Oxford (1977), pp. 6-7.

history. In fact, the theme of the ordeal of the negative runs through the philosophical culture of the early twentieth century, in varied ways, sometimes more explicitly and sometimes more subterraneanly, as if to best express the disruptive meaning of "transformation" and "movement," and within them, the drama of subjectivity. The point of discussion for us today is certainly not to propose a "constellation" of philosophers dialogically "internal" to tradition itself, but rather to turn our attention to that "power of the split" that permeates the whole of Hegelian philosophy—emphasizing what makes thought restless and shifting from within. It is precisely this "power of the split" that makes the twentieth century not representable *after* Hegel, after the total dissolution of the system, but rather *from* Hegel, in a kind of *contamination* that is generated at every step. Thus, far from being able to claim and place itself after absolute knowledge, contemporary thought contaminates itself and gets nourished by it, in the awareness that it can no longer "have enough knowledge capable of living up to those objects of thought (being, the transcendental, the foundation), of that kind of knowledge capable of manifesting them, of exposing them, of justifying them."[3] In fact, the Hegelian inheritance is a hand-to-hand struggle with them, a precise intention to trigger the crisis of the ontological-substantialist tradition within the paradigm of the subject. Therefore, such an inheritance passes through the concept of finitude—dialectically mediated by Hegel—lying at the boundary of Husserlian phenomenological reflection, thus intersecting with the themes of intersubjectivity, as well as of language, hermeneutics, and materialist dialectics. The contributions to Hegelian reflection are all harbingers of a "tradition" of Spirit that is also simultaneously its "betrayal," according to that etymology that qualifies betrayal as the act of *"carrying beyond"* while simultaneously retaining, however, the movement of an *Aufhebung* that thankfully "can't be swallowed,"[4] according to that suggestive expression Nancy referred to the body. However, before turning to Nancy's reading of Hegel—particularly in the two works we will focus on here, namely *The speculative remark: one of Hegel's bons mots*[5] and *Hegel: The Restlessness of the Negative*[6]—it is worth going back to the historical-philosophical context preceding Nancy's encounter with Hegel, characterized by a veritable rebirth of Hegelian studies in France. It will then be possible to fully understand within what humus of thought Nancy's reflection arises and how it both relates to and simultaneously distances itself from interpretive perspectives that find, from the 1930s–1940s onward, a pivotal point of reference in the Stuttgart philosopher.

That is not all. Indeed, the renunciation of systematicity, wholly encompassed within its logical structure and confined to the realm of pure thought, as well as Hegel's interpretation mediated, or rather, crossed by Kierkegaard, Jaspers, and Heidegger, will allow the French philosopher to open a new interpretive path in the

---

[3] Cortella, L.: Dopo il sapere assoluto. L'eredità hegeliana nell'epoca post-metafisica. Guerini & Associati, Milan: (1995), p. 18 (my translation).

[4] Nancy, J.-L.: Corpus. Fordham University Press, New York (2008). p. 5.

[5] Id.: The speculative remark: one of Hegel's bons mots. Stanford University Press, Stanford, Calif. (2001).

[6] Id.: Hegel: The Restlessness of the Negative. University of Minnesota Press. Minnesota (2002).

direction of a marked deepening of the concepts of consciousness, reason, dialectics, and history. It is precisely in these key concepts of the *Phenomenology of Spirit*[7] that—as we shall see shortly—the restlessness of the negative is concealed, which will become in Nancy an outstanding or essential point of reflection on the subject understood no longer as *positum*, but as *ex-peau-situm*. Other French thinkers such as Kojève, Hyppolite, Bataille, and Merleau-Ponty moved the direction of that unprecedented Hegel glimpsed by Jean Wahl—all authors who should be kept in mind against the background of Nancy's analyses. From that moment on, in fact, they all began to focus their attention on what was still to be thought of in Hegel: *depuis* Hegel, "starting from Hegel," precisely, as Merleau-Ponty[8] expressed during that lapse of years. The intent to restore the deep sense of such a condition and to further question the experience of the negative in order to discern its disruptive elements has been continuously pursued—as already mentioned—by Maurice Merleau-Ponty[9] as well. Indeed, Hegel's presence plays a very complex role within his reflection for it is intertwined, among other things, with the intensive reading of the second Husserl and the consequent theme of *Lebenswelt*, which Merleau-Ponty himself was developing in those same years and which would lead him to the ontology of the *chair*.

The need to rethink Hegel, or rather, to rethink the whole fruitfulness of the "travail of the negative" starting from the relationship between Absolute and phenomenon, between thought and reality, leads Merleau-Ponty to speak of *Aufheben* in the terms of a double movement of negation that is continually folded on itself. From this perspective, then, it is only possible to understand the Absolute as the other part of the phenomenon: "There is no absolute *Ansich*, and no absolute für uns"[10] but

---

[7] Hegel, G. W. F.: Phenomenology of spirit, quot.

[8] The reference is to the last course of lectures given by M. Merleau-Ponty at the Collège de France, Philosophie et non-philosophie depuis Hegel, in 1961, published in *"Textures"*, 74 (8–9), 1974, pp. 83–129 - first part - and 75 (10–11), 1975, pp. 145–173 - second and last part; t. The English version is dated 1976 and is entitled Philosophy and Non-philosophy Since Hegel, Telos: Critical Theory of the Contemporary 1976 (29):43–105 and 1988, Philosophy and non-philosophy since Hegel. In Philosophy and non-philosophy since Merleau-Ponty. Northwestern University Press, Evanston. Here the French philosopher expresses with brilliant theoretical rigor the need to re-discuss negative philosophy precisely starting from Hegel as the eminent site of the disintegration of the positive Absolute.

[9] Not surprisingly, in one of the most famous passages the French philosopher dedicates to Hegel, we can read that "interpreting Hegel means taking a stand on all the philosophical, political, and religious problems of our century." The quotation is taken from Merleau-Ponty, M.: *Sense and Non-Sense*: Northwestern University Press, Evanston (1964), p. 110. Merleau-Ponty's words also echo E. Weil's ones, who, in the volume dated 1954, entitled Hegel et l'État ("Revue Philosophique de la France et de l'Etranger", 144, pp. 463–464), writes: "Hegel's philosophy is the last of the greatest philosophies and, consequently, it is also the first contemporary philosophy in the sense that it has not been replaced by any other. [...] His philosophy still speaks of our world today, not only to us, but about us. It thus constitutes a node in history" (my translation; the original quotation can be found at p. 127).

[10] Merleau-Ponty, M.: Philosophy and non-philosophy since Hegel. In Philosophy and non-philosophy since Merleau-Ponty, quot., p. 39.

rather—as the French philosopher writes plainly—"their reciprocal relativization, their 'mutual intertwining' [*Ineinander*]."[11] Merleau-Ponty holds firm to the Hegelian principle of the negation of negation: the Absolute is not the plenum consolidating the negation within itself, but is the unfounded result of the negation that "travails" it. Finite and mortal absolute within which the movement of the negative is held. Therefore, it is a matter of having "a conception of the negative that does not transform nature, man and history, into abstractions, a conception of the negative which is their very fabric."[12] In short, it needs to return to the basic problem of the relationship between thought and reality, "between philosophy and non-philosophy," that is, between the Absolute and phenomenon (*Erscheinung* of the Absolute), between Being and entities.[13] Thus, it needs to hold the Hegelian principle of the "negation of negation" firmly so that it does not end up being stiffened up into a "negativism or positivism" that would reduce movement into a motionless "identity."[14]

It is thus a matter of seeing not a reconciliation of positive and negative in the Hegelian dialectical movement, but rather a double movement that both suppresses the firm, full adherence of immanence to itself and at the same time the referral to the otherness of transcendence. "The most conspicuous result of all this is that the concept of the Absolute comes out, indeed, completely 'upset,' overturned. This is because not only can it no longer be conceived as a Founding or Constituent Positivity, but on the contrary, it reveals itself exactly as the negative that "travails" ("works") every "determinate negation," that is, every "phenomenon" or established world. In the sense that the Absolute - as the "other side" of the phenomenon - delimits it, defines it, meaning that it establishes it as an emptied fullness, a hollowed-out whole, a broken " whole" that can never absolutize itself. Thus, as an irreducibly finite institution."[15] This, then, shows how Hegel has indeed been "rediscovered" and "positioned" on the threshold of transcending traditional metaphysics; this is how Hegel can be a "participant" in a movement of thought that surrounds nihilism at various levels and somehow smashes it down, alongside Nietzsche and Heidegger paving the way for what, a few decades later, Nancy would call "finite ontology." This target, reached in particular by Merleau-Pontyan philosophical reflection, can give us a better understanding of the analysis focused by Nancy in relation to the need to rethink Hegel today. This once again means leaving behind

---

[11] Ibid.

[12] Therein, p. 76.

[13] On this need for thought in Merleau-Ponty - which characterizes, on closer inspection, the whole of Western culture, from Plato to the present day - we refer to the analyses by Lisciani-Petrini, E.: La passione del mondo. Saggio su Merleau-Ponty; quot., (see, in particular, pp. 156–178).

[14] "Aufheben. The negation of negation must be maintained. However, the surpassing must be a true one and not a conserving negation (i.e. in raising the object to the level of thought)" - we can read in Merleau-Ponty, M.: Philosophy and non-philosophy since Hegel. In Philosophy and non-philosophy since Merleau-Ponty, quot., p. 70.

[15] Lisciani-Petrini, E.: La passione del mondo. Saggio su Merleau-Ponty, quot, p. 165 (my translation)

the pacifying vulgate that had come to terms with Hegel, as well as returning to thinking about the sub-jectum, the "Subject"—precisely with Hegel, but also beyond Hegel—as that which is already always defined, cut off, delimited, spotted, and identified by the other, by the "outside" of oneself. In order to do so, Nancy recovers the tragic dimension of Hegelian thought, making it resonate to the point where—we might say—there is no longer any substance at all. A recovery that appears quite evident in the works that the French philosopher devotes entirely to Hegel, such as *The speculative remark: one of Hegel's bons mots* and *Hegel: The Restlessness of the Negative* that we have previously mentioned; texts in which Nancy assumes the limit of the double gesture that bears "only one 'name', aufheben."[16] The double gesture of the negative, which is configured as both absence and permanence, is the reaching depth of thought.[17]

Along this perspective, Nancy writes—making it immediately clear, without mincing words, the interpretive key he intends to attach to Hegel:

> The Hegelian subject [...]is in no way the self all-to-itself [...] it reveals itself as other, infinitely in the other. [...] It is not only the passage from a "one" to an "other," but the one, in this passage, finds its truth in the other, and thus touches upon [toucher à} and unsettles its own ground. [...] The Hegelian ground is neither fundament nor foundation, neither groundwork nor substrate. It is the depth in which one is submerged, into which one sinks and goes to the bottom. More precisely, this ground founds only to the extent that it sinks in itself: for foundation should be a hollowing out. [...] this hollowing neither attains nor brings to light a secure groundwork. It hollows out the point of passage, and the point itself is such a hollowing out: work of the negative, but right at the surface.[18]

The relationship between *Grund* and *Ab-Grund* is thus understood by Nancy as the sign of an unassimilable excess. Here it is not a matter of displacing the *Grund* differently, but of sinking it, and it is clear that this extreme displacement can define itself, on the one hand, only in relation to the *Grund*, forced to speak negatively of the *Ab-Grund*; on the other hand, in the *Ab-Grund*, the intention, the will that moved it cannot resurface in any way. *Impensement* is the negative excess of thought, its sinking into itself. As Nancy writes, "if A=A, it is because A posits itself as other than itself. And this is precisely what 'I=I' exposes.";[19] "I is an other", to quote Rimbaud.[20]

However, precisely because of this, and here is the key passage, "Logos is subject, which means the exposing of the infinite exposition of identity."[21] In this sense,

---

[16] Nancy, J.-L.: The speculative remark: one of Hegel's bons mots, quot., p. 127.

[17] See, in this regard, the excellent essay by: Goria, G.: L'ellisse speculativa. Nancy, Hegel e il passo del pensiero, in "Shift. International Journal of Philosophical Studies", 2/2021–1/2022, pp. 253–266.

[18] Nancy J.-L., Hegel: The Restlessness of the Negative, quot., pp. 4, 6, 14, 15.

[19] Therein, p. 21. The theme of contradiction and the splitting of the identical in Hegel - albeit from an entirely different perspective than Nancy - is brought to radical consequences by Vitiello, V., *Topologia del moderno*, quot. On this issue, in particular, see also Donà, M.: Sull'Assoluto. Einaudi, Turin: (1992); and Id.: Sulla negazione, Bompiani, Milan (2004).

[20] Rimbaud, A.: Opere. Mondadori, Milan (1975). pp. 450 and 452 (my translation).

[21] Nancy, J.-L.: Hegel: The Restlessness of the Negative, quot., p. 21.

the restlessness of the other—of that non-A which lies within A itself, "inhabits" it from within—is the very "restlessness of the negative" that defines identity, that travails it from within, and constitutively and continuously exposes it to its outside. The "immense power of the negative," far from being resolved into an all-encompassing Absolute, tears and shatters the whole system. Such "power" characterizes Hegel as well, using famous words that are taken up and commented on both by Kojève and Nancy, affirming that:

> But the life of Spirit is not the life that shrinks from death and keeps itself untouched by devastation, but rather the life that endures it and maintains itself in it. It wins its truth only when, in utter dismemberment, it finds itself. [...] on the contrary, Spirit is this power only by looking the negative in the face, and tarrying with it. This tarrying with the negative is the magical power that converts it into being.[22]

"Tarrying with it" thus means posing the terms of one of the most decisive questions of our time: the essential finitude of being. In short, it is a matter of coming to terms with the submission of thought to finitude, to the limit, to the "negative that works"—in one word, to death. As Nancy explains, "With Hegel, philosophy attempts neither to represent the Whole nor to found it; but it does have the task of opening for itself the totality of relation such as it opens itself in every thing-but as it opens itself, each time, here and now."[23] The subject of such a philosophy would be therefore not an abstract subject contemplating hunger, distress, and anguish, having on its side the sense and the ultimate truth of the world, but the "name of its own passing out"[24] that manages to think "the powerlessness of all thought."[25] This means that.

> If spirit "finds itself" in "death;' it is because death is not before it, and not outside of it, neither as the death of an other, nor as the death of self that would remain outside of itself as the simple exterior cessation of the sense of self. Spirit is not a given that looks upon and suffers death as a given other or as another given-and, in this sense, nowhere, not even Literally in Hegel himself, is there a spirit of the world that would coldly contemplate the passing procession of deaths and annihilations as the spectacle of its own sense. Spirit is not something finite that would have its own end - its absolute dismemberment-before it as an object, a representation, a duty, an idea, or an absurd contingency.[26]

The spirit is "[...] the finite that finds itself to be infinite in the exposition of its finitude, this is what is to be thought-which is to say, this is what it is to 'think.'"[27] To think the spirit as infinite in the exposition of its own finitude is the *trembling* "being in itself detachment from self."[28] It means, in other words, to think its infinite tearing, to think the Augustinian *interior intimo meo* or the Cartesian *ego sum*

---

[22] Hegel, G. W. F.: Phenomenology of spirit, quot., p. 19.
[23] Nancy, J.-L.: Hegel: The Restlessness of the Negative, quot., p. 28.
[24] Therein, p. 29.
[25] Therein, p. 30.
[26] Ibid.
[27] Therein, p. 31.
[28] Therein, p. 45.

"undoing, unraveling all consistency of the *interior or of the ego*."[29] A return to Kojève is not extrinsic at this point:

> Now, only by becoming aware of his finitude and thus of his death, does man truly become aware of himself. Indeed, he is finite and mortal. On the other hand, the spirit obtains its own truth only by finding itself in absolute laceration.[30]

If "Hegel is the inaugural world,"[31] this is because he radically thinks about the meaning of finitude and death. The *sum* unravels from within or, to put it better, "the subject is the experience of the power of division, of exposition or abandonment of self."[32] Here is the *alter* of the *ego sum*. Here is the beginning of negativity. It "makes all determinateness tremble, all being-all-to-itself."[33] However, what "makes the self tremble" exactly? What is the lack rooted within it? What lays bare (*dérobe*) its imposing "determinateness"? What unrest is unsettling in the self of the sum? In the self of the sum arises the presence of negativity as desire and here "The heart trembles because the self is indeed bound to disappear."[34] It is bound to disappear and end up in the desiring becoming of the other. In Hegel's words, "*Self-consciousness achieves its satisfaction only in another self-consciousness*."[35] The incidence of this statement, placed by Hegel in the first pages of the chapter on self-consciousness, flows through the entire early twentieth century and presents itself as the point of greatest tension within philosophical reflection on the question of the Self/other relationship. Nancy writes:

> In the famous "dialectic of master and slave" the mastery of the master remains an abstraction precisely insofar as the master himself does not tremble in the imminence of death. But the slave is just as much the one who trembles before the master. Their struggle is that of the consciousness that exposes itself of itself to its own desire to be recognized and to be desired by the other: but the other as such, and as the other self subsisting outside of me, imperils my subsistence, this being-all-to-myself that I thus know can only be affirmed in risking it. I cannot stop trembling before the other, and even further, at being in myself the trembling that the other stirs up.[36]

The exposition to the other is the very being of the subject, its concrete negativity. Moreover, it can certainly be stated—following Nancy—that Hegel was the first to bring thought out of the realm of identity and subjectivity.

> The concretion of negativity begins with the other. The self that negates itself, instead of coming back to itself, throws itself into the other, and wills itself as other. This is why the other is not second, does not come after. If the other, by the simple fact that I name it

---

[29] Therein, p. 36.
[30] Kojève, A.: Introduzione alla lettura di Hegel (G.F. Frigo, Trans.). Adelphi, Milan (1996), p. 680 (my translation).
[31] Nancy, J.-L.: Hegel: The Restlessness of the Negative, quot., p. 3.
[32] Therein, p. 43.
[33] Therein, p. 45.
[34] Therein, p. 59.
[35] Hegel, G. W. F.: Phenomenology of spirit, quot., p. 110.
[36] Nancy, J.-L.: Hegel: The Restlessness of the Negative, quot., p. 45.

"other;' seems to presuppose the "one" or the "same" and thus only to come later, this is the effect of a still abstract thought that has penetrated neither into the one nor into the other. The one does not begin: it begins with the other. With the other means near to the other, with the other at his place. I am first the guest of this other: world, body, language, and my "twin" (mon "semblable").[37]

Again, in a very intense passage from *The Inoperative Community*, Nancy moves to the realm of existence, due to his critique of subjectivity. To exist means.

> To hold one's selfness as otherness, and in such a way that no essence, no subject, no place can present this otherness in itself - either as the proper selfness of another, or an "Other," or a common being [...] The otherness of existence consists in in its non-presence to itself [...] We are others - each one for the other and each for him/herself - through birth and death, which expose our finitude. Finitude does not mean that we are noninfinite [...] but it means that we are infinitely finite, infinitely exposed to our existence as a non-essence, infinitely exposed to the otherness of our own 'being' [...] We begin and we end without beginning and ending: without having a beginning and an end that is ours, but having (or being) them only as others, and through others.[38]

However, precisely that being near the other is the establishment of the "us." The subject takes shelter in the desire for the "us," in the being-in-common that is the radical dispossession of the self from itself. This is because such being-in-common is not the homogeneous *wholly-full* subject understood as presence to himself, but rather the place of original openness, of the *il y a,* of the offering of oneself to the other and of the other to oneself.

Here, the French philosopher declines in an ethical-political key the theme of the community of being, the experience of an impossible sharing of sense, of that which, by escaping any undue signifying operation and staying originally outside communication, grounds singularity in finitude. Community is not made up of individuals, but of finite singularities that welcome the limit within themselves and do not leave it outside a supposed unity. Nancy outlines a communitarian dimension that does not claim to make itself absolute, to assimilate within itself all the dimensions of man, but which displays precisely what, by eluding the concept, the total transparency of sense, makes the being-in-common as an inappropriable *other.* Therefore, the dimension of community is not that of the *Geist*, of a substance that becomes a subject by producing the world of meanings, values, and norms; it is rather that of a finitude capable of exposing itself to its own limit, of standing on its own boundary in order to grasp that excess which, by crossing it, breaks it and makes it impossible for it to control itself. It is in this sense that "death irremediably exceeds the resources of a metaphysics of the subject."[39] The existential dimension of death is thus turned by Nancy towards the direction of the excess, the inoperativeness theorized by Bataille—the community of death. In fact, the latter subtracts the notion of sovereignty from the exercise of power and knowledge to link it instead to the crisis of the unitary, homogeneous subject, confident in the domain of

---

[37] Therein, p. 57.

[38] Nancy, J.-L.: The birth to presence. Stanford University Press, Stanford, Calif. (1993)., p. 155.

[39] Id.: The Inoperative Community, quot., p. 14.

knowledge and the power of reason. Instead, the sovereign instant is that in which the subject, by dissociating himself from his own conceptual activity, accomplishes an operation that, not being teleologically oriented or determined by anything, exposes him to non-knowledge, to discontinuity, to that excess that prevents him from dominating himself even before he dominates others or the world. At the extreme limit of knowledge, Bataille discovers the limitless depths of non-knowledge. In this way, every laugh, every cry, every erotic relationship, and every death reveal the abyss that tears every supposed unity of the subject, laying bare its original fragmentation. Hence the opposition of Bataille's community to any thought of intersubjectivity, since it is the very identity of the subject to have failed;[40] in this sense, it can be shared/partitioned (*partagée*) simply in an existence, in a finitude experienced in the sovereign moment in which dispossession, the exposure to the other, occurs. For Bataille, in fact, "Communication cannot proceed from one full and intact individual to another. It requires individuals whose separate existence in themselves is risked, placed at the limit of death and nothingness; the moral summit is the moment of risk taking, it is a being suspended in the beyond of oneself, at the limit of nothingness."[41] In *The Inoperative Community*, Nancy takes up the concept of Bataille's sovereignty as an exposition to unlimited alterity. Indeed, it is still Bataille's thesis of the "unemployed negativity" that he embraces when affirming that community is "neither a work to be produced, nor a lost communion, but rather as space itself [...] of the outside-of-self."[42]

> Sacrificing existence in order to preserve it: it is this tragic paradox that dissolves any idea of community and individual that philosophy and politics fail to think about. It is from this threatening and terrible destructive power that philosophy and politics fail to immunize the community and the individual.[43] This because the enterprise is absurd (it is the absurdity of a thought derived from the individual). Death is indissociable from community, for it is through death that the community reveals itself-and reciprocally [...] A community is the presentation to its members of their mortal truth.[44]

Community is this very impossibility. Within a community, individuals experience their finitude, their constitutive mortality. The impossibility of community is given by the fact that it can be experienced "concretely" only in the death of others. Therefore, community always reveals itself to individuals *through* others and *for* others. It is not the space where individuals meet, but the space where the individuals are always others. The space where they disappear. If community manifests itself in the death of others, then this means that death is the only possible community of individuals who are no longer such. There can only be a community insofar as individuals end being individuals. Let us put it differently. Death is not a

---

[40] The issues related to Bataille's "community" have been explored in depth by Esposito, R.: in Categorie dell'impolitico, quot. pp. 245–312.

[41] Bataille, G.: On Nietzsche. Paragon House, New York (1992)., p. 19.

[42] Nancy, J.-L.: The Inoperative Community, quot., p. 19.

[43] Cantarano, G.: La comunità impolitica. G. Giappichelli Editor, Turin (2018). p. 137 (my translation).

[44] Nancy, J.-L.: The Inoperative Community, quot., pp. 14–15.

communion that "merges the selves into a higher Self or Us. It is the community of others. The true community of mortal beings, or death as a community, is their impossible communion." As an impossible communion, community is the impossibility of its own immanence. The impossibility of conceiving the individual as a communitarian individual. Community bears witness to the very impossibility of community. According to Nancy, therefore, thought must withdraw from the immanentism of the idea of a common substance, give up the worship of the hypothesis of any "essential communion" understood as a sharing of origin and end (as a purpose) or of a community pre-understood in the presuppositional act of being or of a "being." However, in order for the "withdrawal" of thought to take place, it must surrender itself to the apparent return to the question of essence and thus of the subject or of subjectivity. This is why—to complete the circle from which we started—Nancy cannot but "return" to Hegel. The "unresolved Hegelism" that permeates such a large part of contemporary philosophy—which therefore seems not to have come to terms with Hegel and has not definitively taken distance from him, appears here to be the foundation of both Nancy's philosophical reflection and of his unceasing hand-to-hand struggle with his thought. In an interview that Nancy granted me in 2005, he asserted: "As for Hegel, the Subject, which is absolute self-generation in him, is such only insofar as it is simultaneously absolute self-movement towards itself through the other - and the passage through the other, through its outside, is so essential to it inasmuch as it is infinite in itself [?]. Infinity which infinitely returns to the subject as his own truth. Nevertheless, precisely by infinitely returning to it, it unceasingly places it back outside of 'itself.' The Hegelian subject is the first to open his 'in-itself.' And his 'being-for-itself' relates him to himself exclusively *in the very measure of his difference to himself*. Consequently, Derrida's '*difference*' can be understood as an explication and unfolding of the self-relation as conceived by Hegel. I shall add," Nancy continues, "a final consideration; these are only 'some folds' of Hegelian thought - it lies entirely in these folds, which articulate it by folding and unfolding it into itself."[45] Nancy's "path of restlessness," from the interweaving of *Grund* and *Abgrund*—"foundation" and "abyss"—generates, in the mark of an ontology of the negative,[46] a concept of community that is nothing but the finitude exposed to its own limit—to death—thus opening up to that excess in which it is—at the same time—singular and "shared." This path of restlessness is the one traced by Hegel, and is the path from which we cannot look away.

In conclusion, therefore, I refer back to the words of a recent dialogue I had with Nancy about Hegel and his presence in contemporary philosophical reflection:

---

[45] Calabrò, D.: Dis-piegamenti. Soggetto, corpo e comunità in Jean-Luc Nancy, con un'intervista al filosofo e un'Appendice di testo inedito. Mimesis, Milan (2005, 2006²). p. 152 (my translation).

[46] On the topic of the ontology of the negative, we refer to the mighty and comprehensive monograph by Villani, M.: Arte della fuga. Estetica e democrazia nel pensiero di Jean-Luc Nancy. Mimesis. Milan (2020).

"La pensée nous attend" et elle ne porte aucun nom - ou bien elle peut porter tous les noms de la philosophie ... [The thought awaits us all, and it bears no name - or it can bear all the names of philosophy].[47]

Appendix

"The Thought Awaits Us All"... After and Beyond Hegel

Daniela Calabro in Conversation with Jean-Luc Nancy

Foreword

It is in *La remarque spéculative. Un bon mot de Hegel*[48] that Jean-Luc Nancy begins his struggle with Hegel. We are in 1973 and the legacy of the thought of the philosopher who wrote *Phenomenology*, *Logic*, and *Encyclopedia* has not yet finished its questioning. The thought on 'tradition of the Spirit' in the Hegelian meaning thus crosses both the first and the second half of the '900, until reaching us today.

In this work, we are going to introduce the dialogue with Jean-Luc Nancy, the subject of which is, once again, Hegel.

D.C.

To begin our conversation, and of course, before focusing our attention on the issues raised starting from *Hegel. The Restlessness of Negative*,[49] I would like to submit to you a fragment of "Hegel's Existentialism" by Maurice Merleau-Ponty:

> All the great philosophical ideas of the past century-the philosophies of Marx and Nietzsche, phenomenology, German existentialism, and psychoanalysis-had their beginnings in Hegel; it was be who started the attempt to explore the irrational and integrate it into an expanded reason which remains the task of our century. He is the inventor of that Reason, broader than the understanding, which can respect the variety and singularity of individual consciousnesses, civilizations, ways of thinking, and historical contingency but which nevertheless does not give up the attempt to master them in order to guide them to their own truth. But, as it turns out, Hegel's successors have placed more emphasis on what they reject of bis heritage than on what they owe to him. If we do not despair of a truth above and beyond divergent points of view, if we remain dedicated to a new classicism, an organic civilization, while maintaining the sharpest sense of subjectivity, then no task in the cultural order is more urgent than re-establishing the connection between on the one band, the thankless doctrines which try to forget their Hegelian origin and, on the other, that origin itself. That is where their common language can be found and a decisive confrontation can take place. Not that Hegel himself offers the truth we are seeking (there are several Hegels, and even the most objective historian will be led to ask which of them went furthest), but all our

---

[47] Calabrò, D.: «The Thought Awaits Us All» ... After and Beyond Hegel. A Dialogue with Jean-Luc Nancy, in "Estetica. Studi e ricerche", vol. X, 2/2020. Il Mulino, Bologna, p. 513.

[48] Nancy J.-L.: La remarque spéculative. Un bon mot de Hegel. Galilée Paris (1973),; eng. Transl. The speculative remarke: one of Hegel's bons mots, Stanford University Press, Stanford (2001).

[49] Id.: Hegel. The Restlessness of Negative, quot.

antitheses can be found in that single life and work. There would be no paradox involved in saying that interpreting Hegel means taking a stand on the philosophical, political, and religious problems of our century.[50]

This text, which was first published in 1946 in "Les Temps Modernes," presents the Hegelian debt of the philosophical thought of the '900. Based on this, my question is: are we still in debt with Hegelian thought? What would our debt consist of? If, moreover, being in debt means accepting an inheritance, and this inheritance leads us to talk about the future-to-come [à-venir], then... Hegel is not yet behind us...

J.-L. N.
Of course, we are in debt and/or we are inheriting it. The two things are different; it seems to me that inheriting does not involve having a debt. We receive something that is, and was intended to be, passed on to us.

Somehow, I agree entirely with Merleau-Ponty's view. But on the other hand, Merleau-Ponty himself is today part of our inheritance—like Heidegger, Bataille, Derrida, and Hamacher, just to name a few important figures in the readings and revivals of Hegelian thought. We are in another era. Merleau-Ponty's reproach to "Hegel's heirs" is no longer so accurate about these four names—which are only a very narrow selection!

It is not just that a deficiency or injustice should have been remedied. It is more complex: I believe that, through readings and reinterpretations by authors like the four philosophers I have mentioned—and thus through the actual, concrete history that separates us from 1946 (the date of the text you are quoting), Merleau-Ponty speaks of the "hope for a new classicism and an organic civilization." Such a statement could be well understood in 1946: it is based on a confidence and a hope in the possibility—and the necessity—of regaining a spiritual project after a disastrous and frightening interruption.

It supposes that history starts again and in a way that opens it up to a future. It is, of course, a confidence implying that Hegel did not close history off and that the adventure of the Spirit must be tirelessly taken up—which was already a way of parting with those who denounced the Hegelian enclosure. But today we are in a very different situation: history has indeed moved forward impressively—in a way that Merleau-Ponty would have never imagined—but after less than half a century and up to today, it has begun to indicate that it is perhaps no longer "The History," the realization of the *Spirit*, but that leaving its course and becoming a succession of shocks, accidents and upheavals, it has become a wandering with no future. Hegel himself would find it difficult to speak of the "cunning of reason" because the "Reason" does not allow us to recognize cunning, detours, and circumnavigations in what, since 50 years now, has been disintegrating and dispersing all the forms or figures which could explore like in a gallery, as it does at the end of the *Phenomenology of Spirit*.

---

[50] Merleau-Ponty, M.: Hegel's Existentialism, in Id.: Sense and Non-Sense, trans. by H.L. Dreyfus and P.A. Dreyfus, Northwestern University Press, Evanston (Ill.),1964, pp. 63–64.

Maybe we should concentrate on the last words of the book, on the foamy overflow of infinity, which should be understood as an overflow that overflows the Spirit itself, or the reason.

To some extent this is what Heidegger does when he speaks of the "technique" as the "last delivery of the Being" and of this last delivery as the complete absorption of the "Being" into the "beings" (In this sense, by the way, I think Heidegger has remained quite Hegelian about history).

It can be said, as I wanted to do 23 years ago (in the book you mentioned), that it is a "restlessness" that is always open-ended and alive. But it is not enough to interpret the overflowing of the infinite as a sense that is still to come. Today (23 years later, not much time and a lot of it too, if you think about what has happened within it: digital revolution, global reshaping of capitalism and climate change) it is clear that if the Spirit carries on its operations through history it may lead to a dissolution of not just the Spirit itself (in Hegelian terms this would make no sense), but at least of the whole civilization of which Hegel, in fact, may have been the most powerful expression.

Hegel himself was undoubtedly the first to know something about it: when he wrote about the "gray on gray" that philosophy paints, he meant that the epoch of the "concept" "lacks the colors of life," as he stated in the *Aesthetics*. Hegel was not triumphant: he had a mixed and worried feeling of his own present. His legacy is probably in there too. He is the last philosopher of a System—that is to say of an "organic" vision (I take up Merleau-Ponty's word) but he is also the first disenchanted philosopher…

D.C.

Thank you… Your definition of Hegel as a disenchanted philosopher interests me very much and reminds me of an extremely significant passage from your *Pli deleuzien de la pensée*: "Tout se joue par rapport à Hegel: ou bien on commence à l'écart de lui, ou bien on l'écart en lui-même, on le défonce".[51] This gives me the opportunity to reflect on what Hegel himself suggested in the appendix to paragraph 396 of the *Encyclopedia*: "the most reasonable thing that children can do with their toy is to break it." Here, in my opinion, Hegel is "sinking in himself." This gesture represents the "non-organic" encounter with the external object, i.e., the encounter with the world as a loss, and therefore as the presence of the negative, which in this case is not the mediation, but is the immediate and irremediable.

Is this the opening to the path of restlessness? The restlessness? that comes from the emergence of the world, from its coming in presence or absence; as You say: "an upheaval, a gap, a disjunction, a breakdown - as well as a divine surprise"[52]?

---

[51] Nancy J.-L.: Pli deleuzien de la pensée, in Alliez, E.: G. Deleuze. Une vie philosophique, Institut Synthélabo, Paris (1998), p. 122.

[52] Id.: Un avenir sans passé ni futur, International. Conférence, Oxford, 30 mars 2019.

J.-L. N
First of all, I would like to warn you that it is probably not so simple to distinguish or oppose mediating negativity and immediate negativity. It should not be forgotten that the second dialectical moment, that of the negation of the first negation, can (and perhaps even must) divide itself in two (as Hegel pointed out almost at the end of his *Logic*), thus it is not obvious that one reaches a final conclusive term, but rather that the movement does not stop. I don't want to go back to this technical analysis now, but this is one of the aspects I believe to be very important in Hegel: the sense of an endless outburst that somehow does not come to a conclusion. It certainly has the form of a process that will come to an end, but any completion is just a new beginning. The spirit is *a perpetual motion*, so much that it risks overwhelming the system itself. But I don't want to dwell on it any further, because it is not something which happened inside Hegel—for there is an "interior": it happened outside of him, in his exterior, which he indicated without being able to get through it, because we probably never get through to the exterior...

I would rather go back to the "gray." Re-read the entire introduction to the aesthetics courses: you will see how Hegel was worried about his time. He saw it as the time of the intellect deprived of affect. A time of administration and management where he did not see the birth of any art that would express the Spirit. It has often been said that he ignored Beethoven and Goya. It is true: he himself was late... But it is very complicated because the art that was being renewed also marked the beginning of a nineteenth century, which was going to be very complex because the arts, all the arts, were going to be shaken by powerful upheavals and divisions...

The important thing is this sense of "gray" that Hegel had. It is the reign of explanation and administration. Everything must be explained and traceable in a management. There is a domination of the rational and the reasonable—not in the Hegelian sense of Reason at all. But today it is even more powerful: everything is calculated, everything is turned into statistical data or neurological circuits. And everyone is involved in it, without protesting.

In the wording of the *Introduction to Aesthetics*, which is the most striking in this respect, the world of the reflected and conscious universal is a world that has *lost* something (the word is in the text), namely the vitality and liveliness of the sensitive life: this cannot be recovered voluntarily.

I feel like Hegel's owl at the end of the day. Hegel, or the beginning of twilight, of our twilight! The restlessness of the negative is also the restlessness of the one who knows that the passage from the world of reflection to that of speculation perhaps occurs only for the philosopher—just like at the end of the *Philosophy of Right* (thus at the other end of what has opened up onto the twilight...) it would be said that only philosophy can contemplate the majesty of the prince—in other words, the sensible truth of the "Ethical Idea in act," that is the State.

Kant was fully experiencing a tension towards a "must-be." Hegel thought of resolving this tension through the rationality of the real. But this thought remains in the restlessness of its own effectivity, which overflows infinitely. And it is perhaps here that philosophy achieve itself, in the sense that Heidegger wanted to replace it with "the task of thinking"… (which perhaps means going around in circles, but this is not what I want to analyze here).

Today we have exhausted both the "must-be" and the speculative truth. It is precisely this double exhaustion that characterizes the dissipation of the long progressive and socialist/communist expectation—a long expectation that was the joint legacy passed on to Kant and Hegel by Marx.

D.C.
Hegel announced the "end of art."

Your thesis is that—on the contrary—Hegel presented us with the birth of art: "With Hegel comes the birth of « a completely independent concept of art, namely that of the 'sensitive' presentation of the Idea.» You explained this well through three passages contained in *Les poids d'une pensée, l'approche*, which I quote almost entirely for our readers:

> 1.Hegel refuse à l'art toute finalité d'expression ou d'enseignement – en général, toute finalité externe. L'art a au contraire pour fin (la fin de l'art, il y a fin et fin, c'est de quoi nous parlons) la fin dialectique elle-même, la "conciliation des contraires", c'est-à-dire de l'Idée (moralité, sublimité, etc.) et de la forme (sensible, présentable) – ou plus largement: la négation de la généralité infinie de l'Idée, l'affirmation de sa particularité finie, et la seconde négation qui affirme l'universel *dans* le particulier.
>
> 2.Si l'art est déclaré passé, l'*Esthétique* répète aussi avec insistance que c'est là une *perte:* perte de la vie, de l'animation, de la fraîcheur—perte d'une proximité de la nature, perte des Grecs. Certes, c'est tout d'abord la perte d'un immédiat, et comme telle elle doit être dialectisée—ce que doit opérer la philosophie (dans la *Phénoménologie,* la religion révélée, puis la philosophie). Alors, la vie devient vie de l'Esprit.
>
> Pourtant il y a aussi une "non-dialecticité", qu'on remarque trop peu, et qui distingue l'art par rapport à d'autres immédiatetés relevées. Par exemple, pour faire un contraste rapide: dans l'État, deux formes d'une vie plus immédiate de la conscience, et deux formes du reste elles-mêmes en rapport de contradiction, sont relevées: la lutte des consciences, et l'amour. Une fois relevées, il ne reste rien de leurs immédiatetés. Mais l'art, l'art en tant que vie, n'est pas aussi manifestement relevé (ni donc relevable): car notre présent, celui qui succède au passé comme l'époque du concept et de la pensée, est aussi "une époque sans vie", plutôt qu'une époque qui s'élève à la vie de l'Esprit. "sans vie" et "triste".
>
> Il y a un hiatus entre la Vie du Concept – que promet la pensée – et la vie bourgeoise de l'âge du concept, une vie prosaïque et sans goût. Or dans l'art, pour Hegel, il y a d'abord vie – mais vie ni immédiate, ni dialectisée. Disons, quitte à anticiper et à aller trop vite, qu'il y a ce "dimanche de la vie" que Hegel salue dans la peinture flamande – et que le dimanche […] ce n'est pas la dialectique de la vie, c'est son suspens, et sa présentation.
>
> Et puis, rappelez-vous, la philosophie de la chouette qui s'envole au crépuscule, c'est aussi, dans le même texte, "la philosophie qui peint son gris sur le gris" de la fin d'une époque. L'époque de la philosophie est la fin d'une époque plutôt qu'une nouvelle époque. Et la peinture philosophique s'avère ainsi comme peinture nulle, ou comme annulation de la peinture. Or la peinture est l'art hégélien par excellence: on peut montrer qu'elle occupe dans l'*Esthétique* la place exacte de l'art à son point d'équilibre (de l'art qui n'a pas entamé sa fin…).
>
> 3.Si "la tâche de l'art consiste à concilier, en en formant une libre totalité, ces deux côtés: l'idée et la représentation sensible", alors l'art ne fait qu'exécuter une nécessité *intrinsèque* de l'Idée. En effet, "la manifestation constitue un moment *essentiel de l'essence*". Ainsi, "la beauté n'est pas une abstraction de l'entendement, mais le concept absolu en soi-même concret, ou, de manière plus précise, l'Idée absolue dans son apparition conforme à elle-même".

Il faut retenir cette indication avec la plus grande attention. Car si la beauté est de l'ordre du "concept concret", elle est de l'ordre du savoir spéculatif lui-même. Or il se pourrait bien que ce savoir spéculatif n'ait pas d'autre régime *effectif* de présentation que celui-là – que l'art, par conséquent. Car sur le registre de la philosophie, le spéculatif semble mal – dans l'*Esthétique* – se détacher, sinon ne pas se détacher du tout, du discours et de "l'abstraction de l'entendement".

Il se peut donc qu'il y ait une contradiction entre la résolution dialectique dans la spéculation, ou dans la "pure pensée (philosophique), et la nécessité de la manifestation (artistique). Il se peut que cette nécessité soit *elle-même* spéculative. Et que, par conséquent, la contradiction don il est question soit une contradiction que bloque, en somme, le mouvement dialectique, et qui *maintienne* l'art là même où il devait disparaître – ou pour dire mieux sans doute: *là même où il disparaît*. L'art pourrait apparaître, selon la loi même de l'Idée, comme irréductible à quoi que ce soit d'autre, religion, État ou philosophie [...]

Ces trois remarques de survol représentent en fait, pour peu qu'on s'y arrête, le programme de toute une lecture de l'*Esthétique*. Je veux dire, une lecture de son texte, de ce qu'il dit et de ce qu'il écrit entre ses lignes, et un déchiffrement de son statut: là où le système, (dans l'*Encyclopédie*) assigne à l'art une place bien *déterminée* (premier, et seulement premier, moment de la triade supérieure de l'esprit, art-religion-philosophie), les leçons de l'*Esthétique* imposent irrésistiblement le constat que Hegel ne peut pas en *terminer* avec l'art. Comme si, dans l'art, un passé immémorial ne cessait de naître à nouveau. [...] Ce passé immémorial, dont le "passage" se répète, serait-il le moment répété d'une incessante *venue en présence*? D'une *venue que le savoir de Hegel ne peut pas, ne veut pas savoir – et ne peut pourtant pas éviter?*

C'est de cette venue, c'est de cette naissance de l'art qu'il serait question dans Hegel et malgré lui. Ou bien, c'est d'une naissance de présence pour laquelle le mot "art" serait encore insuffisant, s'il doit être entendu au sens où Hegel *veut* l'entendre".[53]

In my opinion, the most interesting path of your "struggle" with Hegel begins here. And it is through the *Aesthetics* that it takes place. Is it necessary to accomplish/substitute the word "art" for *vestigium*? In *Portrait de l'art en jeune fille* we find the edge from which Hegel leaned... or perhaps his secret...

> It is the butterfly, the Psyche, which in the sunlight of its heaven hovers even over withered flowers.[54]

J.-L. N.

Yes, I absolutely agree with everything you say.

Let's clarify a little more: before saying that art is behind us, Hegel claimed that our times do not favor it. It is the age of the abstract universal, of reflection, and in short, of discourse. So there is a more or less visible rip between two meanings, if I may say so, of "philosophy": on the one hand it is the "grayness" of the "concept" (where "concept" means "notion," "meaning"); on the other hand it is the color of

---

[53] Id.: Les poids d'une pensée, l'approche, La Phocide, Strasbourg (2008), pp. 39–42.
[54] Hegel, G.W.F.: Aesthetics. Lectures on fine Art, trans. by T.M. Knox, vol. II, Oxford University Press, Oxford (1975), p. 875.

life, and in that respect the Concept has the strongest meaning, i.e., the unity of two identities or substances that remain distinct, even opposed, in this unity. (We can find this explanation on the colors in the *Encyclopedia*—and gray is not really a color but a "simple" overlapping of light and dark).

What strikes me then is that Hegel was the first to speak of our society as rational in the sense of understanding (and not of Reason). He was the first to feel something that soon after him artists would feel too. There is something of Baudelaire's spleen in him. Closely related to this is, in the *Introduction* to the *Aesthetics*, even a critique of the modern artist who wants to isolate himself to escape the isolation of the understanding. I believe that Hegel his thinking of Beethoven, without naming him, because he knows his symphonies (and of course his ninth too…), and Fidelio, rather then works such as his quartets. He therefore criticized a search for meaning in the name of art. (This is only a hypothesis, but there is enough reason to support it).

There is thus a division between the thought of the Concept and the discourse of the concepts. What happens in the thought is only accessible to the thought that communicates—that vibrates—with the copresence of the diverse that art implements. What happens in the discourse does not reach this vibration—even in Hegel's own oral or written discourse.

The same occurs at the end of the *Philosophy of Right*, when Hegel asserted that only philosophy can contemplate the majesty of the Prince, for this majesty is the copresence of the very Idea of the State (I would dare say, without further explanation, of the community) with a contingent individual who is there only through a dynastic contingency.

Not only did Hegel believed that philosophy has no need to direct the future (this is one of the lessons of the Owl), but it can only present its truth—the truth—to itself and within itself. It does not deal with the must-be, but with the being. It lets the being present itself in its divided unity, in its unified division.

Hegel is undoubtedly always in the tension between discourse (which has to be raised) and thought, which precisely raises discourse. This thought escapes the discourse. This is the truth.

This is why I do not trust any question about "what can Hegel bring us today?". Today he can bring us no more than yesterday, in his time, which is no longer ours but which marked the beginning.

In this he also indicated that the same goes for any philosophy: none is available as a discursive tool even though, of course, we can make use of it. Each one is offered as a singular, significant way of welcoming what is and what is not. Otherwise each becomes a kind of art…

D.C.

If today, 250 years after his birth, Hegel is still being discussed, it is because his philosophy, that of the "grayness of the concept," as well as that of the "color of life," continues to propose horizons of meaning to our reflection. As you say in *Le poids d'une pensée, l'approche*: "As the girl raises the tray of fruit to the right of the painting, her gaze turns towards the viewer [Tandis que la jeune fille lève le plateau de fruits vers la droite du tableau, son œil se tourne vers le spectateur]";[55] in this turning of gaze—I believe—the thought awaits us all… and it is not a conclusion….

J.-L.N.
What you feel about Hegel is certainly due to the fact that he was the first thinker of a modernity, which in his time (and in his own home) was rushing, quivering but was not yet in the race forward, which would begin around 1850 and would be felt by Nietzsche and Kierkegaard (by Marx as well, of course, but not with such a worry in his case… a future was already defined).

Yes, the girl who presented the art of the past is a fascinating figure since Hegel perceived her as a living, young, and graceful form, while at the same time he found her in a Roman drawing. Hegel recaptured our whole past—but after him, little by little, this past itself lost its living character. This is why Hegel cannot but be "a thing of the past" for us, even though he was also the first to worry about the "grayness" of universality.

However, in fact, it cannot be otherwise: after Hegel we have had a completely different experience of the past; we really cut loose from him, Hegel and Plato—but I would also say from Nietzsche, Heidegger and Wittgenstein as well. Contemporary thoughts—Derrida, Deleuze, Lacan—all bear very clear marks of these fractures, of the ordeal of these fractures.

But "fracture" does not mean "abandonment": it is another relationship that is being forged with all of our somewhat philosophical, even with philosophy as "something of the past." It is then Heidegger that we would have to deal with. But Heidegger himself has undoubtedly remained, at least in part, in the philosophy he considered to be finished. This is not the place to talk about it, but at least it can be said that Derrida is probably the one who most precisely and effectively dissociated these two aspects in Heidegger.

But neither Derrida nor any other—Hegel or anyone else—can be said to be a resource to be employed (Whether it can be unexpectedly reinterpreted, like Stanislas Jullien is doing, but that is another matter). As you rightly said: "Thought awaits us all" and it bears no name—or it can bear all the names of philosophy…

---

[55] Nancy, J.-L.: Le poids d'une pensée, l'approche, quot., p. 63.

Chapter 3
Ontological Partition

1 The Unfolding of the Body

"I am first the guest of this other: world, body, language."[1] *The guest of this other* is the very experience of bodily existence—as Nancy states several times in his text dedicated to Hegel. There, as we have had the chance to see, the philosopher rethinks the servant-master relationship not to enclose it within a dialectic of the negative, but rather to open it up to the singular constitution that every other—being an other—shares. From the deconstruction of the paradigm of the subject—raised by Nancy's critique of the Cartesian *ego cogito*—to the analyses carried out on the other as the inoperative outside standing out against the sense of the inside, we are led to the place where precisely the inside/outside of existence unfolds and is exposed, namely the body.

Thus, it is no coincidence that Nancy addresses the question of the other[2] by undertaking an involutional path (so to speak), or better, a path in which the other presents itself in the guise of an outside (my body) that is simultaneously an inside (it is from my body that I access the outside and it is inside my body that my existence unfolds). To think of the body as a constant fluctuation between inside and

---

[1] Nancy, J.-L., Hegel. The Restlessness of the Negative, quot., p. 57.
[2] The "question of the other" is, for all intents and purposes, today a minefield, a "rough territory"that—to quote P. A. Rovatti—"has always inhabited philosophy but today concerns any kind of knowledge and even any social practice. Thus, "whether it is the stranger outside us or the foreign part within ourselves, the 'other' cannot be suppressed by an intellectual expedient nor can it be reduced by assimilation to just a variant of the 'same.'" The 'other' remains an other, a difference, an elsewhere, a 'there' which is never completely attainable. [...] Otherness always remains parasitic, improper." The reference is taken from the Foreword to the volume—edited by P. A. Rovatti, entitled Scenari dell'alterità, Bompiani, Milan (2004), pp. 7–8. On this topic see also, again by Rovatti, P. A.: Abitare la distanza. Per un'etica del linguaggio, Feltrinelli, Milan (1994).

© The Author(s), under exclusive license to Springer Nature Switzerland AG 2024
D. Calabrò, *The Thought Awaits Us All*,
https://doi.org/10.1007/978-3-031-75401-2_3

outside, to think of both its immunization and contamination,[3] and to think of it as the very unfolding of the skin, viscera, limbs, and senses, means to experience the other. The "corporeal," as a constitutive medium, draws an inner/outer line, as if to say a double that escapes the objectivist and conscientialist grasp. There, the transparency of the cogito touches its limits and the thought sinks—as Merleau-Ponty would say—into the sensibility of the flesh. This is precisely the point from which we must start over in order to understand the change of meaning marked by Nancy to the concept of "body."

However, before delving into Nancy's reflection, it is appropriate for us to focus on Husserl's "fundamental research concerning the phenomenological origin of corporeality"[4]—contained in the manuscript D 17 entitled *Grundlegende Untersuchungen zum phànomenologischen Ursprung der Ràumlichkeit der Natur.*[5] Indeed, this is where we can glimpse how the original relationship between the self and the world[6] unfolds and makes sense from the reconsideration of the concept of Nature as soil (Boden) and as body (*Leib* and not *Körper*).

From the very first lines of Husserl's manuscript, a key point becomes quite clear: the whole of Nature—as Husserl writes—is not given "as perfectly conceived but as a horizon already implicitly formed."[7] This assertion, which—as we shall see shortly—marked the break from the traditional representation of the world, echoes in one of the last courses held by Merleau-Ponty at the Collège de France. These are the words of the French philosopher:

> For the Copernican human, the world contains only "bodies" (Korper). Through meditation we must again learn of a mode of being whose conception we have lost, the being of the 'ground' (Boden), and that of the earth first of all — the earth where we live, that which is this side of rest and movement being the ground from which all rest and all movement break

---

[3] On the issues related to contaminations/immunizations of/by bodies—furthermore, also in dialogue with issues addressed by Nancy himself—see the important work by Esposito, R.: Immunitas. The Protection and Negation of Life, transl. by Z. Hanafi, Polity Press, Cambridge (2011), and the chapters II and V of the book by Esposito, R.: Bios. Biopolitics and Philosophy, transl. by T. Campbell, Minnesota Press, Minneapolis (2008).

[4] The expression takes up part of a note placed in the epigraph of Husserl's manuscript dated 1934, preserved in the Husserl archives in Leuven and registered as D 17. The manuscript in question was transcribed in the late 1930s by Landgrebe, L., and was later published under the title Grundlegende Untersuchungen zum phänomenologischen Ursprung der Räumlichkeit der Natur, in the volume edited by M. Farber, Philosophical essays in memory of Edmund Husserl, Harvard UniPress, Harvard (1940). The Italian translation edited by G.D. Neri, containing also a nice introduction, is entitled Rovesciamento della dottrina copernicana nell'interpretazione della corrente visione del mondo, "aut aut," 245, 1991, pp. 3–18.

[5] See above.

[6] This relationship, on closer inspection, was the focus of investigations throughout the Twentieth Century in the fields of philosophical anthropology, biology, medicine, physics, and psychology. Suffice it to think of the research works carried out by Scheler, Plessner, Uexkull, Goldstein, Straus, Weizsäcker, Einstein, Planck, Schroedinger, Köhler, Koffka, Bühler, and Vigotski.

[7] See Husserl, E.: Foundational Investigations of the Phenomenological Origin of the Spatiality of Nature, 1934, in McCormick, Peter & Elliston, Frederick A. (eds.), Husserl, Shorter Works. University of Notre Dame Press, Notre Dame (1981), p. 222.

away, which is not made out of *Kòrper* being the "source" from which they are drawn through division, being the source which has no "place," being that which lifts all particular beings out of nothingness, as Noah's Ark preserved the living creatures from the Flood. There is a kinship between the being of the earth and that of my body (*Leib*) which it would not be exact for me to speak of as moving since my body is always at the same distance from me. This kinship extends to others, who appear to me as other bodies, to animals, whom I understand as variants of my embodiment, and finally even to terrestrial bodies since I introduce them into the society of living bodies when saying, for example, that a stone 'flies.' To the degree that I adopt the Copernican constitution of the world, I leave my starting situation; I pretend to be an absolute observer, forgetting my terrestrial roots which nevertheless nourish everything else, and I come to consider the world as the pure object of an infinite reflection before which there are only objects which can be substituted for one another. But such an idealization cannot provide its own foundation, and the sciences of the infinite are experiencing a crisis. The type of being which our experience of the earth and the body reveals to us is no curiosity of external perception but has a philosophical signification. Our implantation envelops a view of space and temporality, a view of natural causation, of our "territory." It envelops an *Urhistorie* which binds all existing or possible societies insofar as they all inhabit the same "earthly" space, in the broadest sense, and finally it contains a philosophy of the world as *Offenheit der Umwelt,* in opposition to the "represented" infinite of the classical sciences of nature.[8]

Hence, here "the nonobjectifiable objects"-which in the DI7 manuscript correspond to the terms *Erde* and *Leib*—bend to become mere *correlates*—namely, "joints" and "membranes" of being. More precisely, the question revolves around the possibility of describing the communication between the body Husserlianly redeemed to *Leib*—a lived unity of perception and motion—and Nature acknowledged also as "an enigmatic object, an object that is not an object at all," since "it is really set up in front of us. It is our soil (sol), not what is in front of us, facing us, but rather, that which carries us."[9] In other words, as Merleau-Ponty adds, we can say that "If Nature is not an object of thought, that is, a simple correlate of a thought, it is decidedly not a subject either, and for the same reason: its opacity, its enveloping. It is an obscure principle."[10] It is precisely because it is an obscure principle that it is not possible to pin Nature down to the categories of substance, accident, cause, end, power, object-act, and subject. In other words—as Husserl himself would say—it is not possible to carry out a "rigorous" study around the concept of Nature from the so-called "matter of facts" that characterize modern science.[11]

---

[8] Merleau-Ponty, M.: Husserl at the Limits of Phenomenology, edited by L. Lawlor and B. Bergo, Northwestern University Press, Evanston, Illinois (2002), pp. 9–10. See also, in this regard, the essay entitled Il filosofo e la sua ombra, almost contemporary with the course mentioned above, later published in Segni, it. transl. by G. Alfieri; Il Saggiatore, Milan (1967), pp. 211–235, the conclusion of which highlights the extremity of thought reached by Husserl.

[9] Id.: Nature. Course Notes from the College de France, Compiled by D. Seglard, transl. by R. Vallier, Northwestern University Press, Evanston, Illinois (2003), p. 4.

[10] Therein, p. 120.

[11] Cf. Husserl, E.: The crisis of European sciences and transcendental phenomenology, transl. by D. Carr, Northwestern University Press, Evanston (1970). See especially pp. 4–18.

Herein lies the stake of philosophy[12] in being able to subvert the "natural" framework of Western culture. Natural because precisely—as previously mentioned—it is grafted within a metaphysical-ontological process that has turned Nature into the place of geometric definition of being. In opposition to such a definition space within which Nature lies, and in the wake of the Twentieth Century scientific revolution, which succeeded in dismantling deterministic and finalistic regrets built up by Newtonian physics, Merleau-Ponty wants to leave behind the so-called "natural laws" regulating the world according to the universal and necessary principle embedded within them. Such "universal natural laws," in fact, are anything but "laws of nature," in the sense of laws dictated by nature; rather, they are laws that modern scientific knowledge has set within nature from the outside, actually concealing the unnaturalness of experimental procedures. Nature becomes the object of analysis of the *Subject-Kosmotheoròs*, an absolute spectator. This is undoubtedly too far from Merleau-Ponty's vision: thinking and speaking of Nature "without explaining it."[13]

It would need to be "unfolded," as Nancy would say a few decades later—meaning by that word the internal/external movement of introflexion and extroversion from which the world unravels—as we shall see later. Therefore, is this the "residue" of Nature of which Merleau-Ponty speaks, its "grey zone"[14]? It would seem so. Indeed, it is from the perspective of a residual condition that—pursuing Merleau-Ponty's philosophical reflection again:

> Things are no longer there simply according to their projective appearances and the requirements of the panorama, as in Renaissance perspective; but on the contrary upright, insistent, flaying our glance with their edges, each thing claiming an absolute presence which is not compossible with the absolute presence of other things, and which they nevertheless have all together by virtue of a configurational meaning which is in no way indicated by its 'theoretical meaning'. Other persons are there too (they were already there along with the simultaneity of things). To begin with they are not there as minds, or even as "psychisms", but such for example as we face them in anger or love—faces, gestures, spoken words to which our own respond without thoughts intervening, to the point that we sometimes turn their words back upon them even before they have reached us, as surely as, more surely than, if we had understood—each one of us pregnant with the others and confirmed by them in his body. This baroque world is not a concession of mind to nature; for although meaning is everywhere figurative, it is meaning which is at issue everywhere.[15]

It is a sense that folds and unfolds in an oscillation that traces a movement, a rhythm, a fall or, in a word, a turning. The world, as well as our bodies, is naturally turned to, turned toward, in a kind of dispossession that continually exceeds its

---

[12] On the stake of philosophy and the risk inherent in it, see the volume by Rovatti, P.A.: La posta in gioco. Heidegger, Husserl, il soggetto, Bompiani, Milan (1987).

[13] Carbone, M.: Presentazione in Merleau-Ponty, M.: La natura. Lezioni al Collège de France (1956–1960); Raffaello Cortina, Milan 1996, p. 22.

[14] Merleau-Ponty M.: Nature. Course Notes from the College de France, quot. p. 109.

[15] Id., Signs, quot., p. 181.

geometric contours.[16] Thus, the process of rectifying nature, established by Euclidean logic, comes to be challenged; what arises is the sense of a research fully aimed at grasping, among "the sprouts and brushwood of the everyday spectacle,"[17] the intimate co-belonging of the Earth as Boden and the Kòrper as Leib, i.e., of an ambiguous, indirect, allusive world precisely because it springs, or rather originates, from a movement of implication, refraction, retraction, subtraction.[18]

It is by following this line of thought that Merleau-Ponty leads us to reflect on the ontological meaning of corporeality according to which "[...] the thing is the correlate of my body and, more generally, of my existence of which my body is merely the stabilized structure."[19] Subject and object, consciousness and world, body and things undergo a deep reinterpretation at this point: the synthesis of the object is achieved through the synthesis of the body proper, and this synthesis does not take place between two external elements—one being the subject, the other the object—but is accomplished in every moment of the relational movement of existence. Moreover, from all that has been said so far, we can see that the concept of "knowledge" turns out to be completely reset: we "know" not despite our body, but because of our body. In other words, our finitude is exactly that for which we "know." The body drags the intentional threads binding it to the surrounding world. It is the latent horizon of our experience, constantly present before any determinate thought, and it is what reveals to us both the perceiving subject and the perceived world. In the very depths of the body, we can find the perceptive life as the medium connecting the body to the pre-individual feeling, to the physiological and somatic life of others; a life that sinks into sexuality, nourishment, sleep, into a hidden and purposeful shared feeling, into an *allowing* and thus a *coexisting*. Each body, each "Ego" feels the other body, the other self, insofar as—just like it—it lives the life of sensibility, of dreaming, of waking, of nurturing, in a common involvement within an original horizon of meaning. Therefore, the body is not a duplicate of consciousness, but it is consciousness itself; it is not one of the means by which we relate to the world, but it is the only way to access it. The phenomenological subject would not be consciousness if it were not inherent in a body, if it were not a body, or in other words, identified in a historical situation that it experiences firsthand as an original and inalienable starting point.

In other words, it is necessary to think about "the double inscription outside and inside"[20] of the body. The dialectic *du dedans et du debors*—on which we need to

---

[16] On this topic, we refer to the interesting volume by Leoni F.: Del corpo, del mondo, del ritmo. ETS. Pisa (2005).

[17] Merleau-Ponty, M.: Notes de cours 1959–1961, Gallimard, Paris (1996), p. 56 (my translation).

[18] On the themes of subtraction and retraction see the volume by Nancy, A finite thinking, within which, in a particularly consonant way with respect to Merleau-Ponty's perspective, the author deals with issues related to the abandonment of the imposing and "calculating thinking".

[19] Merleau-Ponty, M.: Phenomenology of Perception, transl. by C. Smith, Routledge, London-New York (2002), p. 334.

[20] Id.: The Visible and the Invisible: Followed by Working Notes, transl. by A. Lingis, Northwestern University Press, Evanston, Illinois (1968), p. 261.

dwell in order to fully understand Nancy's consequent detachment from Merleau-Ponty's phenomenological/ontological proposal—represents the full extent of Merleau-Ponty's reflection and covers all its stages. The analyses of oppositional figures (exteriority/interiority, body/soul, man/world, figure/background, sense/nonsense, visible/invisible, philosophy/nonphilosophy) have one specific aim, which is the search for a *"Being in indivision"*[21] in *promiscuity*[22] in *overlapping*[23] which is always in such a relationship of *conjunction, adherence, belonging* that allows no *overlook* or *fusion,* but—simultaneously—it grants *distance* and *proximity:*

> Consider the right, the left: these are not simply contents within a relational spatiality (i.e. positive): they are not parts of space (Kant's reasoning is valid here: the whole is primary), they are total parts, cuts in an encompassing, topological space. Consider the two, the pair, this is not two acts, two syntheses, it is a fragmentation of being, it is a possibility for separation (two eyes, two ears: the possibility for discrimination, for the use of the diacritical), it is the advent of difference (on the ground of resemblance therefore, on the ground of the "ομου ην παντα".[24]

Thus, it is not a matter of a rediscovered immediacy, of a real merging, but of a merely partial coincidence, of a "coincidence from afar," of a constitutive gap that incessantly differentiates into "from inside" and "from outside." A reversibility which is unfinished by essence, "always imminent and never realized in fact."[25] Indeed, "its realization would mean the loss of the world, the closure in an inside without an outside."[26]

In other words, and continuing Merleau-Ponty's intensive analysis, the privileged site of the metamorphic experience of inside-out and outside-in is—as mentioned at the beginning—the body, understood now as the "carnal junction" between self and world. In fact, while the body is that which is always on my side, it is also that which is on the side of others, exposing both itself and myself.

> The body catches itself from the outside, [...] it tries to touch itself while being touched, and initiates 'a kind of reflection' which is sufficient to distinguish it from objects, of which I can indeed say that they 'touch' my body, but only when it is inert, and therefore without ever catching it unawares in its exploratory function.[27]

---

[21] Therein, p. 218.
[22] Therein, p. 253.
[23] Therein, p. 246.
[24] Therein, pp. 216–217.
[25] Therein, p. 147.
[26] Cf. Dastur, F.: Merleau-Ponty et la pensée du dedans, in Vv.Aa., Merleau-Ponty, phénoménologie et experiences. Edited by M. Richir & E. Tassin, Millon, Grenoble, (1992), pp. 50–51.
[27] Merleau-Ponty, M.: Phenomenology of perception, quot., p. 107.

1 The Unfolding of the Body

In taking up Husserl's words[28] and moving forward with the reflection on the singular phenomenon of the touching hands, Merleau-Ponty further deepens the investigation of corporeality. Again, in *Phenomenology of Perception*, we can read:

> My body, it was said, is recognized by its power to give me 'double sensations': when I touch my right hand with my left, my right hand, as an object, has the strange property of being able to feel too. [...] in passing from one rôle to the other, I can identify the hand touched as the same one which will in a moment be touching. In other words, in this bundle of bones and muscles which my right hand presents to my left, I can anticipate for an instant the integument or incarnation of that other right hand, alive and mobile, which I thrust towards things in order to explore them.[29]

In the phenomenon of the touching hands,[30] the body doubles, and at the same time, chiasmatically wraps itself in the active/passive imminence of reversibility:

> My left hand is always on the verge of touching my right hand touching the things, but I never reach coincidence; the coincidence eclipses at the moment of realization, and one of two things always occurs: either my right hand really passes over to the rank of touched, but then its hold on the world is interrupted; or it retains its hold on the world, but then I do not really touch it— my right-hand touching, I palpate with my left hand only its outer covering.[31]

In the movement of reflection constituted by the active/passive passage of the two hands touching each other, what remains is an unquenchable gap, a space of absence, a persistent otherness. As if to say that in the self of the body proper abides the other from/than the body. Therefore, there is no longer a *corpus individuationis* capable of separating and separating itself from other bodies, but rather a generic "flesh," an "element"—as Merleau-Ponty stated in *The Visible and the Invisible*— that has nothing to do with the body proper, insofar as every relation of existence is given as a seam and tear of the same "flesh," of the same "pulp" of the world. It is impossible to designate, identify, or locate the corporeal—as extensively emphasized by the philosopher in his long dialogue with Cézanne.[32] In the essential ambiguity of the carnal texture—and it is worth emphasizing here the *inhuman* dimension ascribed to the notion of flesh[33]—the incompleteness and finitude of the human–

---

[28] See, in this regard, the book by Husserl, E.: Ideas Pertaining to a Pure Phenomenology and to a Phenomenological Philosophy—in particular, second Book: Studies in the Phenomenology of Constitution, transl. by R. Rojcewizc and A. Schuwer, Kluwer Academic Publishers, Dordrecht—Boston—London (1989), pp. 63–78.

[29] Merleau-Ponty, M.: Phenomenology of perception, quot., pp. 106–107.

[30] On this issue, see Lisciani-Petrini, E.: La passione del mondo. Saggio su Merleau-Ponty, quot., especially pp. 86 and ff.

[31] Merleau-Ponty, M.: The Visible and the Invisible: Followed by Working Notes, quot., pp. 147–148.

[32] See, in this regard, Id.: Cezanne's Doubt in Sense and Non-Sense, Northwestern University Press, Evanston, Ill, (1964), pp. 9–25; and Id.: Eye and Mind, in The Primacy of Perception, quot., pp. 159–190.

[33] On the inhuman character attributed by Merleau-Ponty to the notion of flesh, R. Esposito rightly writes: "Inscribing the threshold that unites the human species with that of the animal in the flesh of the world, but also the margin that joins the living and the non-living, Merleau-Ponty contributes

world relationship is given. In this way Merleau-Ponty marks the distance from all philosophical anthropology and all transcendental phenomenology; it is precisely this emptiness, this absence, this passivity of the other and from the other that prevents any identification with the perfectly whole and accomplished wholeness. Therefore, the flesh, far from being the *plenum*, the *substantia*, is the unreflection within which man and world *bend*—as if to say, the articulation of the sharing, or rather, of the annexations/expropriations of/from the body. This is a very contemporary line of thought that alludes to the grafts or intrusions of bodies into bodies and that penetrates the webs of philosophical culture throughout the post-World War II period up to the most recent debates in the ethical, scientific, religious, and biotechnological spheres,[34] about which we will discuss in the next sections.

It is clear, then, the huge scope of Merleau-Ponty's work, which—moving from the theme of the body proper to the ultimate theme of the flesh of the world—has opened up a new path for thought. It is a path that—to borrow Merleau-Ponty's famous expression—leads "to the limits of phenomenology."[35] Nancy walks on this threshold, or this edge of thought, and—precisely in order to mark his own advancement with respect to the phenomenological tradition—he makes one of the most powerful attacks against it, including Merleau-Ponty.

As we shall see shortly, the discourse on inhuman flesh, in the theoretical proposal outlined above, takes on the features of a misunderstanding by Nancy—which, in my view, however, turns out to be the only apparent in the end. The flesh of the world, "that butchered, deformed, slaughtered skin"[36] of which Merleau-Ponty speaks, does indeed seem to get very close to the place of the *partition* of Being, a finite and mortal place within which bodies unfold and emerge. All bodies, whether living or nonliving.

> Every thing outside all the others, every thing according to the stretching that spaces them and without which there would be just one indistinct thing gathered into the point at which it would annul itself, a thing untinged, a de-realized res, a perfect, syncopated subject turned back in on itself without its having ever reached itself, an extinct, noiseless trinket, a

---

to the deconstruction of that biopolitics that had made man an animal and driven life into the arms of non-life" in Bíos: Biopolitics and Philosophy, quot., p. 162.

[34] La vita nell'epoca della sua riproducibilità tecnica is the title of the very recent volume by M. De Carolis, published by Bollati Boringhieri, Turin, (2004), which cleverly fits within today's debate on human technosciences, namely the technique applied to the reproduction and manipulation of life forms, including human life. In fact, according to De Carolis, nowadays we need to think about a redefinition of the problem of technique, since it has now become a "technique of life." "The greatest difficulty is that—to quote the author's words—in the contemporary forms of technique, scientific evolution becomes more and more closely intertwined with the various dimensions of social dynamics, giving rise to a network of relations and conditionings of which the theories of the early Twentieth Century could at best guess the outline, but without yet knowing its structural nodes. [...] Technique now invests, reproduces, and optimizes the natura naturans, and no longer just the natura naturata. Yet it is this qualitative leap that distinguishes contemporary biotechnology from traditional techniques." References can be found on pp. 171–172 and 182.

[35] The expression is taken from the title of one of the last lecture courses given by Merleau-Ponty at the Collège de France in 1959: Husserl at the Limits of Phenomenology, quot.

[36] The expression is taken from Esposito's book, Bíos: Biopolitics and Philosophy, quot.

one annihilated without its being dead: every thing, then, touching every part of every other thing, touching me in the same way, piece by piece, here and there, always, from time to time, exposing the infinity of our relations. Things: the first stone that's thrown, a sheet of paper, galaxies, the wind, my television screen, a quark, my big toe, a trapped nerve, prostheses, organs planted or grafted beneath my skin, placed or exposed inside, all things exposing themselves and exposing us, between them and between us, between them and us, together and singularly.[37]

2 Ex-peau-Sition: The Expropriation of/from the Body

In a paper by Derrida, *Le toucher*, Jean-Luc Nancy, an important survey of the latest outcomes of phenomenology in France is carried out, almost bearing further witness to the incidence of Husserlian reflection not only on Merleau-Ponty, but on most contemporary thinkers. Therefore, questions related to touching, to the touch, as well as consequently to one's own body and flesh, become nodal in this text. First of all, the ambivalent relationship of phenomenology with the whole Western tradition deeply fueled by Christianity, a relationship that comes into play precisely in the way of understanding the "body," that is, the "flesh" (and the related "incarnation").[38] Derrida's interest in Nancy can be explained from this point of view, and he intends to break precisely this relationship. In fact, Nancy not only wants to bring the axis of philosophical reflection back to the concept of the "body" again, by progressively depriving it of any residual revelatory path of the transcendent or *imago Dei*, but also marks a real turning point with respect to the other authors who, by privileging the theme of the "flesh," remain confined within the optics of Christianity.[39] As shown in the texts *La déconstruction du Christianisme*,[40]

---

[37] Nancy, J.-L.: A finite thinking, quot., pp. 315–316.
[38] See, on this topic, the major book by Franck, D.: Chair et corps. Sur la phénomenologie de Husserl, Minuit, Paris (1981); as well as—in an opposite direction—Henry, M.: *Incarnation. Une philosophie de la chair*, Éditions du Seuil, Paris (2000). See also the following texts: Watkin C.: Phenomenology or Deconstruction? The Question of Ontology in Maurice Merleau-Ponty, Paul Ricoeur and Jean-Luc Nancy, Edinburgh University Press, Edinburgh (2009); Balibar, É.: Incarnations, Postface in Jean-Luc Nancy. Anastasis de la pensée, quot., pp. 245–246.
[39] On this topic, see Esposito, R.: Chair et corps dans la déconstruction du christianisme, in Vv. Aa., Sens en tous sens. Autour des travaux de Jean-Luc Nancy, Paris: Galilée, 2004, pp. 153–164, and the pages by M. Carbone contained in Carbone, M. and Levin, D. M.: La carne e la voce. In dialogo tra estetica ed. etica. Mimesis, Milan (2003), pp. 11–65; Calabrò, D.: Dis-piegamenti. Soggetto, corpo e comunità in Jean-Luc Nancy, quot.; Recchia Luciani, F.R.: Corpus, Amore, Sessistenza: critica della ragione tattile e ontologia aptica a partire dalla "filosofia del corpo" di Jean-Luc Nancy, in "Teoria", XLI,/2021/2, pp. 77–98 and Ead. Jean-Luc Nancy, Feltrinelli, Milano (2022); Villani, M.: Arte della fuga. Estetica e democrazia nel pensiero di Jean-Luc Nancy, quot.
[40] Nancy, J.-L.: La déconstruction du christianisme, in "Les Etudes Philosophiques" 1998, (4), pp. 503–519.

Corpus[41] and *La Déclosion*[42]—he identifies a pronounced metaphysical and spiritualistic connotation of the concepts of flesh and incarnation, from which it needs to break free in order to achieve an authentic "deconstruction of Christianity" and point to a renewed way of experiencing the body. Therefore, a deconstruction that must go through a new way of thinking, an "ecotechnics" of the body according to a perspective that goes beyond Husserl and Merleau-Ponty's phenomenology. The deposition of the concept of "body proper" (*Leib*)—still surreptitiously understood as a *positum*—is what Nancy strives for. Thus, in Corpus, far from being understood as "proper," the body becomes the place par excellence of the "improper," or rather, of the "inappropriate." In other words, the body can no longer be understood as *positum* but rather *as ex- peau-situm*, that is, as skin already exposed to the world. In this sense, Nancy writes that the.

> Body is certitude shattered and blown to bits. Nothing's more proper, nothing's more foreign to our old world. The body proper, the foreign body: *hoc est enim* displays the body proper, makes it present to the touch, serves it up as a meal. The body proper, or Property itself, Being-to-itself embodied. But instantly, always, the body on display is foreign, a monster that can't be swallowed. We never get past it, caught in a vast tangle of images stretching from Christ musing over his unleavened bread to Christ tearing open his throbbing, blood-soaked Sacred Heart. This, this … this is always too much, or too little, to be that. And all thoughts of the "body proper," laborious efforts at reappropriating what we used to consider, impatiently, as "objectified" or "reified," all such thoughts about the body

---

[41] Id.: Corpus, Fordham University Press, New York (2008).

[42] Id.: La Déclosion. (Déconstruction du christianisme I), Galilée, Paris (2005). On the themes related to the Deconstruction of Christianity, particular attention should be given to the following textes: Alexandova, A., Devisch, I., Kate, T.L., Rooden V. A., Re-opening the question of religion: Dis-enclosure of religion and modernity in the philosophy of Jean-Luc Nancy, Preface in Re-treating Religion. Deconstructing Christianity with Jean-Luc Nancy, (A. Alexandrova, I. Devisch, L. T. Kate, and A. van Rooden, eds.), Fordham University Press, New York, (2012) pp. 22–42; James, I.: Incarnation and Infinity, in Re-treating Religion. Deconstructing Christianity with Jean-Luc Nancy, quot., pp. 246–250; Kate L.Ten.: God Passing by: Presence and Absence in Monotheism and Atheism, in Re-treating Religion. Deconstructing Christianity with Jean-Luc Nancy, quot., pp. 132–144; Kate L.Ten.: The impossible encounter. Creation, Incarnation, Trynity and Miracle in Nancy and Pontormo, in "Shift. International Journal of Philosophical Studies", 2–2021/1–2022, pp. 89–104; Kesel de M.: Deconstruction or Destruction? Comments on Jean-Luc Nancy's Theory of Christianity, in Re-treating Religion. Deconstructing Christianity with Jean-Luc Nancy, quot., pp. 63–79; Liviana Messina A.: Apocalypse et croyance en ce monde. Monde, finitude et christianisme chez Nancy et Blanchot, in J. Lèbre, J. Rogozinski, Jean-Luc Nancy. Penser la mutation, Presses Universitaires de Strasbourg, Strasbourg, (2017), pp. 153–168; Loose, D.: (2012), The excess of Reason and the return of religion: Transcendence of Christian Monotheism in Nancy's Dis-enclosure, in Re-treating Religion. Deconstructing Christianity with Jean-Luc Nancy, quot., pp. 163–181; Maia, T.: Dieu exsangue—Le Caravage et la Résurrection, in Jean-Luc Nancy. Anastasis de la pensée, quot., pp. 165–174; Manchev B.: Ontology of Creation: The Onto-aisthetics of Jean-Luc Nancy, in Re-treating Religion. Deconstructing Christianity with Jean-Luc Nancy, quot., pp. 261–274; Mohan, S.: Decostruzione e anástasis, in "Post-filosofie", n° 15, pp. 129–135; Mohan, S.: Déconstruction et Anastasis, in Jean-Luc Nancy. Anastas de la pensée, quot., pp. 27–32; Raffoul F.: The self-Deconstruction of Christianity, in Re-treating Religion. Deconstructing Christianity with Jean-Luc Nancy, quot., pp. 46–62; Rooden, van A.: «My God, my God, why hast Thou forsaken me? » Demytologized Prayer; or the Poetic Invocation of God, in Re-treating Religion. Deconstructing Christianity with Jean-Luc Nancy, quot., pp. 189–202.

proper are comparably contorted: in the end, they only expel the thing we desired. The anxiety, the desire to see, touch, and eat the body of God, to be that body and be nothing but that, forms the principle of Western (un)reason. That's why the body, bodily, never happens, least of all when it's named and convoked. For us, the body is always sacrificed: eucharist. If *hoc est enim corpus meum* says anything, it's beyond speech. It isn't spoken, it's exscribed-with bodily abandon.[43]

This is where the whole of Nancy's reflection on the deconstruction of Christianity[44] and the consequent question regarding the resurrection of the flesh rightfully finds its place. Indeed, the *levée du corps* reveals an unavoidable paradox: the presence of a body—that of Christ—which is both human and divine at the same time, or rather, the presence of a tangibility that is very far from the sensible; *noli me tangere* is precisely the actual impossibility, an interdiction, a lack of, a *discard of*. It is a subtracted body—that of Christ, a body stolen from the human and which nevertheless accesses the divine just as a body. In *Noli me tangere*, we discover an impasse that reveals the expropriation from/of the body of Christ and can be effectively summarized by the two main evangelical propositions: *hoc est corpus meum* on the one hand, and *noli me tangere* on the other. Nancy goes straight to the point by analyzing the episode—repeatedly taken up as a theme in Christian iconography—of the *Noli me tangere* found in the fourth Gospel, known as John's Gospel. The Risen Christ appears to the Magdalene who, after recognizing him, reaches out to touch him. However, and herein lies all the strangeness of the gesture, Christ evades that touch—"*noli me tangere*." An entirely contrasting request to that of the Last Supper, in which Christ invites the apostles—his fellow diners—to eat his body and drink his blood—*hoc est corpus meum*, from which the rite of the Eucharist will be taken—as a pledge of eternal life. On the one hand, the body of Christ is converted into bread and wine (and thus is made humanly tangible); on the other hand, at the moment of the resurrection, it is made inviolable and untouchable; the tangible presence must vanish, slip into absence, into the non-tangible.

> But this point is precisely the point where touching does not touch and where it must not touch in order to carry out its touch […] Christ expressly rules out the touching of his arisen body {son corps ressuscite\ . At no other moment had Jesus either prohibited a touch or refused to let someone touch him. Here, though, on Easter morning and at the time of his first appearance, he suppresses or prevents Mary Magdalene's gesture. What must not be touched is the arisen body. We could just as well understand that it must not be touched

---

[43] Nancy, J.-L.: Corpus. quot., pp. 5–7.
[44] "With deconstruction of Christianity", as Nancy writes, "I am attempting to designate a movement that would be both an analysis of Christianity–from a position presumed to be beyond it –as well as the displacement, with modifications, proper to Christianity, itself moving beyond itself, inclining toward resources (ones to which it gives access) that it both conceals and recuperates. It is essentially a matter of the following: not only does Christianity detach and exempt itself from the strictly religious, but it also marks out intaglio, beyond itself, the place of what will finally have to abandon the simplistic alternative of theism or atheism. In fact, this deconstruction is at work, in various modalities, throughout the monotheism of the "Religions of the Book" as a whole. This work always corresponds to the following: the "One" god is no longer precisely "one god." The quote is taken from Nancy, J.-L.: Noli Me Tangere: On the Raising of the Body. New York: Fordham University Press, 2009, note 4, p. 108.

because it cannot be: it is not to be touched. Yet that does not mean that it is an ethereal or immaterial, a spectral or phantasmagoric body. What follows in the text, to which we shall return, clearly shows that this body is tangible. But it does not present itself as such here. Or rather, it slips away from a con¬ tact that it could have allowed. Its being and its truth as arisen are in this slipping away, in this withdrawal that alone gives the measure of the touch in question: not touching this body, to touch on [*toucher a*] its eternity. Not coming into contact with its manifest presence, to accede to its real presence, which consists in its departure.[45]

The resurrected body, according to Nancy, is not a symbol of victory over death and access to eternal life. Death is not defeated, as religion assures. Death spreads far and wide. Christ dies indefinitely, and *noli me tangere* represents the sense of this death removed from the limit of mere death; or yet, it is the presence of an indefinitely renewed or prolonged absence or disappearance. What the resurrection reveals is the inevitability of death. Only in the mirror of absence is our being restored to us for what it is: earthly, mortal, sorrowful, fragile, joyful, fearful, cruel, elusive, indefinable, or simply free. The truth of Christ is thus in his disappearance, in his going away to join his Father—as he himself says. However, his Father is nothing but the absent. Resurrection, therefore, is not a return to life, but is the glory at the earth of death. It depends on the unveiling of the truth of death.[46]

"The resurrection is not a resuscitation: it is the infinite extension of death that dis places and dismantles all the values of presence and absence, of animate and inanimate, of body and soul."[47] In short, the infinite otherness of/from the body, its subtraction from itself is revealed in the resurrection. Instead, a body unfolds this presence by presenting itself, by putting itself outside itself, by separating itself from itself, by dispossessing itself. The body is all in its "highlighting," all in the surface of *exposition*, as in a painting.[48] This is why, at this stage, Nancy prefers to speak of "*ex-peau-sition*."

Ex-peau-sition as the skin that stands outside, as covering, an exposition precisely. Exposition of one's own body to self and other. A skin that represents both an exposition and a covering; a nakedness that declines according to the intimacy of its inside, of its retraction and that at the same time exposes itself to the intrusion of the other as being other than itself. Therefore, there is a sort of

> Something true right at the skin, skin as truth: neither the beyond-the-skin sought by desire, nor the underside that science aims for, nor the spiritual secret of flesh revealed. For us, the nude is neither erotic nor anatomical nor authentic. It remains on the edge of or beyond these three postulations. The truth right at the skin is only true in being exposed, in being offered without reserve but also without revelation. After all, what the nude reveals is that there is nothing to be revealed, or that there is nothing other than revelation itself, the

---

[45] Therein, pp. 13–15.

[46] Cf., therein, pp. 17–19.

[47] Therein, p. 44.

[48] On this topic we refer to Nancy's reflections in his recent volume dated 2005: The ground of the image, Fordham University Press, New York.

revealing and what can be revealed, both at once. It doesn't have the power to lay bare; that is to say, it is naked only in this very narrow place-the skin-and for this very brief time.[49]

Nancy dismantles any idea of exposition understood as full manifestation, elimination of concealment, readiness for grasping and knowing. Superficial nakedness, we might say, or rather, a nakedness that explicates itself, exposes itself, coagulates into a surface image; it is all there, always available. A skin that then stretches, unfolds, folds back into its own surface of *ex-peau-sition*.[50] Almost like the music conceived by Jankélévitch, which is all given in the superficiality of listening.[51] Therefore, it is no coincidence that Nancy, in order to demonstrate in a precise bodily place what he wishes to bring to evidence, turns to the experience of listening. In the latter, in fact, even more than in viewing, that surface existence which is like skin *provoked* on the outside, is realized; an outside that has no meaning, neither as signification nor as

---

[49] Nancy J.-L. & Ferrari, F.: Being Nude. The Skin of Images, Fordham University Press, New York, (2014), p. 2.

[50] On the major themes related to corporeality, nudity, and exposure-body-theater in Jean-Luc Nancy, please refer to the following texts: Ariemma T.: Il nudo e l'animale. Filosofia dell'esposizione, Editori Riuniti, Roma (2006); Calabrò D.: Ex-peau-sition. Dal corpo alla dismisura dell'essere-con, in «B@belonline/print», 10–11, (2011), pp. 41–47; Calabrò, D.: La peau du monde: finitude et existence, in Jean-Luc Nancy. Anastasis de la pensée, quot., pp. 55–64; Carbone M.: Il corpo improprio, in VV. AA., Incontro con J.-L. Nancy, Cortina, Milano (2003), pp. 180–188; Cariolato A.: Posizione, messa in posizione e differenza, in A. Potestà, R. Terzi (eds.), Annuario 2000–2001. Incontro con Jean-Luc Nancy, quot., pp. 189–208; Giugliano, D.: « Non c'è una società senza spettacolo ». Una riflessione su Nancy, presupponendo Debord, in «Shift. International Journal of Philosophical Studies», 2–2021/1–2022 pp. 65–74; Mascia V.: Scenari della corporeità in Jean-Luc Nancy, in "Quaderni di Inschibboleth", n°0, (2012), pp. 67–84; Mascia V.: La messinscena del vivente. A partire da alcune riflessioni su Jean-Luc Nancy, in Architetture del vivente. Studi e narrazioni, D. Calabrò and V. Mascia eds., Le Lettere, Firenze (2015), pp. 153–167; Montévil, M.: Remarques sur le corps, in Jean-Luc Nancy. Anastasis de la pensée, quot., pp. 93–100; Moscati A.: Corpi di nessuno, in J.-L. Nancy, Corpus, quot., pp. 101–108; Pelgreffi I.: Il corpo-teatro fra Nancy e Derrida, in U. Perone (ed.), Intorno a Jean-Luc Nancy, Rosenberg & Sellier, Torino, (2012), pp. 83–94; Piazza V.: Jean-Luc Nancy e il pensiero dell'esposizione, in A. Potestà, R. Terzi (eds.), Annuario 2000–2001. Incontro con Jean-Luc Nancy, quot., pp. 114–126; Piromalli S.: Nudità del senso, nudità del mondo. L'ontologia aperta di Jean-Luc Nancy, Il Poligrafo, Padova (2012); Ponzio, J.: A corpo perduto" tra Nancy e Derrida: il desiderio ellittico della filosofia, in «Post-filosofie», 15, (2022), pp. 136–152; Villani M.: Al di là di paura e coraggio. Tre note sull'esposizione di Jean-Luc Nancy, in «Epékeina. International Journal of Ontoloy History and Critics», 2, (2013), pp. 283–305; Vozza M.: Jean-Luc Nancy e la filosofia del corpo, in U. Perone (ed.), Intorno a Jean-Luc Nancy, quot., pp. 95–102.

[51] As Jankélévitch writes, "Considering its naïve and immediate truth, music does not signify anything other than what it is: music is not an exposé, revealing some nontemporal truth; rather, it is exposition itself that is the only truth, the serious truth [...] As sonorous presence, music could be said to correspond, in its entirety, to the superficial actuality of the process of hearing it. In other words, music could occupy its phenomenal aspect as appearance perceptible to the senses: in this initial sense there would be nothing to look for behind the façade, no conclusion to be drawn, no consequence to deduce; the magic has a natural end since it is its own meaning and raison d'être. Music, from this standpoint, is exactly what it appears to be, without secret intentions or ulterior motives. [...] Music does not say what it says, or better, does not 'say' anything, to the extent that 'to say' means to communicate a meaning." The passage is taken from the book by Jankélévitch, V.: Music and the Ineffable, Princeton University Press, Princeton, 2003, p. 59 and ff.

direction. Just like the music to which we have just referred and on which Nancy himself focuses his attention in one of his last writings, entitled *Listening*. Here, in fact—by overcoming the phenomenological approach, all oriented on the logic of the eye—he finds in sounds, and therefore in music itself, the unattainable and inappropriable place within which its uncatchable nakedness is expressed:

> Sound has no hidden face; it is all in front, in back, and outside inside, inside-out in relation to the most general logic of presence as appearing, as phenomenality or as manifestation, and thus as the visible face of a presence subsisting in self [...] To listen is to enter that spatiality by which, at the same time, I am penetrated, for it opens up in me as well as around me, and from me and me as well as toward me: it opens me inside me as well as outside, and it is through such a double, quadruple, or sextuple opening that a "self" can take place. To be listening is to be at the same time outside and inside, to be open from without and from within, hence from one to the other and from one in the other. Listening thus forms the perceptible singularity that bears in the most ostensive way the perceptible or sensitive (aisthetic) condition as such: the sharing of an inside/outside, division and participation, de-connection and contagion.[52]

Therefore, according to Nancy, it is a matter of making ourselves sensitive to the relational texture to which we are already forever exposed and surrendered ... with no closures or pauses: "The ears have no eyelids."[53] In short, "listening makes us clearly see how the body is always grasped and open on every side in a 'partitioning' produced by endless referrals. This reveals it, far from a property, as the locus of the most radical expropriation from (the) self, insofar as it is dislocated, grafted into a circuit of contacts and contagions that continually 'bend and unfold' it inside and outside itself."[54]

Thus, the reflection on listening fits fully within the "trans-phenomenological ascent" made by Nancy throughout his works, with the intention of "further validating that problematization of the body which he has been carrying out for years and which has marked the beginning of a completely different way of encountering—and inhabiting—the body."[55] In fact, it is precisely listening that succeeds in generating "a singular mode of opening of and within the listener's body, since sound, by resonating around him, simultaneously resonates in him, enters and widens his body, putting him outside himself, creating a kind of cross-reversal—of condivision—between the internal and the external, the inside and the outside."[56] Not

---

[52] Nancy, J.- L.: *Listening*. Fordham University Press, New York (2007), pp. 13–14.

[53] As Nancy himself points out in Note no. 30 of his book cited above, the expression is taken from Quignard, P.: La Haine de la musique, Calmann-Lévy, Paris 1996, p. 107.

[54] Lisciani-Petrini, E.: Noi: diapason-soggetti, Introduction to Nancy, J.-L.: All'ascolto, Cortina, Milan (2004), p. XXVII.

[55] Ibid. p. XXVI.

[56] Ibid. p. XXVII. On the theme of sound and listening and voice, starting from Nancy, it refers to the following texts: Cavarero A.: L'orecchio di Nancy, in «aut aut», 316–317, (2003), pp. 68–76; Lawrence F.: The Art of Listening, in L. Collins, E. Rush (eds), Making Sense. For an Effective Aesthetics, Peter Lang AG, Bern, (2011), pp. 77–86; Lisciani-Petrini, E.: quella voce 'che s'effonde ...di selve e d'onde', in «aut aut», 316–317, quot., pp. 57–67; Matassi E.: "Esposti al suono", in «B@belonline/print», n. 10–11, quot., pp. 159–167; Morazzoni A.M.: Nei margini

surprisingly, the "sound movement" that constitutes the "skin of the real" is unbroken or uninterrupted. Ultimately, it is a movement that once again binds itself to the *ex-peau-sition*—as that which inseparably intertwines the outside with the excess, something that does not allow itself to be absorbed or blocked. It is thus, precisely, that it

> always feels himself feeling a "self" that escapes [s'éch-appe] or hides [se retranche] as long as it resounds elsewhere as it does in itself, in a world and in the other. [...] the "self" is precisely nothing available (substantial or subsistent) to which one can be "present," but precisely the resonance of a return [renvoi]. For this reason, listening—the opening stretched toward the register of the sonorous, then to its musical amplification and composition—can and must appear to us not as a metaphor for access to self, but as the reality of this access, a reality consequently indissociably "mine" and other, "singular" and "plural," as much as it is "material" and "spiritual" and "signifying" and "a-signifying".[57]

In this sense, leaving the self is not an unveiling, it does not mean making oneself fully transparent, but it is a surrendering to existence, to its deferring from the self and thus to the relationship with the other in which only we meet or touch each other without ever being able to grasp ourselves, to enclose ourselves in a stable and unified entity. This nonadherence to the self, this impossibility of presence, which gives way to the ever-new gesture of the introduction, to the event, is what Nancy calls "finitude." However, it is a finitude that does not hold the infinite beyond itself—and therefore does not lean toward it as if it were a perfection or a fullness that it lacks. The infinite is in the very deferring of the self from itself, in its subtraction, but also in its partitioning and therefore in its openness. No "catastrophism or even the apocalypse of a swallowing up. [...] Neither purpose nor end of the world. But perhaps exactly the opposite: unreserved and, in this case, endless existence. Existence: the *Dasein*, the being-there that perpetually returns to its here and now, which means: endless here and now."[58]

The *ex-peau-sition* as nudity shows the excess of the finite: its being endless, unfulfilled, or that "absence of finality" that "all totalitarianisms, all identitarianisms, and basically all '-isms' want to fill with all their might."[59] Here, as Nancy explains, the dimension of nakedness is ontological; a nakedness of being and of thinking-of-the-being, the "undressing" of thought. Undressing does not therefore mean unveiling, manifesting or unmasking oneself; on the contrary, the "undressing" of thought stands for the deposition of its very object, as that in which its momentum settles down, the deposition of the purposes, of the guarantees of logic and, more radically, of knowledge itself. In this undressing of knowledge, the thought shows itself in its character of tension, of mobility, of restlessness, which brings it closer to desire than to a theoretical act. Thus, there is something of passion,

---

musicali dell'ascolto, in «aut aut», 316–317, quot., pp. 85–92; Rovatti P.A.: Cerchiamo tutti un occhio che ascolti, in «aut aut», 316–317, quot., pp. 93–96; Manchev, B.: Le surgissement de la voix, Jean-Luc Nancy, in Jean-Luc Nancy. Anastasis de la pensée, quot., pp. 211–220.

[57] Nancy, J.-L.: Listening, quot., p. 9 and 12.

[58] Id.: La pensée dérobée, Galilée, Paris (2001), p. 162 (my translation).

[59] Therein.

of sensuality and not only of sensibility in the thought that is given as a relationship to the other. A relationship, however, that is no fusion nor reduction to one at all, but is rather the opening up of difference; it is the exposition to an otherness that does not allow itself being grasped, and which rather disconnects identity itself. This is why

> Today nudity has become a relentless motif of thought [...] The preoccupation occurs in different registers, from the horror of bodies thrown onto the charnel heap to the desperate desire to make bodies their own icons, and it always leads us back in the direction of stripping bare and coming undone. This ambiguous proximity is also an opportunity for thought, if: for thought, it is a matter above all else of remaining stripped bare of all received meaning and figures that have already been traced. The nudes of painters and photographers expose this bareness and suspense on the edge of a sense that is always nascent, always fleeting, on the surface of the skin, and on the surface of the image.[60]

Thus, we are still referred back to the dual dimension of "intrusion"/"ejection" which is the nakedness of thought, the "chenosis"—as Nancy writes—in which the emptying of ends and principles takes place. It is not a matter of abandoning meaning, but of seeing meaning in the openness and incompleteness of the present, in its strangeness, in its being never consistent with what we can see or know about it. It is not a matter of going beyond, for the beyond is already here; it is precisely in the instability and opacity of the present, in its inexhaustibility. The dualisms, the oppositions, with which we are used to think, no longer work. The nakedness of thought also means its "detheologization",[61] the abandonment of the gods, or rather of any perfection, or of any reason, any foundation, that comes to fill the gap of the here and now, even when we refer to this fullness as something lost. As it empties itself of knowledge, subtracts itself from itself as an intellectual act, the thought thus does not find mysticism, which reinforces its dimensions, but rather ethics; it becomes relationship, relation to the other, openness of meaning and not its establishment. Nakedness, our subtracting ourselves from each other and from ourselves, is what unites us, binds us and at the same time banishes all appropriation, all identification and all generalization. Nancy seems to say that the relationship is born where knowledge fails, where a remainder (or an excess) emerges; this is the (hidden) place of thought, the responsibility of which is not to reach a conclusion. Therefore, the thought must restrain itself in this nakedness and maintain plurality and irreducibility to a single sense. Just as in Rembrant's *Bathsheba*.[62] There, indeed, we are met with a headless nakedness, open to endless questioning. Not a meaning to be

---

[60] Nancy J.-L. & Ferrari, F.:, Being Nude. The Skin of Images, quot., pp. 3–4.

[61] Nancy, J.-L.: *The Creation of the World, or, Globalization*, New York: State University of New York Press, 2007, p. 51.

[62] Significant, in this regard, are Ferrari's analyses: "There is no response to the letter that Bathsheba holds in her hand and that asks to be deciphered, to receive a sense and an unequivocal response: words fail her. All that remains is the nudity of a wounded and disoriented woman, which becomes the crisis of every "metaphysics" of the sign, every will to hyper-signification, classification, systematization, granting of sense, and manifestation of essence. The question gets lost in the singularity of the flesh. It is the very essence of the nude that is lost. Short of and beyond every essence there remains the immanence of a body, its being there with no answers, totally exposed, and with

deciphered and uncovered behind signs and features, but a truth directly on the skin. Yet here, finally, what remains is:

> ... a skin, variously folded, refolded, unfolded, multiplied, invaginated, exogastrulated, orificed, evasive, invaded, stretched, relaxed, excited, distressed, tied, untied. In these and thousands of other ways, the body makes room for existence (no "a priori forms of intuition" here, no "table of categories": the transcendental resides in an indefinite modification and spacious modulation of skin). More precisely, it makes room for the fact that the essence of existence is to be without any essence. That's why the ontology of the body is ontology itself: being's in no way prior or subjacent to the phenomenon here. The body is the being of existence.[63]

No body proper: no inside, no interiority; *se toucher toi*, "to self-touch you," instead of *se toucher soi*, "to touch oneself." The body is an objection to the self, it is an objection to the appropriation of the body... "a monster that can't be swallowed." The body is atomized, fragmented, pulverized and reassembled, reimplanted, regrafted onto still possible corners of skeleton, in an entirely performative perspective of existence.[64] Profusions of nature and proliferations of technique; this is how all things hang together, this is how they all simultaneously touch and mutually expose each other, in an intangible "grain" that unravels and exceeds the identity image of an immovable Ego.

> A corpus would be the registration of this long discontinuity of entries (or exits: the doors always swing both ways). A seismograph with impalpably precise styluses, a pure literature of breaching bodies, accesses, excesses, orifices, pores and portals of all skins, scars, navels, blazon, pieces, and fields, body by body, place by place, entry by entry by exit. A. body is the topic of its every access, its every here/there, its *fort/da*, its coming-and-going, swallowing-and-spitting, breathing in /breathing out, displacing and closing.[65]

The ecotechnics of bodies mentioned by Nancy is—so to speak—the epochal expression that meshes with the deconstruction of Christianity addressed at the beginning of this section. Hence, in such a view

> "God is dead" means: God no longer has a body. The world is neither the spacing of God nor the spacing in God: it becomes the world of bodies. The other world is dissolved as the body of Death, as Death in Person: a rotting where space is abolished, a pure concentration, crushing, dissolving body into the suave ineffable, crawling with *this thing that as no name in any language*, this beyond of the cadaver where Tertullian and Bossuet, and so many

---

no protection." This passage is taken from the book by Nancy and Ferrari, Being Nude. The Skin of Images, quot., p. 14.

[63] J.-L. Nancy, *Corpus*, quot., p. 15.

[64] Examples of performative medical practices are cosmetic surgery, treatments against baldness, and hormone therapies to reduce the effects of the menopause. As De Carolis writes, "In all these cases, medical intervention is not based on the identification of a pathological state, but on the simple and neutral distinction between different possible ways of being, linked to technically reproducible conditions, which may or may not be desirable with no apparent legitimacy in considering one more or less 'natural' than the other". This passage is taken from the book by De Carolis M.: La vita nell'epoca della sua riproducibilità tecnica; Bollati Boringhieri, Turin,quot. p. 176 (my translation).

[65] Nancy, J.-L.: Corpus, quot., p. 55.

others, make us see the end of the world. An unnamed God disappears with this unnameable thing: he disappears into it, he's revealed dead there, as Death in Person, in other words, *no body*. It may be that all entries into all bodies, all ideas, images, truths, and interpretations of the body, have disappeared with the body of God-and perhaps we're left only with the corpus of anatomy, biology, and mechanics. But even this, and precisely this, means: here, the world of bodies, the worldliness of bodies, and there, a cut off, incorporeal discourse, the orientation, entry, or exit whose sense we no longer decipher. Such, henceforth, is the condition of sense: lacking entry or exit, spacing, bodies.[66]

On these issues, which are as decisive and topical today as ever—given the biogenetic advances which increasingly invasively involve our being and its branches with no solution of continuity between organic and inorganic—Nancy insists on several occasions while never stopping to question the classical philosophers. Moreover, here emerges the "truth" of the deposition of the cogito discussed in the first part of this volume. In fact, at this point, we can see that the barriers posed by traditional thought, which Descartes himself seemed to have respected, are somehow put to the test:

> The early Descartes was well aware of this when he attributed a quite different reality to the union of the two things, from an evidence as powerful as that of the ego (cogito), but from an evidence that is entirely ordinary and immanent to the course of things, from an evidence present on the very surface of the most everyday experience of existence; an evidence that is given without thinking. There's nothing to prove; there's nothing but the test of the real [*il n'y a pas à prouver, il n'y a qu'à éprouver le réel*]. The first and last real, the ground of the real and the ground of the res in all its modes, ultima res, is the identity and difference of relation and exposure: more accurately, it is this identity in its difference and this difference in its identity (and here, in obviously means outside). The two are the same, the same *thing* - insofar as they turn things toward one another; but they differ absolutely-have nothing in common-since relation refers to an inside and exposure co an outside. They never encounter one another; rather, they pass through one another. The fact that one moves in the other, and vice versa, doesn't change anything; they are oblivious to one another and exclude one another as they change roles. All of which means, then, that the "inside" and the "outside" of the World, the self and the outside-the-self, subject and thing, are strangely, paradoxically even, the same.[67]

There is no *self* of the world, no universal subject, no transcendence. The world shrinks, presents, subtracts, touches, and bends itself; it folds into and from its outside, which has no place and at the same time is all the places, because it is the exposure of its inside.

> There is not "the" body, there is not "the" touch, there is not "the" res extensa. There is that there is: creation of the world, *techne* of bodies, [...] topographical corpus, geography of multiplied ectopias and no utopia. No place beyond place for sense. If sense is "absent," it's by way of being here - *hoc est enim* -and not by way of being elsewhere and nowhere. Absence- here, that's the body, the extent of psyche. No place before birth or after death. No before/after: time is spacing. Time is the rising up and absenting, the coming-and-going into presence: it's not engendering, transmission, perpetuation [...] No place for an Other of places, no hole, no origin [...] No place for Death. But places are dead bodies: their spaces, their tombs, their extended masses, and our bodies coming and going among them,

---

[66] Therein, p. 59.
[67] Id.: A finite thinking, quot., p. 317.

2 Ex-peau-Sition: The Expropriation of/from the Body

among ourselves. The between-bodies reserves nothing, nothing but the extension that is the res itself, the areal reality through which it happens that bodies are exposed to each other. The between-bodies is their images' taking-place. The images are not likenesses, still less phantoms or fantasms. It's how bodies are offered to one another, it's being born unto the world, the setting on edge, the setting into glory of limit and radiance.[68]

So is death. Figureless and subjectless. It is not that which stands against life or is expected at the end, and which will place a mortal self where the vital self stands. It is all there, "from the moment that I am 'here,' at once and immediately my flesh and bones, the extension of what exposes me, the *res extensa* that opposes the *res cogitans* only to the extent that it exposes it, exposes it to itself."[69] The locus of death is the constitutive alteration of the self as well as of the whole world. It is to be found where it is: "in things, in the general connection and exposure of things, and so in the world, rather than in the hideous outside of a disfigured Subject (disfigured by the very hope of its transfigurarion). Neither from within nor from without does death concern a self."[70]

Nancy points to death as the very exposition of which all the existing is made up. Therefore, not the final act to which everything would be destined or Christianly consigned, but the absolute exposition of all things in which time stretches or extends, "Cracks without having begun, compresses and breaks open a mass of present with no past, opens wide a moment with no precedent, and bursts out of nothing."[71] The time of death, the mortal time, spaces existence just like the cracks space out the walls: out of nothing. For there is nothing in that spacing but precisely the very exposure of irreducible finitude. To think death is to think such essential, absolute finitude: absolutely detached from all completeness, from all infinite and senseless circularity. Therefore, "not a thinking of limitation, which implies the unlimitedness of a beyond, but a thinking of the limit as that on which, infinitely finite, existent arises, and to which it is exposed. Not a thinking of the abyss and of nothingness, but a thinking of the un-grounding of being: of this "being," the only one, whose existence exhausts all its substance and all its possibility."[72] Death is not the time to come of the end or of the fulfillment of an ultimate meaning, as we are accustomed to think of it from a Christian perspective based on the archeological and teleological circle of the final eschaton. Death is the very exposure of the self, of every self to the other that is always already here, like a crack, like a rift, like the blade of a knife. Understood in this way, death exceeds the sense of the universal end, of the cosmic nothingness by which we would be swallowed up according to an eschatological image of time; it is the infinitely finite death that has already joined or is rather joined to things, like a syncopation, a halt, a partition.

---

[68] Id.: Corpus, quot., pp. 119–121
[69] Id.: A finite thinking, quot., p. 315.
[70] Ibid.
[71] Id.: Ex nihilo. Vacarme, 10, (1999). p. 67. https://doi.org/10.3917/vaca.010.0067
[72] Id.: A finite thinking, quot., p. 17.

This is what thought must strive for, what it cannot constitutively escape: the exposure of the self to the other than itself can only be thought of as the blade of a knife that tears the skin and lays it bare, and literally opens it up. In this very opening lies the inside/outside of our existence. With no secrets; such is the exposition, such is the nakedness.

> What renders itself naked makes itself an image, pure exposition. It is no accident, then, nor a matter of objective, or sensual curiosity, that the image devotes itself to the nude. The image of the nude replays its own nudity each time; it plays its own skin of the image: the complete presentation there in the foreground, on the only plane of the image, of what has precisely no other plane, no dissimulated depth, and no secret. The secret is on the skin (the secret and the sacred). Painting, drawing or photographing the nude always poses the same challenge: how to represent the unrepresentable fugacity of stripping bare, the instant modesty that comes to conceal revelation, and the indecency that comes to reveal the evasion. The one and the other take turns exposing just this: here is a subject in the strict sense of the word, *sub-jectum:* there is nothing beneath it, and it no longer hides anything else. It rests on itself and this "self" is the skin, the thinness of skin and its flesh color. What painting paints when it colors itself with "flesh" and what the photo captures when it takes a "body" is the transparency that plays on the skin, or that makes skin. This is an appearing that makes nothing appear, a luminosity that sheds light on itself alone, a diaphanous touch that allows one to make out nothing but its touch itself.[73]

This is what happens in the love relationship as well. As Nancy writes: "The heart lives - that is to say, it beats - under the regime of exposition."[74] Being offered to the "outside" it exposes and is exposed. In the statement "I love you," the "I" stands as an exposure to the other; not as an identity subject, but as an "I to itself broken."[75]

The heart thus longs for the place of its sameness in the other, longs for this kind of decentralization, dispossession, détour from itself, from the compact sameness of the self. Such a desire "is unhappiness without end: it is the subjectivist reverse of the infinite exposition of finitude."[76] The heart exposes itself to such unhappiness, longs to be splintered by the other, to feel its bleeding scar, to suspend its own sameness, to hold itself within the other, and to end up in the other. But,

> Desire is therefore not merely unhappy relation to the other. In the unhappiness of lack, just as in the satisfaction of possession or of consummation, there is but one isolated side to desire. The truth of desire itself is still other: it is precisely to the other, it is alterity as infinite alteration of the self that becomes.[77]

In this alterity "Love unveils finitude. Finitude is the being of that which is infinitely inappropriable, not having the consistency of its essence either in itself or in a dialectical sublation of the self."[78]

---

[73] Nancy, J.-L. & Ferrari, F.: Being Nude. The Skin of Images, quot., pp. 2–3.
[74] Nancy, J.-L.: A finite thinking, quot., p. 252.
[75] Therein, p. 261.
[76] Therein, p. 263.
[77] Id.: Hegel: The Restlessness of the Negative, quot., p. 61.
[78] Id.: A finite thinking, quot., pp. 262–263.

Precisely because love comes from the outside, it keeps an ever-singular opening with me that is like the alterity of a "blade thrust in me, and that I do not rejoin, because it disjoins me."[79] Therefore, according to Nancy, it is ultimately a matter of indicating in the love relationship a missed transcendence, an impossibility of fulfillment: "love takes place, it happens, happens endlessly in the withdrawal of its own presentation."[80] Here lies the difference between love and desire: in fact, the latter is that which, being lacking in the subject (the subject who desires, precisely), irremediably appropriates it. Love, on the other hand, fails precisely in such appropriation; it is that which does not tend toward an end insofar as it always passes through it, by touching it and marking its limit.

That is why love's ultimate paradox, untenable and nonetheless inevitable, is that its law lets itself be represented simultaneously by figures like Tristan and Isolde, Don Juan, or Baucis and Philemon—and that these figures are neither the types of a genre nor the metaphors of a unique reality, but rather so many bursts of love, which reflect love in its entirety each time without ever imprisoning it or holding it back. When the promise is kept, it is nor the keeping, but it is still the promise that makes love.[81]

Appendix

The Skin of the World: Finitude and Existence

First of all, I would like to thank Divya Dwivedi and Jérôme Lebre and all the other organizers of this volume celebrating Jean-Luc Nancy.[82] With great emotion I am going to briefly draw up his profile, without forgetting that Jean-Luc Nancy, the philosopher of the « democracy to come, » of « singular/plural freedoms, » of « corporeity, » and the « touch, » had the merit of forming several generations of young students to whom he dedicated much of his time during the debates that followed his lessons. All this in a resonant gathering of looks, words, bodies, gestures, and thoughts. In fact, the questions were the ones that always pushed his philosophical reflection further and further, on the threshold, the sense of our finite existence.

In autumn 2021, at the University of Salerno in Italy, he would speak on the theme of vulnerability and care. The idea, once again, started from one of his most recent books, *La peau fragile du monde*,[83] on which the conference would be based,

---

[79] Therein, p. 261.
[80] Therein, p. 262.
[81] Therein, p. 265.
[82] I am refering to the Congress titled "Anastasis de la pensée", held on January 22–23, 2022 in Paris, which was organized in memory of Jean-Luc Nancy. This text was published in French by the Hermann publishing house in Paris in November 2023.
[83] Nancy J.-L., La peau fragile du monde, Galilée, Paris (2020); engl. Transl. by C. Stockwell, The fragile Skin of the world, Polity (2021).

and which—in Nancy's words—aimed to « join to our worries for tomorrow a welcome for the present, by way of which we move towards tomorrow. Without this welcome, anxiety and frenzy devastate us. Yet we would remain stupid if we didn't worry. » We should all be « oriented towards the same concern about what is currently happening to us—we, late humanoids. What happens to us when we ourselves arrive at an extremity of our history, whether this extremity should turn out to be a stage, a rupture, or quite simply a last breath. »[84]

Concern and care are the resonant terms here, and which Nancy proposes to us; in this sense, this « attraction » for care involves us all, like a magnet, like a mineral the life of which seems so far away and distant from us. It is this world that we have to take care of, to worry about, otherwise we « remain stupid, » or inert, frozen. Instead, care is action, an action directed towards something or someone. If we pay attention and listen carefully, it is the original movement of all forms of existence: human, vegetable, animal, and mineral.

However, we cannot speak of care without dealing with the theme of corporeality to which, as I said before, Nancy dedicated much of his philosophical reflection.

Thus, in one of his most important works, *Corpus*, Nancy wrote: « A body is an image offered to other bodies, a whole corpus of images stretched from body to body, colors, local shadows, fragments, grains, [...] tendons, skulls, ribs, pelvises, stomachs, meatuses, foams, tears, teeth, droolings, slits, blocks, tongues, sweat, liquors, veins, pains, and joys, and me, and you ».[85]

In this intense passage, we can find all the sense that the French philosopher attributes to the concept of body. A body that that bends itself—*from body to body*—in an existence that has always been exposed, laid bare, open, and staged.

The existence to which the French philosopher refers is not a possession, nor an incorporation, but rather it is the proximity as such, the imminence and the emergence, the rhythmic, the constant singularity that makes every determination and every consistency of the ego, of the ego cogito tremble, in that original opening of the self to the other self that is the experience of the power of division, finiteness, exposure or self abandonment. It is the continuous breakthrough of every formed, closed-up body, identical to itself; it is continuous birth, agitation, concern, pain and joy, visceral unconsciousness clinging to a body, the other body, and upset time, crossed by slurred speech, smells, and tastes. This in an emergence of skin, lips, and touches that disconnect the dialectical system and are produced in a « *diastole without systole.* »[86] In its continual stretching, ripping and cracking, the skin, the skin of each body, of each ego, opens up to its own dislocation, becomes an « areal » surface, touches the *sublimitas* of a touch that does not touch, of a *body-to-body* that tends to infinity, that stretches to the bodies, that borders on them, continuously exposing them to the limit of the partition. A skin that puts at *risk/saves that of the other*. Thus the existence is the open presence of an image of desire that is always

---

[84] Ibid., p. 9 (my translation).
[85] Nancy, J.-L.: Corpus, quot. p. 121.
[86] Ibid., p. 39.

Appendix

Fig. 3.1 Paul Cézanne, *Afternoon in Naples*, 1872

renewed and always awaited, like the one masterfully offered to us by Cézanne's painting dated 1872, *Afternoon in Naples*, on which Nancy invites us to reflect in another extraordinary and evocative text, entitled: *Being nude—The skin of images* (Fig. 3.1)

> The scene that is shown is a scene of desire. […] The desire to see, to share or to touch the desire that is shown. What is shown, is the caress of two bodies […] One body is lying on top of the other, but as if lightly elevated above it, posing rather than posed, the whole in a fragile equilibrium. They are lying down but also suspended, capable of slipping or of a sort of leap […] Everything here touches and transmits the contact or contagion of desire and its arousal and satisfaction, its light touch and embrace, which is not, however, an interlacing. It is a light touch, with barely any pressure. It is the impression of skin against skin, right next to the skin.[87]

Everything here becomes a scene: « the undone sheets, the discretely erectile teapot, the ewer in the niche, the mirror that reflects and invites us to look at the image of the image, »[88] or rather a *skené* that, paradoxically, returns to its *proskén*. As we all know, in fact, the proscenium—the front part of the theatre—is somehow the outside of the stage, which instead is the shelter, the curtain, the inside, the place from which something is staged, which therefore appears to existence. Therefore, Nancy explains the theatre to us in this sense. Far from being understood as the spatial-temporal manifestation of a deception, of which the actors and the masks

---

[87] Nancy J.-L. and Ferrari F.: Being Nude. The Skin of Images, quot. p. 17.
[88] Ibid., p. 23.

would become conscious proponents, it is the staging of the world, the body of which is placed before us without secrets, without intimacy.

> In front of the intimate shelter, which somehow falls outside of space, into the blind spot, opens the space in which one is supposed to step forward, in which the body pushes itself before itself—for its entire presence is here, in this outside of oneself which is not detached from an "inside" but which evokes it only as an impossibility, as a void outside of space, time and sense. This is how a "self" becomes: a character, a role, a mask, a way or an air, an exhibition, a presentation—in other words, a singular variation of the dehiscence and distinction by which there is a body, a presence.[89]

The image of the nude—as it presents itself in Cézanne's painting and as it always presents itself to us—replays its own nudity, its own image skin each time: an integral presentation in the foreground, on the only plane of the image, of the fact that there is no other plane, no dissimulated depth, and no secret. The secret is on the skin (the secret and the sacred). According to Nancy's indication, in the nude it is shown, from time to time, that a subject—in the strict sense of *sub-jectum*[90]— carries nothing beneath it, and no longer hides anything. The subject rests on itself and the « self » is its skin, the thinness of its skin and of its embodiment. When the painting is colored with « flesh » or the photo takes a « body, » there is a « *transparency that plays on the skin, or that makes skin. This is an appearing that makes nothing appear, a luminosity that sheds light on itself alone, a diaphanous touch that allows one to make out nothing but its touch itself.* »[91]

We are in the dis-closure of our own existence, in the *anarchy* of an indefectible dislocation, in the hyperbolic opening of the finite: breach, tear, caress, mouth, and kiss. And, again, *you and me*. A skin that announces and promises enjoyment through a touch:

> Never abolishes the distance between us, but turns the gap into an approach. Not in the sense of being in contact, but in the sense of being about to approach. Not in presence, but in appearance. Not as a being there, but as a way to go through, to pursue, to meet [...] The touch meets the skin: it approaches it, visits it, and observe.[92]

Here lies the prohibition of all touches, its taboo, but also, and again, its promise; the one for which every taboo pronounces: « *ne me touche pas, touche en moi plus loin que moi.* »[93] The Skin-to-skin is such an impossible big hole to fill, a bleeding wound that finds no healing, and a frontier that does not rival any border.

> The areas are tickled, stimulated, induced to twitch, quiver, laugh and get irritated. [...] They are sonorous, rumbling, moaning, shouting, blowing skins. Skins that rub and mix

---

[89] Nancy, J.-L.: Body-Theatre, translated by S.E. Lindberg and M. Luoto, in Figures of Touch. Sense, Technics, Body, The Academy of Fine Arts at the University of the Arts Helsinki, Helsinki 2018, p. 24.

[90] Hence Nancy's entire critique of the vice of thought that, from Descartes onwards, has only produced identity drifts.

[91] Nancy, J.-L.: The skin of images, quot., p. 3.

[92] Id.: Peau essentielle, "Estetica. Studi e ricerche", vol. IV, (2016) p. 76. (my translation).

[93] Ibid.

their sweat, their humors, their dirt. Skins excited, exaggerated, exasperated, delighted: exorbitant existences, nudities.[94]

All the nudities, all the *peaux*, teguments which texture constitutes what we are, our cortex, are differentiations that develop not according to a gender (male/female), but according to multiple, pluriverse differentiations within the self/of the self, according to those *zonal* partitions that ex-tend (stretch out) every singular existence. An exorbitant existence, which is out of every orbital zone, of every link to a self, of a body, of an ego. That of every skin is an eccentric existence, like a painting that does not reveal, but evokes a coexistence of colors, thicknesses, depths, interweaving, attractions, and intensifications « on the surface of the skin ». It is in this direction that Jean-Luc Nancy's aesthetic ontology moves: it is in the work of art, in fact, that the staging of the body, of its nudity, of its complexion replays, « at the heart of the being, » not a possession nor a revelation, but the « faux bond »[95] that has always mocked the portrayed faces, the silent presences, the figurations of the world: here the vice of Western thought is unhinged. That vice of the thought that, as Nietzsche taught us, should be unmasked by challenging modern subjectivity, since it is precisely within the Apollonian vision of reality that the abyss of the Dionysian opens up. *Mundus est fabula* therefore tells us that the mundus, understood as what is pure, clean, and transparent, is nothing more than a deception, thus precisely a *fabula*. The *mundus* as *cosmos*, built on the apodictic certainty of the Cartesian ego cogito, no longer has « a place to be. » It remains the *cosmos* of a *teatrum mundi* that puts on stage « bodies that meet, distance themselves, attract, repel one another, and reveal one another by simultaneously showing behind them, and around them, the incorporeal night of their origin. »[96] Touches, sketches, subtracted profiles, lost casts, like an « approaching" which is the very exposition of the figures in the scene, the birth and death of every body in the world, the threshold *like* the skin.

Our existences are lived on this threshold, on this liminal edge that thickens its borders and at the same time binds us to itself, because perhaps we ourselves are this edge and this limit. We can better understand this passage by making further reference to another essay by Nancy, entitled « On the Threshold ». Here, the French philosopher makes us approach Caravaggio's masterpiece « Death of the Virgin » (Fig. 3.2):

> So, we have entered there where we will never enter, into this scene painted on a canvas. All at once, there we are. We cannot exactly say that we have penetrated there, but neither can we say that we are outside. We are there in a manner older and simpler than by any movement, displacement, or penetration. We are there without leaving the threshold, on the

---

[94] Ibid., p. 78 (my translation).

[95] Nancy, J.-L.: L'autre portrait, Galilée, Paris (2014), p. 107–109.

[96] Lorelle, Y.: Le corps, les rites et la scéne—des origines au XX$_e$ siècleI, Edition de l'Amandier, Paris (2003), p. 37 (my translation).

Fig. 3.2 Caravaggio, *Death of the Virgin*, 1605–1606

threshold, neither inside nor outside – and perhaps we are, ourselves, the threshold, just as our eye conforms to the plane of the canvas and weaves itself into its fabric.[97]

The scene offers itself, unfolds before our eyes, with no explicit request made by us. In this unfolding we find ourselves already caught and grasped, wrapped up like the velvety drapery that introduces us into the scene, inside it. So we are literally parted—both a « part of" and at the same time « divided from »—in a place that is not our own; indeed, we are in a place that absolutely does not belong to us.

As Nancy said, we are never « in front » of the painting, but it is *en avant*, is « prominent » for our gaze. And this « being in evidence » with which we « enter » into the painting and with which we « make the painting » is the condition for which

---

[97] Nancy, J.-L.: The muses. Translated by P. Kamuf, Stanford University Press, Stanford (1996), p. 57.

the gaze emerges from the painting as « something. » However, in this « coming to, » in this approaching that is the exposure of the figures of the scene, there is our correspondence to what we are required to do: entering and looking at it. This is what we are allowed to and promised in this exhibition of the world. A place of election par excellence, the canvas shows us a sign: unveiling and coming out (of the canvas) are offered to us

> Come and see. Exhaust your looks until your eyes close, until your hands are raised over them, until your face falls upon your knees. [...]. See the invisible, not beyond the visible, nor inside, nor outside, but right at it, on the threshold, like its very oil, its weave, and its pigment.[98]

Here, however, the invisible seems to be death. This is where we are, this is what we do not see: « we are never there in death, we are always there ».[99] Nancy indicates in death the very exposition of which every existing being is constituted. Therefore, not the final act to which everything would be delivered up by destiny or by Christianity, over which time stretches out or ex-tends itself: « it cracks without having begun, compresses and breaks open a mass of present without past, opens wide an instant without precedent, bursts out of nothing. »[100] The time of death, mortal time spaces existence as cracks space walls: of nothing. This is because there is nothing in that spacing but the very exposition of irreducible finiteness. Thinking death is thinking such essential, absolute finiteness: absolutely detached from any accomplishment, from any infinite and senseless circularity. Therefore

> Not a thinking of limitation, which implies the unlimitedness of a beyond, but a thinking of the limit as that on which, infinitely finite, existence arises, and to which it is exposed. Not a thinking of the abyss and of nothingness, but a thinking of the un-grounding of being: of this "being", the only one, whose existence exhausts all its substance and its possibility.[101]

Death is not the time to come of the end or the accomplishment of a final sense, just like we are used to thinking in Christian optics, founded on the archaeological and teleological circle of a final *eschaton*. Death is the exposition of itself, of each self to what is always already here, like a fissure, a crack, the blade of a knife.

Understood in this way, death goes beyond the sense of the universal end, of the cosmic nothing by which we will be swallowed up, according to an eschatological image of time; it is an infinitely finite death that has already come, or more appropriately expressed, that is joined to things, like a syncope, a stop, a partition. This is what thinking should aim to, something from which it cannot constitutively withdraw: the exposition of the self to another than the self can only be thought of like the blade of a knife that tears the skin and opens it.

In this opening lies the inside and the outside of our existence. Without secrets, as is the exposition and the nakedness of disclosure. We have reached the proximity, we have marked the threshold, we have faced a world, its presences, its absences:

---

[98] Ibid., p. 59.
[99] Therein.
[100] Nancy, J.-L.: La pensée derobée, Galilée, Paris (2001), p. 187 (my translation).
[101] Id.: A Finite Thinking, quot., p. 27.

Inside and outside, at once, but without communication between inside and outside, without mixture, without mediation, and without crossing. Perhaps that is what we have access to here, as to that which is absolutely inaccessible. Perhaps it is to this that we ourselves are the access, we mortals. [...] The threshold that we are, we the living.[102]

Dragged forcefully into this opening, into this time of immemory, into this burdensome space... everything weighs here, everything makes one think. This painting exposes « our access to the fact that we do not accede—either to the inside or to the outside of ourselves. Thus we exist. »[103] This is the « monster that can't be swallowed, »[104] to make our own; this is the disorientation, the outside of the thought.

As rightly stated by Esposito:

> Nancy's philosophical path traces the contours and the possibility of a general disorientation. [...] The extreme possibility of doing philosophy in the era of the end of philosophy. If philosophy can no longer be a conception of the world, if it can no longer grant it its own sense or even any other sense, it can, however, constitute the opening of a space of thought in which the world recognizes itself as the only sense. The world - the relationships that it creates, the knots that it weaves, the encounters that it sets free in the grain of a finite existence because it never coincides with itself, always focused on the other than itself. It is this orientation of existence towards its outside - its appearance in the singular plurality of the world - that characterizes Nancy's thought in a constitutively political key. If the sense coincides with existence, it means that we can finally "present ourselves" to ourselves without intermediaries or mediators - to each other, in the infinite sharing of a common experience.[105]

In a multiple proximity of bodies in which the *us* becomes perceptible, it touches itself and offers itself to be touched... the image multiplies, breaks, crashes, rejects itself.

All this entails a radical reflection on where we come from and our path, in short, on what we want to be: « neither places, nor heavens, nor gods [...] dismantling and disassembling of enclosed bowers, enclosures, fences. »[106] It is therefore necessary to establish a « thought of the shores, » a thought of approaching that makes us available to « listen to the stone, » to « preserve the wide spaces » of the open air, to penetrate into the « sound of the night »—to quote Rilke's verses;[107] it is necessary to wait until the western sun has set in order to finally be-with « the space between

---

[102] Id.: The Muses, quot, p. 60.

[103] Therein.

[104] Nancy, J.-L.: Corpus, quot, p. 5.

[105] Esposito, R.: Libertà in comune, an introduction to J.-L. Nancy, L'esperienza della libertà, it. transl. by D. Tarizzo, Einaudi, Turin (2000), p. X–XI (my translation).

[106] Nancy, J.-L.: Dis-Enclosure: The Deconstruction of Christianity, Fordham University Press, New York (2008), p. 161.

[107] Rilke, R.M.: The Book of Hours, Riverhead Books, New York (1997).

one body and another »[108] and « thus regain the risk of the extremes »;[109] we, who may have realized that « this point, this dust, this seed, and this hole we have discovered ourselves to be, as well as this silence, which we call the *big bang*, whose echo haunts our voice. »[110]

---

[108] Nancy, J.-L.: Dis-Enclosure: The Deconstruction of Christianity, quot, p. 161.

[109] Id., Rives, bords, limites (de la singularité), in Id., Le poids d'une pensée, l'approche, La Phocide, Strasbourg (2008), p. 137 (my translation).

[110] Id.: Dis-Enclosure: The Deconstruction of Christianity, quot, p. 161.

Chapter 4
Compearance

1 Philosophy of Touch

> The caress does not want simple contact; *It Seems* that man alone can reduce the caress to a contact, and then he loses its unique meaning. This is because the caress is not a simple stroking; it is a shaping. In caressing the Other I cause her flesh to be born beneath my caress, under my fingers [...] The caress is designed to cause the Other's body to be born, through pleasure, for the Other-and for myself -as a touched passivity in such a way that my body is made flesh in order to touch the Other's body with its own passivity; that is, by caressing itself with the Other's body rather than by caressing her. This is why amorous gestures have a language which could almost be said to be studied; it is not a question so much of taking hold of a part of the Other's body as of placing one's own body against the Other's body.[1]

To begin with a quotation from *Being and Nothingness* is here intended to be not so much a provocation, but rather a consideration of the fact that the "place" of contact, designated by Sartre through the caress, manifests itself once again under the oppositional dualism between *in-itself* and *for-itself*. Indeed, if we analyze Sartre's passage, we can immediately observe that the "contact" 'is not the place of the *with*, but that of the *against*. Hence, the purported relation of existence is again reduced to the instrumental possession of the other and, correlatively, even the activity/passivity relationship lies in the pure desiring power that vanishes, or rather gets annihilated, in the transcendence of the *Ego*. The Sartrean attempt to escape from the logic of finality, through the analysis of the body, can be deemed to have failed. To some extent, it is as if the supposed vanishing of the *cogito* had suffered a backlash in itself, thus affirming again the hegemonic and totalizing madness of thought. Nevertheless, touching eludes thought; as Derrida wrote,[2] its law is

---

[1] Sartre J.-P.: Being and nothingness, engl. Trans. Haxel Barnes, Philosophical Library, New York (1956), p. 390.
[2] Cf. Derrida, J.: On Touching. Jean-Luc Nancy, transl. Christine Irizarry, Stanford University Press, Stanford (2005).

precisely a law of touch. It cannot be touched or be reached by an exercise of thought that unfolds its meaning. In short, touching the "touching" lies in an impossibility that, rather than reducing it to pure nothingness—and thus once again restoring a vision of essence—defers it ultimately to finiteness. Therefore, surely, rather than Sartre's words, we should dwell—albeit briefly—on Lévinas' ones, which highlight, through dense and vibrant lines, the impersonal and finite character of the touching:

> The caress consists in seizing upon nothing in soliciting what slips away as though it were not yet. It searches, it forages. It is not an intentionality of disclosure, but of search: a movement into the invisible. In a certain sense it expresses love, but suffers from an inability to tell it [...] Beyond the consent or the resistance of a freedom the caress seeks what is not yet, a "less than anything", closed and dormant beyond the future, consequently dormant quite other-wise than the possible, which would be open to anticipation. The profanation which insinuates itself in caressing responds adequately to the originality of this dimension of absence—an absence other than the void of an abstract nothingness [...] In the caress, a relation yet, in one aspect, sensible, the body already denudes itself of its very form, offering itself as erotic nudity. In the carnal given to tenderness, the body quits the status of an existent [...] The caress aims at neither a person nor a thing. It loses itself in a being that dissipates as though into an impersonal dream without will and even without resistance, a passivity, an already animal or infantile anonymity, already entirely at death.[3]

Lévinas' reflections lead us directly to the heart of the matter: to touch is to feel, to indicate a sense, to mark a direction or rather a directionality of movement. It is a "*going toward*" that embeds the unreachability of place, and at the same time, the sensible impression of the desired body that somehow becomes a tangible place. It is in this direction of thought that Nancy moves. Indeed, in one of his most recent works—*Corpus II—Writings on Sexuality*—he took up a particularly intense passage from Paul Celan's *No One's Rose*: "le baiser, de nuit, l'imprime la brulure du sens dans une langue," which he commented on as follows:

> The burning of sense, which is also the burning of the senses, each one taking place in or by the other, is what escapes representation. It cannot be understood as a form or a figure that leads to a ground, or means destined to disappear into an end that is a presence without farm, a fusion, absorption, or consummation. Certainly, the act consummates itself and consumes itself: but not in the farm of entropy surfeit or in the symmetrical farm of the gaping impossibility that lies beneath fantasy. The act consummates itself in not ending; it makes neither one nor two, it has no result, it never stops beginning, and it never stops finishing. In one sense it is confined to the simple sentiment—or simple shock- of existing itself: existing that, to be precise, is neither separate nor fused, for those are two ways of missing the true sense of the term *existing*.[4]

Thus in touching there is an impotence, a limitation, a touching without touching.[5] We should then keep speaking of caressing, which, although it cannot be

---

[3] Lévinas, E.: Totality and Infinity: An Essay on Exteriority, transl. A. Lingis, Duquesne University Press, Pittsburgh, PA: (1969), cf. pp. 257–259.

[4] Nancy, J.-L.: "The 'There Is' of Sexual Relation," in Corpus II: Writings on Sexuality, transl. A. O'Byrne, Fordham University Press, New York (2013), p. 16.

[5] On the question of the philosophy of touching or touch in general, see: Caldarone, R.: Il toccare della filosofia. Jean-Luc Nancy, in "Shift. International Journal of Philosophical Studies",

reduced to mere touching, is nevertheless divided by this contradictory injunction, which is no longer completely that of touch: touching without touching, pressing without pressing, more and more, always too much and simultaneously not enough. Discretion of touch… touching without touching: here is the limit.[6] A limit that presents itself—according to Nancy—in a quite singular way:

> The singular mode of the presentation of a limit is that this limit must be reached, must come to be touched. This is, in fact, the sense of the word *sublimitas*: what stays just· below the limit, what touches the limit […] Sublime imagination touches the limit, and this touch lets it feel "its own powerlessness".[7]

In feeling "its powerlessness," imagination touches its powerlessness. Imagination encounters what it cannot encounter and accesses, as such, the inaccessible itself. It tends toward what it cannot touch and thus it touches itself, in a movement of retraction or refolding. It touches itself the moment it touches the untouchable. In what sense and on what grounds then do we say that it touches itself or that it feels itself touched or touching, that it feels itself to be touched or unto touching? What is then the phenomenological, ontological status, the logical or rhetorical legitimacy of what will no longer be called without trembling, once again, the figure of "touching"?[8] These questions that Derrida poses to himself in his volume on Nancy are echoed by three of his essential indications—which we will find a little further on and on which it is important to dwell: (1) In this context, the "touching" is that of the imagination: sensitive presentation or transcendental scheme. The non-delimitable concept of touching embraces, simultaneously, all that the following words encompass: imagination, presentation, sensitivity, passivity/activity, inner sense/outer sense, time/space, intuitus derivativus, and thus finiteness, schematism, transcendence, and so on. (2) Feeling itself as touching will immediately be a "feeling itself" and thus a "touching itself." We have not finished exploring the endless resources of this singular reflection. In the French grammar (being Derrida arguing) "se toucher" strangely folds this sort of reflection depending on the meaning of the sentence. Thus, if we say "s'attendre," "se toucher," the feeling can turn the subject toward itself or toward the other, according to a mutuality that proves easier being said than obtained: "se toucher toi"—as indeed Nancy himself would say in *Corpus*. (3) All of Nancy's thought concerning syncope is, in this respect, taken up again, reread, relaunched.[9] The passage we quote below concerns precisely the "syncopated

---

2/2021–1/2022, pp. 39–48; Devisch, I.: Geraakt zijn. Derrida's Le toucher, Jean-Luc Nancy, "Tijdschrift Voor Filosofie", 62, (2000), pp. 733–742; Introna, C.: Il t(r)atto tra Nancy e Derrida: come restare in contatto, in "Post-filosofie",15, (2022), pp. 90–112; Recchia Luciani, F.R.: Potere erotico e sessistenza: Jean-Luc Nancy con Audre Lorde, in "Post-filosofie", 15, (2022), pp. 153–164; Recchia Luciani, F.R.: Pour une critique de la raison tactile: de la philosophie du corps à l'ontologie haptique avec Jean-Luc Nancy, in Jean-Luc Nancy. Anastasis de la pensée, quot., pp. 109–120.

[6] Derrida, J.: On Touching—Jean-Luc Nancy, quot. p. 33 and ff.
[7] Nancy, J.-L.: A Finite Thinking, quot., p. 233.
[8] Derrida, J.: On Touching—Jean-Luc Nancy, quot., p. 103.
[9] Cf. Therein, p. 103.

imagination," which is configured as that which opens up the experience of the sublime:

> If presentation takes place above all in the realm of the sensible-to present is to render sensible-sublime imagination is always involved in presentation insofar as this imagination is sensible. But here sensibility no longer comprises the perception of a figure but rather the arrival at the limit. More precisely, sensibility is here to be situated in the imagination's sentiment of itself when it touches its limit. The imagination feds itself passing to the limit. It feels itself, and it has the feeling of the sublime in its "effort" (*Bestrebung*), impulse, or tension, which makes itself felt as such at the moment when the limit is touched, in the suspension of the impulse, the broken tension, the fainting or fading of a syncopation.[10]

What is Nancy telling us here? He is speaking of an experience, perhaps of the experience in general, which would consist in this: there is a *"feeling oneself,* " a *"feeling oneself touching"*; thus, a *"feeling oneself being touched."* However, the experience to which we are exposed—as Derrida again highlighted, in close connection with Nancy's reflection—leads us to "feel ourselves touching a limit," touched by a limit, the very limit of ourselves and of every other one that we encounter. What does touching one's own limit mean? It is also a not-touching, a not-touching oneself enough, a touching oneself too much: impossible sublimity of the touch; the machination of love when it imposes endless renunciation. It is to lose oneself in the moment of touching, it is to lose oneself in the moment when, by touching the other, it *becomes the other* and *is for the other*; it is this interruption that constitutes the touch of self-touching, touching as self-touching, which is precisely the syncopation, the interruption, the stop.[11] There is—as explained by Nancy—a *"corpus of touch"* which is precisely a syncopated corpus, interrupted and mixed with other bodies in the

> skimming, grazing, squeezing, thrusting, pressing, smoothing, scraping, rubbing, caressing, palpating, fingering, kneading, massaging, entwining, hugging, striking, pinching, biting, sucking, moistening, taking, releasing, licking, jerking off, looking, listening, smelling, tasting, ducking, fucking, rocking, balancing, carrying, weighing…[12]

Contacts between bodies, *partes extra partes*, contact with the body "that is engorged, engorging on its own proximity".[13] Irreducible gap between body and *Self*, which implodes the idea of "touching" and leads us immediately to a promiscuity of contacts, of bodies, of body-to-body. Yet, regarding the reflection on the caress, the eminent site of a touching that does not touch, of a body-to-body that tends to infinity, the image of a desire that is always innovated and awaited, through the analysis of a famous canvas by Cézanne -Afternoon in Naples- Nancy wrote:

> The scene that is shown is a scene of desire; on the other, the scene of monstration, or the showing scene, if one can put it that way, is the scene of the desire to see, to share or to touch the desire that is shown. This is because what is shown, what both proposes and

---

[10] Nancy, J.-L.: A Finite Thinking, quot., p. 233.
[11] Derrida, J.: On Touching—Jean-Luc Nancy, quot., p. 105.
[12] Nancy, J.-L.: Corpus, quot., p. 93.
[13] Therein, p. 103.

imposes itself is the caress of two bodies toward which we advance through an entrance created by the lifting of a curtain (an anachronistic reference to an ancient pictorial topos) and by the movement of a servant who leads us in behind the couple, catching them in a caress. (Can a caress be seen, other than by surprise?) [...] One body is lying on top of the other, but as if lightly elevated above it, posing rather than posed, the whole in a fragile equilibrium. [...] Everything here touches and transmits the contact or contagion of desire and its arousal and satisfaction, its light touch and embrace, which is not, however, an interlacing. It is a light touch, with barely any pressure. It is the impression of skin against skin, right next to the skin.[14]

Mixing, contagion, contact of bodies, spacing; body becoming space within another body by duplicating it, multiplying it. But it is not only in the love relationship that all this takes place: the body—as Nancy underlined—is also the place of "hybridizations of the self" and modern "therapeutic cloning." Ecotechnics of the body: explantation, implantation, transplantation. Nancy asserted that:

> Our world's bodies are neither healthy nor ill. Ecotechnical bodies are another kind of creature, pressed in on all sides, by all the masses themselves, across and between themselves, plugged in, echographed, radiographed, one crossing another, communicating their nuclear resonances, controlling their deficits, adapted to their defects, outfitting their handicaps, their trisomies, their collapsed muscles, their broken synapses, coupled, glued, mixed, infiltrated allover by billions of bodies, not one of which stays balanced on a body, all of them sliding, opened, spread out, grafted, exchanged. Neither a healthy state nor a sick stasis: a coming-and-going, a jumpy or smooth palpitation of skins side to side, wounds, synthetic enzymes, synthetic images. Not a single integrated psyche, closed in upon a solid or hollow space.[15]

The very mode of our "being body" consists in being absolutely and necessarily *improper*. This impropriety configures itself as "biologically valid." In this sense, the technique applied to our bodies constitutes the *vital* and no longer *natural* passage for the achievement or prolongation of existence. We have definitely become part of a different meaning regime. As Esposito explained, "While up to a certain point human beings projected themselves into the world, and then also into the universe, now it is the world, in all its components—natural and artificial, material and electronic, chemical and telematic—which penetrates us in a form that eliminates the separation between inside and outside, front and back, surface and depth: no longer content merely to besiege us from the outside, technique has now taken up residence in our very limbs".[16] It is very well understood, then, that today's technical processes—those within medical science in particular—are all aimed at grafting and implanting themselves in our very flesh, and constitute more and more the vital basis for our survival (just consider, by way of example, the cardiac pacemaker). We are faced with a "real paradigm shift in interpretation. If in the 1930s the discursive regime on the body attained its ultimate ideological solidity in the concept of 'race', and around the 1970s it was reconceived by Foucault in terms of 'population', today

---

[14] Nancy J.-L. & Ferrari, F.: Being Nude. The Skin of Images, quot., pp. 17–18.
[15] Nancy, J.-L.: Corpus, quot., p. 107.
[16] Esposito, R.: Immunitas: The Protection and Negation of Life, trans. Z. Hanafi, Cambridge, UK: Polity Press, (2011), p. 147.

it must be looked at from the standpoint of its technical transformation."[17] What emerges here, and what Nancy also argued from his own personal experiences, is a total disconnection of the vital parameters and limits of the body, of every body. This disconnection, which represents the interruption between the biological and the artificial, between the vital and the non-vital, between the organic and the non-organic becomes, on closer inspection, the place where all bodies are partitioned. Alteration of the individual body, which precisely, very literally, becomes other. Perhaps "Never before have we had such an accurate perception of this community of bodies—the endless contagion that combines, overlaps, soaks, coagulates, blends, and clones them."[18] Thus, if in the pages of *Corpus* Nancy confronts us with the body understood as alien, foreign, made of an extension that is always singularly shaped, in the pages of *The Intruder*[19] we are introduced within a profoundly invasive experience of bodily partition, that of cardiac transplantation. This experience, lived firsthand by Nancy, is, in the most peremptory and devastating terms, the exposition of the body integrity of the self carved out by the intrusion of the other (the other heart).[20]

> What penetrates the body of the person who receives a transplant, even before the tubes, pliers and probes traverse it, is not even simply its outside. It is the acute point of intersection between several forms of estrangement that oppose and impose upon each other, each challenged, replicated, and, finally, overwhelmed by the other. The first is the estrangement of our immune system from the transplanted organ. The second, with an equal force of collision, is the estrangement of the immune system of the transplanted organ that strikes against our own. The shared line between the recipient body and the donor heart coincides with the frontline in the clash between these two opposing immune systems: one committed with all its power to rejecting the other while simultaneously not allowing itself to be rejected. For this reason, the resistance on the part of the person receiving the transplant must be redoubled: against the protection system of the other and his or her own; against the maelstrom of estrangement and the impossible demand for appropriation. For this reason, even to distinguish between "self" and "non-self" is no longer admissible, since it is not simply the improper that is the intruder, but the proper as well, inasmuch as it is estranged: "Thus, then, in all these accumulated and opposing ways, myself becomes my intruder".[21]

The transplanted heart makes space for itself and, by spacing apart the receiving body, indefinitely divides it; it is there in contact, but in this contact, it expropriates it, exposes it, exports it. The new heart is something from the outside that brings something outside, that replaces the tranquility of the Self, which fights to the death to implant itself in the acknowledgement of the gift:

> Not because they opened me up, gaping, to change the heart. But because this gaping cannot be sealed back up. (In fact, as every X-ray shows, the sternum is stitched with filaments

---

[17] Therein, p. 146.

[18] Therein, p. 151.

[19] Nancy, J.-L.: "The Intruder," in Corpus, transl. Richard A. Rand, Fordham University Press, New York 2008.

[20] See, in this regard, the essay by Adamek, Ph. M.: The intimacy of Jean-Luc Nancy's "L'Intrus", in «CR: The New Centenniallosionc Review», 3, 2002, pp. 189–201.

[21] Esposito, R.: Immunitas: The Protection and Negation of Life, quot., p. 152.

of twisted steel.) I am closed open. Through the opening passes a ceaseless flux of strangeness: immunodepressor medications, other medications meant to combat certain so-called secondary effects, effects that we do not know how to combat (the degrading of the kidneys), renewed controls, all existence set on a new register, stirred up and around. Life scanned and reported onto multiple registers, all of them recording other possibilities of death. Thus, then, in all these accumulated and opposing ways, my self becomes my intruder. I certainly feel it, and it's much stronger than a sensation: never has the strangeness of my own identity, which for me has always been nonetheless so vivid, touched me with such acuity. "I" clearly became the formal index of an unverifiable and impalpable change. Between me and me, there had always been some space-time: but now there is an incision's opening, and the irreconciliability of a compromised immune system.[22]

Hence, the body—a body of none, singular, partitioned, manifold—turns out to be the point at which Nancy brings to completion the journey that began with the deposition of the *cogito* and continued with the sovereignly mortal exposition to the other. What happens to the self? What remains of it? What happens to Merleau-Ponty's *'body-proper'*? The identity subject discovers itself hopelessly partitioned and poured out in a space that—for the French philosopher—is our only, possible community. A community of bodies, which *makes* the body, which *makes* the existence, and which -as we shall shortly see- *makes* politics.

2 "Being-With and Being-There"

> What does it mean to exist with one another?
> What would it mean to live one another?[23]

The twofold question that Nancy posed as the beginning of the volume *La pensée dérobée* presents itself, in some respects, as arising immediately from reflections on the concept of the impropriety of the body and its exposition to the other. The French philosopher's main concern becomes immediately clear from the very first lines of the Introduction, in the question that echoes the incipit with which we wanted to mark the beginning of this paragraph: how do we relate to one another today, in the era of globalization? As Nancy explained, on this question depends

> our relationship to ourselves, to "nature" or "culture," our relationship to the absolute - our absolute relationship to the absolute (to paraphrase Kierkegaard). What relationship is there between us (and then, what being?)? Neither politics, nor language, nor exchange or partition really seem to answer this question.[24]

It is necessary, before answering such questions, which moreover represent the questions of our time, to take a step back and follow Nancy in his direct

---

[22] Nancy, J.-L.: Corpus, quot., pp. 167–168.
[23] Nancy, J.-L.: Sull'agire: Heidegger e l'etica. Ed. by A. Moscati—my English translation, Cronopio, Naples (2005).
[24] Therein, 7–8.

confrontation with Heidegger and his "fundamental ethics".[25] The French philosopher examined three texts: *Being and Time*,[26] the *Letter on Humanism*,[27] and *Kant and the Problem of Metaphysics*.[28] It is precisely in such texts in fact that Heidegger outlined the essential character of the existential *with*. In its definition, Heideggerian *Dasein* implies the constitutive or original property of being also a *"Being-with"* (*Mitsein*). Indeed, Heidegger also introduced the term *Mitdasein* (*Being-there-with*). But such terms, which in fact are at the origin of existential analytics, are left somewhat overshadowed, overwhelmed by terms such as "cure," "anguish," and *"Being-towards-death."* Nancy's intent was instead to take up the places from which it is possible to reconsider *Dasein* to then get to *Mitdasein*—the core, as we shall see, of Nancy's reflection on community. And it is no coincidence that the title Nancy gave to his recent essay, included in the volume devoted to Heidegger's *The Original Ethics*—republished this year—is precisely *The Being-with of the Being-there*.

The French philosopher's first observation was that

> Mitsein and Mitdasein are posited as co-essential to Dasein's essence, that is, to its property as an existent for which Being is not its ontological foundation but rather the bringing into play of its own sense of Being as well as of the sense of Being itself. Therefore, Being-with, and more precisely Being-there-with, constitutes an essential condition for Dasein's essence.[29]

The essence of *Dasein* is in the *da* of *sein*, or better, in its exposure. The exposure to the outside, which is the *da*, constitutes the opening to the world, or rather it is the opening itself. As exposed being, it is originally brought into play. *Dasein* is thus not to be understood simply as a *"Being-there,"* but rather as a *"Being-the-there."* Therefore, to be in the mode of *"there"* means to be, to exist as being exposed, as being open. However, as we have seen, following Nancy's words, *Dasein* is essentially *Mitdasein*. Moreover, it was Heidegger himself who unequivocally affirmed the essentiality of the *with*, meaning the particle *mit* not as the mere contiguity or proximity of things, but the condition of possibility of human existence. But

> How is Mitdasein possible? First, how should one picture it? As the Being-with of several Dasein, where each opens its own da for itself? Or as the Being-with-the-there, or maybe more precisely as a Being-the-there-with, which would require that the openings intersect each other in some way, that they cross, mix or let their properties interfere with one another, but without merging into a unique Dasein (or else the mit would be lost)? Or else—in a third way—as a common relation to a there that would be beyond the singulars? But what would such a therebeyond be? Thus we have in reality three possible modes of the

---

[25] Id.: L' «éthique originaire» de Heidegger, in Id.: La pensée dérobée, quot. p. 88.

[26] Heidegger, M.: Being and Time, HarperCollins, New York, (2008).

[27] Id.: Letter on Humanism, in Pathmarks, transl. Frank A. Capuzzi, edited by William McNeill, Cambridge University Press, Cambridge; New York (1998).

[28] Id.: *Kant and the Problem of Metaphysics*, transl. James Churchill, Indiana University Press, Bloomington (1966).

[29] Nancy, J.-L.: *The being-with of being-there*, transl. Marie-Eve Morin, in "Continental Philosophy Review", 41, pp. 1–15; quot., p. 2.

"common": the banal *Being-alongside* (a common mode in the sense of ordinary, vulgar), the common as the sharing of properties (relations, intersections, mixtures), or, lastly, the common as downmost structure in itself, and thus as communional or collective.[30]

At the two extremes of the threefold mode of thinking the common (the cum or the *mit* in the Heideggerian sense), according to Nancy's analysis, we have a pure exteriority and an equally pure interiority. The first mode, in fact, "seems to fall back into the simple contiguity of things,"[31] (*partes extra partes*), while the third mode "seems to suppose a single communal *Dasein* beyond the singulars."[32] Now, – and here Nancy's critique is made explicit not only against Heidegger but also and above all against his exegetes and epigones—the intermediate mode of conceiving the mit remains not fully explained; it remains, as the French philosopher stated in the following passage, an "*enigma*":

> It is [...] noticeable that Heidegger never attempted a specific examination of that which had at first been undertaken under the terms of Mitdasein and Miteinandersein ("Being-with-one-another"), since the with had been declared essential to the existent's essence (an assertion that nothing in the development of the work can lead us to believe has been forgotten or minimized: Heidegger has never stopped thinking in a collective or common dimension and nothing in his thinking even approaches solipsism). Some will say at this point: that is precisely the problem! He has always been a communautaristic or communional thinker in the hypernational and hyperheroic style that Lacoue-Labarthe qualifies as "archi-fascism". [...] This is true, but it is no less true that no other thinking has penetrated more deeply into the enigma of Being-with, and that during Heidegger's time as well as today, no object of thought remains more unthought than this enigma (which is an enigma exactly because thinking has kept it at a distance for so long). Nowadays, the decline of politics, as well as the re-emergence of all sorts of communautarisms over at least 20 years, are sufficient testimony to a shortfall in thinking regarding this matter. And this shortfall betrays without a doubt a fundamental disposition of our whole tradition: between two subjects, the first being "the person" and the second "the community," there is no place left for the "with".[33]

The *with* thus seems to have been "subtracted,", "hidden," "removed." The "'original ethics" fails to think through to the end the sense of "the responsibility of one's own exposure (to others, to the world), which nevertheless constitutes its authentic logic."[34]—According to Nancy's affirmation, Heidegger remained bound to the very humanism he intended to reject, and the analytic of *Mitdasein* appears in this sense a missed opportunity:

> As much as Heidegger felt with peculiar acuity the necessity of the primordiality of the with (he is probably the first one, after the relation of consciousnesses constituting the Hegelian subject, to aim at this in such a clear way), he himself has erased the possibility he opened: namely, the possibility of thinking of the with exactly as he had indicated, as neither in

---

[30] Ibidem.
[31] Therein, 4.
[32] Ibidem.
[33] Therein, 5.
[34] Nancy, J.-L.: L'éthique originaire' de Heidegger: L'être-avec de l'être-là, in La pensée dérobée, quot., my translation, p. 112.

exteriority, nor in interiority. Neither a herd, nor a subject. Neither anonymous, nor "mine." Neither improper, nor proper.[35]

When the essential *with* is revealed to be destined to the *Being-towards-death*, and when it is caught in the property of the community and not in the impropriety of the itself until it rises—as a people—in a kind of historical superexistence, Heidegger did not question the very destination of the *with* destined to the *Being-towards-death*. And it is in this intentionally eluded questioning that lies the gap between the German philosopher and Nancy. The inclusion of the *mit* "into a destinal unity in which there is no room for the contiguity of the theres, nor consequently any logical, ontological or topological room for the *with* as such"[36] does not allow to think of a mit as an exposition or rather as a "co-exposition can be thought, which would in sum expose itself to nothing other than itself, and not to the hyper-existence of a community"[37] so that "exposition to death would not constitute a sacrifice, but would share between all existents, between us, the eternity of each existence."[38] But then, as Nancy wondered, "How can death between us, or even death as the co-opening as such of the there, be thought?"[39] In other words, how can we think of a shared death?

> Heidegger came very close to this question when, within the analytic of Being-towards-death, he considered the following point: in grasping its ownmost possibility from death as the end of any possibility, the existent "dispels the danger that it may, by its own finite understanding of existence, fail to recognize that it is being outstripped by the existence-possibilities of others" (§ 53). Hence, "death individualizes—but only in such a way that, as the possibility which is not to be outstripped, it makes Dasein, as Being-with, have some understanding of the potentiality-for-Being of others." Could this understanding of the possibilities of others [...] be transformed directly into the "sacrifice in accordance with the demands of some possible Situation or other" that I quoted earlier? Of course, in the context of § 53 "self-sacrifice" was suggested to be the "uttermost possibility," and the mention of the "the potentiality-for-Being of others" follows directly upon the one about sacrifice.[40]

However, as explained by Nancy, this link does not seem sufficiently clear since, first of all, there is nothing in *Being and Time* that designates sacrifice as "the privileged mode of an 'understanding of the possibilities of others';[41] and 'the others,' not being characterized in any way, cannot be identified as 'the people.'[42] So that, in conclusion, between 'sacrifice' and 'understanding,' as well as between 'the people' and 'the others according to Being-with,' a gap remains which is neither indicated

---

[35] Jean-Luc Nancy, The being-with of being-there, in "Continental Philosophy Review", 41: 1–15, quot., p. 11.
[36] Therein, 13.
[37] Ibidem.
[38] Ibidem.
[39] Ibidem.
[40] Therein, pp. 13–14.
[41] Therein, p. 14.
[42] Ibidem.

nor analyzed, but on the contrary overlooked, be it intentionally or not."[43] Here, once again, the *with* remains outstanding. Perhaps, therefore, it might be useful to refer—as the French philosopher expressly did—to the correspondence between Heidegger and Hannah Arendt in the years contemporary with the writing of *Being and Time*, in which it is possible to discern a reflection on love that has the proper/improper character of *Being-with*. A character that the German philosopher—according to Nancy—failed to thematize in his work:

> [...] love is [...] qualified as the genuine space of a "we" and of a world that can be "ours," and represents the genuine "taking care" of the other, since its formulation, borrowed from Augustine, is volo ut sis: "I want that you be what you are." Thus, love is a mitglauben, a shared faith in the "story of the other" and a mitergreifen, a shared grasp of the "potential of the other," in such a way that love is always a singular with: "your love" since "Love as such does not exist."[44]

What emerges from these few lines is the fundamental core of the singular/plural essence of the existential *with*. Therefore, to Nancy's questions, which we wanted to quote in this paragraph—"What does it mean to exist with one another?" and "What would it mean to live one another?" We cannot but answer that by using the words of the last of these letters, "your love. Love as such does not exist." Indeed, here lies wholly the partition of existence to which Nancy alluded: there is nothing but your love; therefore, not general, absolute love, but that one which is infinitely singular—and therefore also infinitely finite. The *with* is just that, the happening of being, the *il y a* of the relationship, its exposition, its *Being-there*. In other words, it is the place where the singular/plural being of every existing Being is given.

> Being singular plural means the essence of Being is only as coessence. In turn, coessence, or Being-with (Being-with-many), designates the essence of the co-, or even more so, the co- (the *cum*) itself in the position or guise of an essence.[45]

Being-with is the inclination to existence, the clinamen as the "inclination or an inclining from one toward the other, of one by the other, or from one to the other."[46] It is this clinamen that must be understood as the spacing of the *Being-in-common* that partitions us: the singular partition of Being, the originality of the partition of Being is the infinitely repeated spacing of the singularity, of each present singular, present not to itself but to the other singular:

> Community is the community of others, which does not mean that several individuals possess some common nature in spite of their differences, but rather that they partake only of their otherness. Otherness, at each moment, is the otherness of each "myself," which is "myself" only as an other. Otherness is not a common substance, but it is on the contrary

---

[43] Ibidem.
[44] Ibidem.
[45] Nancy, J.-L.: Being Singular Plural. Trans. R. D. Richardson and A. E. O'Bryne, Stanford University Press, Stanford, CA: (2000), p. 30.
[46] Id.: The Inoperative Community, quot., p. 4.

the nonsubstantiality of each "self" and of its relationship with the others. All the selves are related through their otherness [...] They are together, but togetherness is otherness.[47]

If we say we experience a relationship, what we in fact experience is this *with*, understood as an irreducible and non-appropriable contiguity. The latter is the figure of the exposition, of con-tact—as seen above. Touching here does not mean belonging to one another, or belonging to the other, whoever the other is. We are in touch, we touch each other, but this touching remains an infinite distance, the *touching-at-a-distance* is the exposure to others, the appearing or showing up, neither beside nor juxtaposed. If hands seek each other, if they intertwine, they only encompass a distance: a twofold, but consequential movement of bridging and confirming that *Being-in-proximity*. Bodies are instruments that measure us in the distance, yet they confirm us that they witness us. If there were no distance to bridge, there would be no reason to give or demand the bridging of a distance that is such only because there are feeling bodies. In this regard, Nancy wrote:

> Even in love, one is "in" the other only outside the other. The child "in" its mother is also exterior in that interiority. [...] The logic of the "with" —of the Being-with, of the Mitsein that Heidegger makes contemporary and correlative with the *Dasein*—is the singular logic of an inside-outside. [...] It would thus be the logic of what belongs neither to the pure inside nor to the pure outside. [...] A logic of the limit pertains to what is between two or several, belonging to all and to none—not belonging to itself, either.[48]

Therefore, not individual, for the individual is the undivided, while the singular has always been divided between inside and outside. Each is nearby the other or others, but never where the other is: "And in the most assembled crowd, one is not in the place of the other."[49] Bataille called this a distinction separating "the principle of insufficiency" or "the principle of incompleteness." It is still about the mode of the unfolding of Being, but above all—as Blanchot reminded us: "what commands and organizes the possibility of a being is a principle."[50] In this sense, "a being," "an existence" does not want a response from the other to this incompleteness or unfulfillment or insufficiency, it does not seek the other "to make up a substance of integrity";[51] it needs precisely the other to be enacted. This is what "*Being-in- common*," "*Being-with*," "*Being singular/plural*,', or finally "*Being shared/partitioned*" mean. Therefore, if there is other mode of Being other than the *with* it is because it cannot come into presence unless in the mode of sharing/partitioning (*partage*).[52]

---

[47] Id.: The Birth to Presence, quot., p. 155.

[48] Id.: Of Being in common In Miami Collective (ed.), Community at Loose Ends., transl. James Creech, University of Minnesota Press, Minneapolis (1991), p. 6.

[49] Ibidem.

[50] Blanchot, M.: The unavowable community. Transl. P. Joris, Barrytown, Station Hill Press, N.Y. (1988), p. 5.

[51] Ibidem.

[52] On the concept of 'partage' and 'Being-with', see the following texts: Meazza C.: Il tratto del tra-noi in Jean-Luc Nancy, in G. Pintus (a cura di), Relazione e alterità, Inschibboleth, Roma, (2019), pp. 53–70; Nishitani, O.: Jean-Luc Nancy, la pensée du « partage », in Jean-Luc Nancy. Anastasis de la pensée, quot., pp. 199–202; Nishiyama Y.: (2017), L'adresse de l'entre-nous:

2 "Being-With and Being-There"

Being is for many, and is therefore necessarily plural. The object of ontology is then a being that is an *us*, that is, the Being-there with one another. In relation to *Dasein*, the demarcation is the same. It is first in the existence of *Dasein* that being is to be sought. Nevertheless, *Dasein* is essentially *Mitsein*, and therefore it is only in coexistence and based on it that it is possible to speak of the question of *being*. "With" is the essential ontological structure; in other words, it is the truth of all other possible determinations of being. For this reason, it cannot consider itself as *Being-toward*, *Being-for* or *Being-of*, but only as *Being-with*.

> *Cum* is an exponent: it puts us before one another, delivers us to one another, turns us against one another, and all together delivers us to nothing but the experience of what it is. It has no end other than itself: but "it itself" is endless, and with no identity. It is – "it itself" what "we" are: nothing but the proliferation of this singular plural "subject" to mean the coexistence of entities in the world.[53]

Plurality is what specifies the determination of the *Being-with*. In this sense, Nancy stated that being is neither numerable nor numerically defined, but is plural. Indeed, plurality and not multiplicity imply the *Being-with*. Taken together, beings do not constitute a totality, but a wholeness. Being is not a totality of which each is a part. This totality is not original and pre-given, but already always partitioned. The totality, in which one is with another, is original. The plurality of which the philosopher speaks excludes the one and the whole. What is there among beings that constitute plural being? We already know that we must consider them without a presupposed wholeness, and without communication content. This implies a spacing and a displacement of Being, and at the same time, his unfolding. To think of being as a wholeness and a unity or as a subject is to speak of it outside of all spatial and temporal reference, and then to think of it abstractly. On the contrary, to acknowledge that being is plural is to immediately acknowledge its most proper condition. Such condition is that of externality; indeed, plurality presupposes the spacing, the displacement, and the structuring of being as an external mode. This therefore means that all beings are *ex-posed*, meaning that they are placed outside one another. Hence, Nancy's approach to an ontology of *ex-peau-sition* becomes quite evident. It is in this exposition that the plural *Dasein* of *Mitsein* is given.

> Thus the *Mitsein* or better yet the *Mitdasein* whose analysis Heidegger eluded or emptied out […] should not be understood as a "being there with" (in the room, in a train, in life) but rather as a being-with-da, which is to say in the open, thus always elsewhere, in a sense (and in accordance with Being and Time). Being modalized *mit-da*—perhaps its only modalization but at the same time indefinitely plural—is nothing other than a being sharing or dividing itself into shares according to the da which is forced to designate the "open," the "open" of the ex-posed. Being-with is thus the same thing as being-open […] *Mitdasein* would thus be a sort of stammering or tautology of thought, concealing everything that is difficult to think: being-with *or* being open *or* being-opening *or* just-plain-being. Or else (forgive me for insisting so emphatically) to be open to the with while being with or in the open. But in

---

l'interpretation platique di Hegel chez Jean-Luc Nancy, in J. Lèbre, J. Rogozinski, Jean-Luc Nancy. Penser la mutation, quot., pp. 127–138; Raffoul F.: (1999), The logic of the with. On Nancy's Être singulier pluriel. Studies in Practical Philosophy, 1,1, pp. 36–52.

[53] Nancy, J.-L.: La pensée dérobée, my translation, quot., 116.

any case a with that is nothing but the effect of an open and an *open* that is nothing but the effect of a with. Finally, an *open / with* that is not added to "being," that does not predicate it, but that is on the contrary the "subject," a subject without substance or support, with no support other than a rapport. Which again is to say an open/with that affects "being," that opens it itself or that makes its opening, that of a circulation of sense. But here again we must ceaselessly beware of the pious resonances of the "*open*" as well as of those of "*community*." "*Open*" is neither simply nor primarily generosity, warmth of welcome, and prodigality of the gift, but principally the condition of coexistence of finite singularities among which—alongside, beside, on the edge of, between "inside" and "outside"—the possibility of sense circulates indefinitely.[54]

Therefore, to say that there is no being without a *with* is to acknowledge a precedence of the *with* over all other possible determinations of being itself. The *with* does not come first in order to become a *Being-with* afterwards. Indeed, this would mean placing back the *with* in the position of the subject, to make it therefore something essential. Instead—for Nancy—the *with* cannot be thought of as subject or substance. We could think of the *with* as a structure that has an a priori, transcendental character in relation to being. However, in this way, the *Being-with* would not be recognized as having the relational order; it would become a property of being. Likewise, if we were to understand it as the transcendental in the Kantian sense and thus see in the *with* a condition of possibility of being, it would be necessary for this condition to be constitutive of a transcendental subject, which would not be possible to affirm if we speak of the *with* instead. The subject itself is such only in relation to the *with*; thus the condition is not given in the subject, but in the relationship of a subject to other subjects. But then: is it possible to speak of a transcendental that comes before any subject and does not itself constitute a subject? Could a given state or relationship be in this position? Nancy seemed to reject the idea of the transcendental: the partition of being is not a transcendental presupposition, but is the symbol of what the philosopher called "compearance."

> [...] compearance is of a more originary order than that of the bond. It does not set itself up, it does not establish itself, it does not emerge among already given subjects (objects). It consists in the appearance of the between as such: you and I (between us)-a formula in which the *and* does not imply juxtaposition, but exposition. What is exposed in compearance is the following, and we must learn to read it in all its possible combinations: "you (are/and/is) (entirely other than) I" ("toi {e(s)tj {tout autre que] moi"). Or again, more simply: you shares me ("toi portage moi").[55]

The ontological status of what is thus presupposed is not further determined, but Nancy's statements consequently allow us to say that the *with* is the condition of being in general, and of the subjects for whom a being exists. Plurality (the space of compearance) and partition are not conditions of possibility for being, but the "topological" condition of being itself.

Following Nancy's words:

---

[54] Id.: *Conloquium*. Transl. Janell Watson, Minnesota Review, 75, (2010)—New Series, 106–107.
[55] Id.: *The Inoperative Community*, quot., p. 29.

[...] the common human condition turns up everywhere, more manifest and bare than ever. Indeed, it is manifest because stripped bare, and vice-versa. The common condition is at the same time the common reduction to a common denominator *and* the condition of being absolutely in common.[56]

These words are undoubtedly echoed by those written again by Nancy himself in his work dated 1993—*The birth to presence*—to which we would like to refer as the closure of this paragraph.

Community therefore is neither an abstract or immaterial relationship, nor a common substance. It is not a common being; it is to be in common, or to be with each other, or to be together. And "together" means something that is neither inside nor outside one's being. "Together" is an ontological modality different from any substantial constitution, as well as from any kind of relation (logical, mechanical, sensitive, intellectual, mystical, etc.). "Together" (and the possibility of saying "we") takes place where the inside, as an inside, becomes an outside; that is, where, without building any common "inside," it is given as an external inferiority. "Together" means: not being by oneself and having one's own essence neither in oneself nor in another self.[57]

In conclusion, what are the real stakes of Jean-Luc Nancy's thought? In his most important works, from *Corpus* to *The Inoperative Community, La pensée dérobée, The Sense of the World, A Finite Thought,* and *Being Nude: The Skin of Images*, the concepts of exposure, corporeality, threshold, limit, finiteness, community, and *Being-with* are the hallmark of the French philosopher's reflection, which bends to the questioning of writing, language, painting, and photography. Nancy's purpose is to literally stage existence, its body, and its excription. To stage the skin of every image, of every world, of all worlds, just like painters do, just as when attending a museum exhibition. In the painters' or photographers' nudes, dispossession is exposed in the mode of suspension, of proximity or approaching, on the brink of a sense which is always on the verge of emerging, always on the run, right next to the skin, right next to the image. Existence is thus compearance in the sense of nakedness, of ever-imminent, ever-rising and never-ending excription. This is where precisely the concept of community as foundation is set aside so as to make sense of the inoperativeness that always underlies it, in a sort of perpetual subtraction of the "cum." I believe that this very subtraction makes sense of a concept of community that opposes any logic of the *positum* and bends in the direction of the singular/plural *ex-peau-sition*. This is how the profusions of nature and the proliferations of technology stand together and create a world; this is how they all simultaneously touch and mutually expose each other, in an intangible grain that disintegrates and goes beyond the identity image of an immovable Ego. Here our existential condition is at stake and made explicit; a condition that is infinitely finite because it has always already been exposed, always lying on its own limit. In this plane of existence we can discover the singular multiplicity of life, whether natural or artificial, actual or virtual. A plural horizon of Nature within which more or less complex constitutions

---

[56] Nancy J.-L. and Bailly, J.-Ch.: La Comparution/The Compearance: From the Existence of 'Communism' to the Community of 'Existence' in "Political Theory 20–3/1992", pp. 371–372.
[57] Nancy, J.-L.: The Birth to Presence, quot., p. 154.

of bodies, existences, and wills unfold eccentrically. All the foregoing shows how Nancy was able to deconstruct, within the framework of that French deconstructionism—of which he remains, as we know, one of the greatest exponents along with Derrida—the occlusive sign of the West, the founding sign of all metaphysics and all transcendence; he was able to deconstruct that sign by reconfiguring the concepts of existence, corporeality and community, opening them up to the disclosure of the outside, to the excription of the world. In an age when we are exposed to contagion with others, with everyone else, on the wave of globalization, a thought of the "exposed body," I think a reflection such as the one Nancy invited us to make on *ex-peau-sition*, on the fact that we are all (starting from the skin itself) exposed and crossed by others, is as important and urgent as ever. The extent to which these reflections can have an impact today, even on a political level, is well evident. Therefore, the dimension of the community outlined by Nancy is not that of a substance which becomes a subject by producing the world of meanings, values, and norms; instead, it is that of a finiteness capable of exposing itself to its own limit, of standing on its own line in order to grasp that excess, that disproportion of the *Being-with* that, by crossing it, breaks it and makes it impossible for it to dominate itself. This community is not made up of individuals, but of finite singularities that welcome the limit within themselves and do not leave it out of a supposed unity. Nancy outlines a community dimension that does not claim to make itself absolute, to reabsorb within it all the dimensions of man, but displays precisely what, by escaping the concept and the total transparency of meaning, configures Being as inappropriable other. In a multiple proximity of bodies, in which the us becomes palpable, touches itself and offers itself to be touched… the image multiplies, splinters, clashes, and rejects itself. All this entails a radical reflection on where we come from and what our trajectory is; in short, on what we want to be:

> […] Neither places, nor heavens, nor gods […] dismantling and disassembling of enclosed bowers, enclosures, fences.[58]

We must then establish a "thought of shores and borders" a thought of approaching and proximity that makes one willing to be "the listener upon the rock," to "be the guardian of the estates, to drift into the sound of the night" to quote Rilke's words.[59] Therefore, it is not simply a matter of erasing borders, redrawing territories, or establishing new identities; indeed, the territorial border is a graft, a complex track that unfolds in multiple contingencies, that opens up to linguistic, philosophical, technological, sociological, historical-political, and other pluralities. Such plurality needs to be taken into account insofar as every existence is the index of a place, a space, a lived topography; but at the same time, this inscriptive and inclusive index opens up to its excription: the border is the passage, the place of crossing, the edge that simultaneously tracks the limit and marks the approaching, like the skin of the body, the liminal exposure of the self. This, in conclusion, is the most

---

[58] Nancy J.-L.:Dis-Enclosure: The Deconstruction of Christianity, quot., p. 161.
[59] Rilke, R.M., The Book of Hours: Prayers to a Lowly God. Transl. A. S. Kidder, Northwestern University Press, Illinois (2002), p. 167.

important contribution (gift) of Nancy's reflection; this is the reason for which, in my opinion, he was a thinker capable of—to quote Hegel—"grasping in thoughts his own time."[60]

Appendix

On Bodies: Perspectives of a Dialogue Between Jean-Luc Nancy and Roberto Esposito

Technique has now taken up residence in our very limbs

R. Esposito, *Immunitas*

Between me and me [...] there is an incision's opening, and the irreconcilability of a compromised immune system

J.-L. Nancy, *Corpus*

Ecotechnics of Bodies

To what extent today, in the era of biotechnology and therapeutic eugenics, artificial insemination and end-of-life, is it urgently necessary to think, or rather rethink, our relationship with the body, and thus with life? Why can life no longer be conceived according to the classical view that understood it—through the body—as a stand-alone living organism? Or rather, why couldn't it be understood as a biochemically and biologically structured "form" of the world, certainly subject to mutation, but always teleologically organized? The answer to these questions emerges from the events characterizing the new modernity, namely, the one in which, as Agamben described it, a "new use of bodies, of technique, of landscape" takes place.[61] In other words, the concept of form-of-life, which replaces the foundational recourse to a subjectivity, takes shape. Moreover, this is how the whole reflection on the categories of person, body, mind, thing, and human life is rethought. The punctum dolens of the Heideggerian view that identified man as the closest being to God than to the animal, for he was the "world-forming" in a kind of scale that relegated the animal to being defined as "world-poor" and the stone as "worldless," is understood precisely from this renewed conception of corporeality.

Stone, animal, man: all are bodies; they are bodies within which sense abides, without privilege of any kind, insofar as each of those bodies is inhabited by, or

---

[60]Cf. Hegel, G.W.F.: Elements of the Philosophy of Right, transl. Hugh Barr Nisbet, Cambridge University Press, Cambridge (1991).
[61]Cf. Agamben, G.: The Use of Bodies. Trans. Adam Kotsko, Stanford University Press, Stanford (2016).

simply "is" sense, which is precisely a gap, a distance, a cut, a postponement or deferral, a composition or a decomposition, and a partition, to borrow Jean-Luc Nancy's cherished lexicon.[62] The nonequivalence of bodies no longer pertains to a matrix defined by the ability to "*form the world*," but far more classically to an *ethos* to be inhabited, in a constitutively singular/plural way.[63] Thinking of such "nonequivalence" as an unquenchable resource of the "form of the world," of its meaning, and of its possibility of existing is what a reflection on the body allows us to do.

In fact, against this background stands out a theoretical horizon which is as timely as ever, namely, that relating to the practices of *grafts* or *intrusions* of bodies into other bodies; in short, to transplants and explants. Indeed, the biomedical approach delivers us a body always *bound* to other bodies, both organic and inorganic, in a sort of latent promiscuity, of permutation and exchange between vital and non-vital, between Self and other. However, let us take a step back. To Nietzsche we owe the most impressive acrobatic leap in the history of philosophical thought, as Esposito rightly observes, "His radical deconstruction of the categories of modern thought coincided with a thought on and of the body (in the sense that the body thinks because it, too, is animate) that was destined to inaugurate a new language. To the question of whether philosophy has not been more than an incessant 'misunderstanding of the body', Zarathustra responds that 'there is more reason in your body than in your best wisdom.' Contrary to thinkers that Nietzsche defines as disparagers of the body, he rereads the whole history of Europe along 'the guiding thread of the body'. [...] The politics of bodies, on bodies, in bodies is the only kind that exists – not in opposition to the 'spirit', but in a weave that integrates the body into the *bios* as an integral form of life."[64]

Starting from here, the theme of life, of *bios*, assumes a decisive importance in the philosophical culture of the entire twentieth century. In addition, today more than ever—namely, ever since biology appeared on the scene of history—it has become more and more the object of extensive and meticulous knowledge, so much so that its preservation—and indeed its unlimited promotion—has become utmost. First and foremost, this has led to increasingly careful, and almost invasive, legislation. An example of this is the so-called population health policy, which has become more and more capable of penetrating into the infinitesimal aspects of the biological-bodily dimension of people's lives, in an often conflicting relationship between the natural and the artificial: from medical therapies to nutrition and fertilization. A typical aspect of this modernity that goes under the now well-known name of bio-politics.[65]

All this profoundly affects philosophical, artistic-literary, political-legal and medical-scientific reflection. What has been brought into play is the identity

---

[62] Cf. Nancy, J.-L.: The Experience of Freedom, quot.

[63] Cf. Id.: Being Singular Plural. Trans. R. Richardson & A. O'Byrne Stanford University Press, Stanford (2000).

[64] Esposito, R.: Persons and Things. Trans. Z. Hanafi, Polity Press, Cambirdge (2015), pp. 115–116.

[65] Cf. Id.: Bios: Biopolitics and Philosophy, quot.

paradigm of the subject, and along with it, the entire relationship with the world. Consequently, the dimension of the human and the "vital" in general has been entirely deconstructed. Hence the need to thoroughly rethink today the "biotechnological" construction of the living being, in order to be able to understand his mighty change of sense.

Reducing the concept of the body to a single level of the subject, as well as linking the natural and the artificial, the real and the virtual, the organic and the inorganic, is what allows us to think of the body as a constant fluctuation between inside and outside and to its immunization and simultaneous contamination.[66] In addition, this makes us understand the body itself as the very unfolding of the skin, viscera, limbs, and senses, all in an ecotechnical profusion of bodies.[67] Hybridizations of the self and therapeutic cloning: accelerations of existence in an impalpable grain that deconstructs and exceeds all "architectures of the living." These transformations, which can be defined as radical without fear of exaggeration, thus require philosophy to question and investigate them, both in relation to the associated change of whole categorical apparatuses (from the scientific to the artistic field) and to their consequences at a more broadly ethical and even political level (i.e., in relation to what is still to be understood by "man" and "world").[68]

If we consider the change to the concept of the body in the twentieth century, we cannot but bring to the fore a new concept of life and explore its entire semantic field: from the purely philosophical to the aesthetic, political, economic, medical, and psychoanalytic spheres. What emerges then are the concepts of "ontology of the living," of "bios and biopolitics," of "person and human life," of "everyday life."[69] Concepts that represent the most problematic governmental faults nowadays, because they are directly implicated or co-implicated in the very structure of the living matter. That "living matter" which is thus ascertained as an "archigonic" fiction/form of inscription to the world, played out precisely from the encroachments and continuous decompositions of all our bodily plexuses.[70]

Therefore, it needs to understand life in its different architectures or "different guises" for it is precisely in the continuous deferral (whether hereditary or abrupt) that each body (whether living or nonliving) frees itself from any preconceived purpose, resists any synthesis, multiplies in irreducible plurality, and destabilizes the temporal-historical continuum, thus disentangling itself from that notion of indefectibly serial time that rests silently on the identity or permanence of the Self; this means thinking the living in its most abysmal *déshérence*. Starting from this backlash in the origin that is precisely the absence of inheritance, the long-distance dialogue between Esposito and Nancy, between *Immunitas* and *The Intruder*, is

---

[66] Cf. Id.: Immunitas: The Protection and Negation of Life, quot.

[67] Cf. Nancy, J.-L.: Corpus, quot.

[68] Cf. Rodotà, S.: La vita e le regole. Tra diritto e non diritto. Feltrinelli, Milan (2006).

[69] Cf. Lisciani-Petrini, E.: Vita quotidiana. Dall'esperienza artistica al pensiero in atto. Bollati Boringhieri, Turin (2015).

[70] Cf. Id..: Risonanze. Ascolto, Corpo, Mondo. Mimesis, Milan (2007).

played out. The essay proposed here is based on all this, aiming to understand how it is no longer man who is projected into the world today, but it is the world to be introjected and implanted in man: as Esposito wrote in *Immunitas*, "technique has now taken up residence in our very limbs."[71] Such a statement recalls the pages of Nancy's Intruder: "Between me and me [...] there is an incision's opening, and the irreconciliability of a compromised immune system."[72] The identity subject discovers itself as hopelessly partitioned (Nancy) and lying on the outside (Esposito), in a space that is our unique possible community.

Immune Bodies?

Nowadays, as we have seen, the body, in its infinite—thus no longer defined and finite—semantic, and speculative extension, poses a problem. Indeed, if biology was once a purely observational and strictly experimental science, today it founds a real engineering of the living being that changes more and more our relationship with our body and with that of others. Roberto Esposito and Jean-Luc Nancy give voice to the ethical-political-philosophical questions revolving around contemporary bodily dynamics: technical and cybernetic existence, artificial or virtual existence, and the ecotechnics of bodies.

Esposito starts from the biopolitical register.

As the Italian philosopher wrote in the introductory pages of *Immunitas. Protection and negation of life*, "the body is the most immediate terrain of the relation between politics and life, because only in the body does life seem protected from what threatens to harm it and from its own tendency to go beyond itself, to become other than itself. It is as if life, to preserve itself as such, must be compressed and kept within the confines of the body."[73] All this—as Esposito explained further on—is not because the body, both singular and collective, is not always exposed to involution and dissolution processes, but because it is precisely there, in the body, that the defense mechanisms intended for its protection are activated. The whole metaphor of the "body politic" in the early modern age—from Hobbes onward—is connected to this mechanism. A framework that is reversed when the prevailing relationships between politics and life are reversed: "The threshold of transformation from the paradigm of sovereignty to that of biopolitics is to be located in the time when power was no longer the subject of inclusion (as well as of exclusion) of life but instead, life – its reproductive protection – became the ultimate criterion for legitimizing power."[74] Life establishes itself, sets off the mechanism of protection by itself and, in this, creates a real immunity paradigm. But here, the whole internal contradiction of the immune paradigm emerges, which Esposito

---

[71] Esposito, R. Immunitas: The Protection and Negation of Life, quot., p. 147.
[72] Nancy, J.-L.: Corpus, quot., p. 168.
[73] Esposito, R.: Immunitas: The Protection and Negation of Life, quot., p. 14.
[74] Therein, p. 15.

unhinges and highlights: "The immune system is actually described as a military device, defending and attacking everything not recognized as belonging to it, and which must therefore be fended off and destroyed. The most striking feature is the way a biological function is extended to a general view of reality dominated by a need for violent defense in the face of anything judged to be foreign. […] the relation between 'I' and 'other' […] is represented in terms of a destruction that ultimately tends to involve both the contrasting terms."[75] A real " self-dissolution impulse" that, in the medical field, is reflected in autoimmune diseases, "in which the warring potential of the immune system is so great that at a certain point it turns against itself as a real and symbolic catastrophe leading to the implosion of the entire organism."[76] The medical metaphor adopted by Esposito highlights all the disturbing features of the ambiguity within which life unfolds. The immunity paradigm as a whole is not something that acts against something, but is rather what reacts to it, in the sense of a counterforce, a backlash, an instance of closure, of blocking; even by reproducing the evil from which one must protect oneself in a controlled way (as vaccines do). In short: protection and negation of life according to a strategy that is not meant to be that of direct contrast, but of avoidance and neutralization. Following Esposito's words once again, "Evil must be thwarted, but not by keeping it at a distance from one's borders; rather, it is included inside them. […] The body defeats a poison not by expelling it outside the organism, but by making it somehow part of the body. […] Of course, this homeopathic protection practice – which excludes by including and affirms by negating – does not consume itself without leaving traces on the constitution of its object."[77] At this point, the path indicated by Esposito is clear: it is a matter of accessing an affirmative biopolitics. The example to which he resorts is that provided by the biological event of birth, where pregnancy exerts a kind of protection of life precisely through that immunity mechanism which should make it impossible, given the different DNAs of both father and mother. Indeed, the child conceived by fertilization, in his intrauterine life, is protected, incorporated, nourished *in his diversity and because of his diversity*, precisely because of his being "other." In short, precisely that "otherness," that diversity which implements and indeed triggers in the mother's organism a complex immunity process, protects the fetus and guarantees his future life at the same time. In this example, according to Esposito, we can trace the paradigmatic movements of a strategy in which we do not purely and simply immunize ourselves from the other, but on the contrary, we protect it by welcoming it—and thus welcoming "life in its different guises." However, in this way, what takes shape is a different philosophy of immunity, as can be seen in a recent work by Esposito entitled *Immunità comune. Biopolitica all'epoca della pandemia* (English translation: *Common Immunity: Biopolitics in the Age of the Pandemic)*[78]—in which the Italian philosopher writes

---

[75] Therein, p. 17.
[76] Ibid.
[77] Therein, p. 8.
[78] Id.: Immunità comune. Biopolitica all'epoca della pandemia. Einaudi, Turin (2022).

that it is a matter of "radically rethinking the constitutive link between immunity and community, building a single common immunity, a co-immunity intended to protect human beings not from each other, but with and for each other. […] Humanity would become not an abstract ideal, but a political concept, a global immune design – something like a forthcoming 'co-immunity'."[79] This is what the recent pandemic, with all the immense power of contagion and death, has taught us. "Today more than ever, in full biopolitical regime, politics has to deal with the protection and development of life. Not only for individual populations, but for humankind as a whole. When community and immunity find an extreme tangency line, the life of each one is protected only by that of all."[80] Therefore, for the first time in history, when the entire world community has required to be safeguarded, immunity seems to have lost its restrictive connotations to require a new interpretation from a biological, philosophical, and political point of view. After the Covid-19 pandemic, the functioning of the immune paradigm has been shaped according to a new interpretation mode. However, if we go back to *Immunitas*, we can understand how much Esposito's lessons, already in unsuspected times, had so much to teach us. The successful exchange with authors such as Alfred Tauber[81] and Donna Haraway[82] led the Italian philosopher to a conception of individual identity and bodily subjectivity completely opposed to the closed and monolithic one of the Western tradition. Certainly, there is no doubt that this has also been inevitable given the developments in genetic technology and bionics that have strongly contributed to changing our usual notion of the body. As Esposito writes, "rather than an immutable and definitive given, the body is understood as a functioning construct that is open to continuous exchange with its surrounding environment. Moreover – this is the argument (a problematic one, to be sure) put forward in the concluding section of this work – the immune system may very well be the driving force behind this exchange. Immune tolerance, understood as a product of immunity rather than as an unraveling or a deficiency of the system, is one of its first expressions. The figure of the implant, whether an artificial prosthesis or a natural implant like fertilized eggs in the mother's womb, provides the most striking case in point. The fact that the genetic heterogeneity of the fetus rather than its genetic similarity is what encourages the mother's immune system to accept it means that the immune system cannot be reduced to the simple function of rejecting all things foreign. If anything, the immune system must be interpreted as an internal resonance chamber, like the diaphragm through which difference, as such, engages and traverses us. As we were saying: once its negative power has been removed, the immune is not the enemy of the common, but rather

---

[79] Therein, p. 147 (my translation).

[80] Therein, p. 180 (my translation).

[81] Cf. Tauber, A.: The Immune Self: Theory or Metaphor?, Cambridge University Press, New York and Cambridge (1994), and the most recent: Immunity: The Evolution of an Idea, Oxford University Press, New York (2017).

[82] Haraway, D.: Simians, Cyborg and Woman. The reinvention of nature. Routledge, New York (1991).

something more complex that implicates and stimulates the common. The full significance of this necessity, but also its possibility, still eludes us."[83]

The concept of the body, unavoidably present, appears again in Esposito's reflection. It is impossible to do without it as it is in the body—as a body—that life is given, and the whole resulting immunity consequence with it.

Phenomenological Grafts: Esposito—Nancy, Flesh and Body

Esposito and Nancy's main objective is to deepen the speculative value and semantic extension of the notion of corporeity in a continuous and close dialogue with ancient and modern tradition, in order to highlight the urgency of a thought of the body in our contemporary times.[84] The latter is increasingly projected toward a conception of it that unhinges the notion of bìos on the one hand, and that of person on the other. Proof of this are the countless scientific, legal, biomedical, and ethical—as well as philosophical—debates around the topic of the vital, the artificial, therapeutic eugenics, and so on.

In the direction taken by Nancy, the sense of the body opens up to its own dissent and exposes itself to a new apex of thought. Here, the concept of decomposition of the body goes hand in hand with that of identity disintegration, in which vital and non-vital, organic and inorganic interplay with each other in a kind of latent promiscuity. "I am first the guest of this other: world, body, language."[85] Being the guest of the other is the very experience of bodily existence—as Nancy writes in one of his most complex and important works, *The Restlessness of the Negative*—the text dedicated to Hegel. Here Nancy rethinks the servant-master/ego-other relationship not to enclose it within a dialectic of the negative, but to open that relationship up to the restlessness, the shifting movement that the other represents in the singular constitution of each self. From the deconstruction of the paradigm of the subject—posed by Nancy's critique of the Cartesian *ego cogito*—to the analyses carried out on the other as the inoperative outside that stands out over the sense of the inside, we are led to the place where precisely the inside/outside of existence unfolds and is exposed, namely the body. Therefore, it is no coincidence that the French philosopher addresses the question of the other by going through a somewhat involutional path, in which the other presents itself under the guise of an outside that is my body itself, and yet is simultaneously the inside from which I cannot distance or detach myself. Thus, it is a matter of thinking of the body as a constant fluctuation between inside and outside—as mentioned earlier—thinking of its immunization and, at the same time, of its contamination. In other words, it is necessary to think of a new way of experiencing and conceiving the body that can no longer be linked to the classical

---

[83] Esposito, R.: Immunitas: The Protection and Negation of Life, quot., pp. 17–18.

[84] On the dialogue between Nancy and Esposito, see the important essay by Fulco R.: Conloquium: il dialogo tra Jean-Luc Nancy e Roberto Esposito, in "Shift. International Journal Of Philosophical Studies", 2/2021–1/2022, pp. 239–252.

[85] Nancy, J.-L.: Hegel: The Restlessness of the Negative, quot., p. 57.

conception which intended it as a living organism in its own right; rather, it is a matter of conceiving it in relation to other bodies, whether organic or not. According to Nancy's words, "Every thing outside all the others, every thing according to the stretching that spaces them and without which there would be just one indistinct thing gathered into the point at which it would annul itself, a thing unthinged, a derealized res, a perfect, syncopated subject turned back in on itself without its having ever reached itself, an extinct, noiseless trinket, a one annihilated without its being dead: every thing, then, touching every part of every other thing, touching me in the same way, piece by piece, here and there, always, from time to time, exposing the infinity of our relations. Things: the first stone that's thrown, a sheet of paper, galaxies, the wind, my television screen, a quark, my big toe, a trapped nerve, prostheses, organs planted or grafted beneath my skin, placed or exposed inside, all things exposing themselves and exposing us, between them and between us, between them and us, together and singularly."[86] Dissent of the body, therefore, by understanding this genitive in a twofold sense: both objective, meaning that it falls on the body (and this is the dissent launched by Nancy)—and subjective, produced by the body itself, meaning a body that is expressed in the plurality which erases, strikes out the sense, i.e., the firm meaning that the philosophical/political/religious tradition has always assigned to it). Dissent of the body because the very body disrupts all defined meaning and endlessly opens itself to the other from itself, to the intruder who goes through it in the guise of a disease or a new donated heart that, like the legendary Trojan horse, brings with it a deceptive new beginning. A symptomatic body always turned to or turned toward, in a kind of dispossession that continually exceeds its subjectivist and objectivist instances.

Nevertheless, already in one of the working notes attached to *The Visible and the Invisible*, Maurice Merleau-Ponty's last work, we can read that we must think of the "flesh of the world – distinct from my flesh: the double inscription outside and inside."[87] It is a significant invite that Merleau-Ponty leaves to future generations, a warning for reflection. Indeed, in my opinion, it is from this outcome that—albeit tacitly—Nancy starts over.[88] Certainly, all this in order to overcome the phenomenological impasse of the proper body and to try to supplant that concept of flesh anchored still too much in the Christian tradition.

However, what does it mean to think of "the double inscription outside and inside"? Moreover, why does the body attest itself as the privileged place of this experience? As Merleau-Ponty writes, "The body catches itself from the outside, […] it tries to touch itself while being touched, and initiates 'a kind of reflection' which is sufficient to distinguish it from objects, of which I can indeed say that they 'touch' my body, but only when it is inert, and therefore without ever catching it

---

[86] Nancy, J.-L.: A finite thinking, quot., pp. 315–316.

[87] Merleau-Ponty, M.: The Visible and the Invisible, quot., p. 261.

[88] See, in this regard, the recent volume by Morin, M.-E..: Merleau-Ponty and Nancy on Sense and Being, At the limits of Phenomenology, Edinburgh University Press, Edinburgh. (2022).

unawares in its exploratory function."[89] While the body is what is always by my side, it is also what, at the same time, is by the side of others, exposing itself and myself. That is to say, the body turns out to be the place of tangibility between me and myself, as well as between the other and me. In this sense, we can say that it is the vector of our being-in-the-world. However, at this point of tangibility that is the body, what is revealed is not a total adherence to (me or the other from me), but rather a space of absence, a principle of incompleteness – as Blanchot would put it. In fact, if we analyze the very famous example of the two hands touching each other (first dealt with by Husserl and later taken up and reworked by Merleau-Ponty), we can see that in the movement of reflection—which is the active/passive transition of their mutual touching – what remains is an unquenchable gap, a space of absence, a persistent otherness. As if to say that in the self of the body dwells the other from/of the body. Therefore, a kind of essential ambiguity of the flesh texture is revealed; it is precisely this emptiness, this absence, this passivity of the other and from the other that impedes the identification with the perfectly integral and fulfilled *Wholly-Full*. If, on the one hand, this line of thought is aimed at overcoming the Cartesian dichotomous instance between res cogitans and res extensa, it turns out to be as very timely on the other, since it already alludes to the practices of grafts or intrusions of bodies from bodies, thus penetrating the meshes of philosophical culture throughout the post-World War II period up to the most recent debates in the ethical, scientific, religious and biotechnological spheres. Thus, it can be clearly understood why Nancy himself embarked—starting from the phenomenological antecedents – on a non-secondary path in the exploration of the concept of the body. This is a path on which Roberto Esposito focuses as well in some extraordinary pages of his *Immunitas*, in which he points out how the line of the body – as understood by Husserl and the early Merleau-Ponty – gains a specific significance with the concept of "flesh." The Italian philosopher writes that "[…] we have to go back to the phenomenological horizon that constitutes its premise and conceptual framework: to be specific, to the theme of carne (flesh), specifically in the version provided by Husserl and later by Merleau-Ponty. For both, albeit stressing different aspects, the semantics of the flesh (German *Leib,* French *chair*) do not coincide with those of the body (German *Körper*, French *corps*) to which it is nevertheless linked by a close relation of implication. Whether involving a singular experience or potentially plural one – such as what Merleau-Ponty referred to with the terms 'flesh of the world' or 'flesh of history' – the process of mutual incorporation of two members of the same body or between several different bodies can never be fully achieved because it is interrupted by an original difference which the author calls 'carnal difference' [*difference charnelle*]."[90] In this carnal difference lies the impossibility of ultimate reversibility between the toucher and the one touched, and makes the chiasma between touching hand and touched hand always suspended, with the consequence that there can be no identification between body and flesh. As Esposito continues,

---

[89] Merleau-Ponty, M.: Phenomenology of Perception, quot., p. 107.
[90] Esposito, R.: Immunitas: The Protection and Negation of Life, quot., pp. 118–119.

"There is something about the flesh, like a hiatus or an original break, that resists incorporation, reversing it into the opposing movement of disincorporation. But, as we were saying, this stubborn resistance of the flesh to being made body cannot come about without aporetic consequences. [...] What finally comes into view is the possibility of bringing to the surface that "primal flesh" no philosophy has yet been able to name, except by negatively deducing it from the element that negated it. [...] there will emerge the silhouette of a flesh that rebels against the One, always already divided, polarized into the Two of the chiasm".[91] Therefore, as Esposito wonders, "How are we to understand 'primordial'? [...] as an ontological alternative that opposes the hegemony of the body from the outside – or the void inside which inhabits it and exposes it to its otherness? [...] is there another flesh beyond the body, or is this not the locus of its constitutive non-belonging – the differential limit that separates it from itself by opening it up to its outside?"[92] By these words, it seems that Esposito definitively silences the category of body for it is unsuitable to respond to a globalized and interconnected, fluid and even cyborg world. The notion of flesh seems to be the most suitable one to correspond theoretically to living institutions. "To fully grasp the meaning of the flesh requires that we be capable of simultaneously conceiving the outside and the inside of the body: one in the other and one for the other."[93] If the flesh is what everts the inverted, then it makes the individual body no longer proper, but improper. In conclusion, "The flesh is neither another body nor the body's other: it is simply the way of being in common of that which seeks to be immune."[94] As previously expressed, if the path chosen by Nancy leads to a tacit dialogue with Husserl and Merleau-Ponty's phenomenology, this is because the French philosopher wants to go beyond the concept of flesh, which is so closely linked to the Christian tradition. Indeed, Nancy deconstructs the spiritualistic and metaphysical residue found within the concept of flesh through the notion of exposition. Hence, the deconstruction of the concept of "proper body" (Leib)—still surreptitiously understood as a *positum*—is what Nancy strives for as well. In *Corpus*, in fact, the body, far from being understood as "proper," becomes the place par excellence of the "improper" or rather, of the "inappropriate." The body, therefore, can no longer be understood as positum, but rather as *ex-peau-situm*, that is, as skin that has always already been exposed to the world. In this sense, he writes that the "Body is certitude shattered and blown to bits." The body, our body is "a monster that can't be swallowed."[95]

Ex-peau-sition as skin that lies outside, a covering, precisely an exposition. Exposing one's own body to oneself and to the other. Nancy dismantles any idea of exposition understood as full manifestation, elimination of concealment, readiness for grasping and knowing. The movement of the *ex* inseparably links the outside to

---

[91] Therein, pp. 119–120.
[92] Therein, p 120.
[93] Therein, p. 121.
[94] Ibid.
[95] Nancy, J.-L.: Corpus, quot., p. 5.

the excess, to an excess that cannot be absorbed nor blocked. To come out of oneself does not mean unveiling oneself, making oneself fully transparent, but rather means surrendering to existence, to differing from oneself and thus to the relationship with the other in which we only meet or touch each other without being able to grasp, enclose ourselves in a stable and unified entity. This nonadherence to oneself, this impossibility of presence, which gives way to the ever-new act of presentation, to the event, is what Nancy calls "finiteness." The *ex-peau-sition* as nudity shows the excess of the finite: its being endless, unfulfilled, or that "absence of finality" that all totalitarianisms, all identitarianisms, and basically all "-isms" want to fill with all their might. The dimension of nudity is that of the intrusion/exposition of the body as such: the being of the body, as a body, exposes itself. Moreover, this exposition of one body to another, this mutual displacement or arrangement of bodies constitutes their sense relationship: the incorporeal element of meaning expressed by language. Therefore, the ontology of bodies is consequently an ontology of the incorporeal as well. That is always, at the same time, an ontology of bodies and an ontology of sense (of being) as an incorporeal element, as a space within which bodies are displaced. Nevertheless, here, according to Nancy, there is no idea of space per se, because it is the body that, as such, spaces existence. As the French philosopher writes, "Bodies aren't some kind of fullness or filled space [...]: they are open space. [...] The body-place isn't full or empty, since it doesn't have an outside or an inside, any more than it has parts, a totality, functions, or finality. It's acephalic and aphallic in every sense, as it were."[96] No body proper: no inside, no interiority; *se toucher-toi*, "to self-touch you" instead of *se toucher-soi*, "to touch oneself." The body is an objection to the Self, an objection to the appropriation of the body, which is still "a monster that can't be swallowed" "There is not 'the' body, there is not 'the' touch, there is not 'the' *res extensa*. There is that there is: creation of the world, *technē* of bodies, weighing without limits of sense, topographical corpus, geography of multiplied ectopias and no utopia."[97]

This is what thought must strive for, what it cannot constitutively escape: the exposure of the Self to the other than itself; it can only think of itself as the blade of a knife that tears the skin and lays it bare, and literally opens it up. In this very opening lies the inside/outside of our existence. Secretless: such is exposure, such is nakedness.

As Nancy explains, there is ultimately a "corpus of tact," which is precisely a syncopated corpus, interrupted and mixed with other bodies. Con-tact between bodies, partes extra partes, con-tact with the body that is obstructed and obstructs itself with its own proximity. An irreducible gap between body and Self, which implodes the idea of "touching" and leads us immediately to a promiscuity of contacts, of bodies, of body-to-body. Mixing, contagion, contact of bodies, spacing; body becoming space within another body by duplicating it, multiplying it; therefore,

---

[96] Therein, p. 15.
[97] Therein, p. 119.

giving rise to hybridizations of the Self, therapeutic cloning, implantation, transplantation, explantation. In one word, to the ecotechnics of the body.

Thus, according to Nancy, "openings for blood are identical to those of sense." The pages of *Corpus* we have followed so far exemplarily introduce us to those of *The Intruder*, namely, where the French philosopher has totally laid bare his own experience of "bodily partition": his cardiac transplantation, that is, the radical exposure of his own integrity carved out by the intrusion of the other (the heart of the other). It is clear that, as Esposito points out in a passage dedicated to Nancy, "What penetrates the body of the person who receives a transplant, even before the tubes, pliers and probes traverse it, is not even simply its outside. It is the acute point of intersection between several forms of estrangement that oppose and impose upon each other, each challenged, replicated, and, finally, overwhelmed by the other. The first is the estrangement of our immune system from the transplanted organ. The second, with an equal force of collision, is the estrangement of the immune system of the transplanted organ that strikes against our own. The shared line between the recipient body and the donor heart coincides with the frontline in the clash between these two opposing immune systems: one committed with all its power to rejecting the other while simultaneously not allowing itself to be rejected. For this reason, the resistance on the part of the person receiving the transplant must be redoubled: against the protection system of the other and his or her own; against the maelstrom of estrangement and the impossible demand for appropriation. For this reason, even to distinguish between "self" and "nonself" is no longer admissible, since it is not simply the improper that is the intruder, but the proper as well, inasmuch as it is estranged."[98]

In this sense, then, that Nancy's peremptory statement: "Thus, then, in all these accumulated and opposing ways, my self becomes my intruder"[99]—represents the figure and scope of his thought. The *ex-peau-sition* is the place where both the dissent of the "body proper" of the phenomenological matrix and the displacement of the ontological dimension of the *Being-with* take place. The transplanted heart makes space for itself and, by spacing out the receiving body, partitions it indefinitely: there it is in con-tact; but in this con-tact it expropriates it, exposes it, exports it. The new heart is an outside that brings outside, supplants the stillness of the Self, struggles to death to implant itself in the recognition of the gift. As Nancy writes: "Not because they opened me up, gaping, to change the heart. But because this gaping cannot be sealed back up. [...] I am closed open. Through the opening passes a ceaseless flux of strangeness [...] I certainly feel it, and it's much stronger than a sensation: never has the strangeness of my own identity, which for me has always been nonetheless so vivid, touched me with such acuity. 'I' clearly became the formal index of an unverifiable and impalpable change. Between me and me, there had

---

[98] Esposito, R.: Immunitas: The Protection and Negation of Life, quot., p. 152.
[99] Nancy, J.-L.: Corpus, quot., p. 28.

always been some space-time: but now there is an incision's opening, and the irreconciliability of a compromised immune system."[100]

Therefore, the body turns out to be constitutively atomized, parceled out and reconstituted, reimplanted on any pieces of skeleton remaining, in a view entirely aimed at a performing existence. Profusions of nature and proliferations of technique: this is how all things stand together; this is how they all simultaneously touch and mutually expose each other, in an impalpable grain that unravels and exceeds the identity image of an immovable Ego. The dissent of the body thus represents our existential condition, which is infinitely finite because it has already always been exposed, lying on its very limit. In this plane of existence, we can discover the singular multiplicity of life, whether natural or artificial, actual or virtual. The plural horizon of Nature within which more or less complex constructions of bodies, existences, and wills unfold—eccentrically. What has been said so far shows how Nancy, in turn, in the framework of that French deconstructionism of which he is (as well-known) one of the greatest exponents along with Derrida, has deconstructed the occlusive gesture of the West, the founding gesture of all metaphysics and all transcendence; he has managed to deconstruct that gesture by literally staging existence, its body, its outside, its excription, its disclosure. In a time when we are exposed to contagion with others, with all others, on the wave of globalization, a thought of the "exposed body," a reflection such as the one Nancy invites us to make on the *ex-peau-sition*, on the fact that we are all exposed and crossed by others, starting from the skin itself, I think is as important and urgent as ever. The extent to which these reflections can have an impact in terms of political thought today as well (of course, in the high and philosophical sense of the term, namely, in the sense of a thought that deals with thinking about the world and what form of it we wish to have) is quite evident. In strong agreement with Nancy, Esposito points out that: "Never before have we had such an accurate perception of this community of bodies – the endless contagion that combines, overlaps, soaks, coagulates, blends, and clones them. Its openings in the flesh and transfusions of blood are identical to those in meaning: every definition of the healthy and the sick, the normal and the pathological, immunity and community, vacillates."[101] If the proper mode of our "being body" consists in being absolutely and necessarily *improper*, then this very impropriety is what constitutes itself as "biologically valid." In this sense, the technique employed on our bodies represents the *vital* and no longer *natural* passage for the conquest or prolongation of existence. We have definitely become part of a different regime of meaning. As Esposito rightly notes in his dialogue with Nancy: "This happens when the body loses absolute ownership of itself through the mode of the technological prosthesis. Only then does a fragment of the body of others, or a non-bodily thing, turn the human body into a space that cannot be fully appropriated, because it is beyond, or before, the dichotomies between subject and object, internal and external, thought and living body."[102] All this, adds Esposito—who quotes

---

[100] Therein, pp. 167–168

[101] Esposito, R.: Immunitas: The Protection and Negation of Life, quot., p. 151.

[102] Id.: Persons and Things, quot., p. 123.

Nancy here—happens "in the philosophical story of his own heart transplant" where the French philosopher expresses himself in these words: "My heart became my stranger: strange precisely because it was inside. The strangeness could only come from outside because it surged up first on the inside [...] The intrusion of a body foreign to thought. This blank will stay with me like thought itself and its contrary, at one and the same time."[103] Inside and outside, internal and external, forward and backward, the magma of existence is concentrated in the body. Artificial, technical, cybernetic existence, implanted in the very flesh of man and "This is not a symbolic surrogate or even a functional extension of a natural limb, but rather, the real presence in the body of something that is not body."[104] A body that carries within itself another body, an outside brought inside. Here Esposito's analyses converge and turn out to be in consonance with Nancy's ones, although the focus on the biopolitical and immune side is at its highest in Esposito. We conclude by letting Esposito have the last word in this long-distance dialogue with Nancy: there is "something non-living that serves to preserve life. We might say that this need for self-preservation is at the root of all contemporary forms of body modification: the body suspends itself – it interrupts and doubles itself – with the aim of extending its duration. It exposes itself to what lies outside it in order to save what it still bears inside. It enters into a problematic relationship with the other in order to protect itself from itself, from its natural tendency to be consumed. On these lines, from this perspective, once again the figure of the immune system rises out of the heart of biopolitics. Situated at the crucial point in which the body encounters what is other than itself, it constitutes the hub that connects various interrelated entities, species, and genera such as the individual and the collective, male and female, human and machine. Precisely because of this power to combine, the immune apparatus has become the point of tangency – of connection and tension – between all contemporary languages [...]."[105]

---

[103] Nancy, J.-L.: Corpus, quot., p. 163.
[104] Esposito, R. Immunitas: The Protection and Negation of Life, quot., p. 148
[105] Therein, p. 149.

Chapter 5
"What Is Missing: The Poem of Our Being-Together"

1 After Communism, to Think the Community

The Inoperative Community, published in an intellectual climate nourished by the teachings of Heidegger, Derrida, and Foucault, contains all the major themes that have animated recent continental philosophy: the end of traditional metaphysics; the decentralization of subjectivity (the cogito); the change of language seen as a repository which is always in "excess of"; and, above all, the conception of human existence understood—according to Heidegger's view—as *Dasein* and *Mitdasein.* Moreover, the political context within which Nancy's work is set fraught with profound changes on a global scale: the progressive fall of official communism, the Cold War, the rise of neoliberalism. Against the latter view, Nancy's book has acquired its distinctive, and even provocative, outlines—outlines manifested already in its title: *The Inoperative Community*, precisely. Following the path laid down by Heidegger and the post-structuralist philosophers,[1] the study thus reaffirms the priority of politics over economics, namely, the primacy of the public place seen as an arena of democratic interactions.[2] With this in mind, the French philosopher enucleates an entirely new notion of "community": as we are about to see, it is a substanceless community and, in this sense, "inoperative" or "nonoperative," thus it is beyond any instrumental control or purpose.

Referring to the gradual decay involving the entire Soviet empire and its satellite countries, as well as the fall of global transformations, Nancy aims to immediately put on the table the implications of this involutional process for political theory in general, and for the conception of community in particular. The most serious and

---

[1] On this topic, we refer to the work by Tarizzo, D., entitled Il pensiero libero. La filosofia francese dopo lo strutturalismo, quot.

[2] In this regard—and in line with Nancy's position—see the work by Arendt, H.: The Promise of Politics, Random House of Canada (2005).

painful experience of our age is "the testimony of the dissolution, the dislocation, or the conflagration of community";[3] a conflagration inextricably linked to the death of communism. According to Nancy's analysis, communism "stands as an emblem of the desire to discover or rediscover a place of community at once beyond social divisions and beyond subordination to technopolitical dominion, and thereby beyond such wasting away of liberty, of speech, or of simple happiness as comes about whenever these become subjugated to the exclusive order of privatization."[4] Despite some merits, communism as a political regime was, from its outset, troubled by a fundamental—and even metaphysical—law: its inclination to reduce everything to production, management, and effective control. Besides the despotic or corrupt teachings of its "leaders," as the philosopher writes, "the schema of betrayal is seen to be untenable in that it was the very basis of the communist ideal that ended up appearing most problematic: namely, human beings defined as producers (one might even add: human beings defined at all), and fundamentally as the producers of their own essence in the form of their labor or their work."[5] In the age of productivity, public community was itself conceived as an operational purpose, that is, as "a community of beings producing in essence their own essence as their work, and furthermore producing precisely this essence *as community.*"[6] Hence comes Nancy's sharp criticism:

> An absolute immanence of man to man-a humanism- and of community to community-a communism-obstinately subtends, whatever be their merits or strengths, all forms of oppositional communism, all leftist and ultraleftist models, and all models based on the workers'

---

[3] Nancy, J.-L.: The Inoperative Community, quot.

[4] Ibid. As Nancy explains a little further on, community cannot be seen as the emblem of a primitive past or a golden age that needs to be recovered. In this sense, the philosopher refers to Rousseau as one of the most significant representatives of a society described as resulting from the loss or degradation of a communitarian (and communicative) intimacy. "[…] at every moment in its history, the Occident has given itself over to the nostalgia for a more archaic community that has disappeared, and to deploring a loss of familiarity, fraternity and conviviality.' 'Regardless of the actual character of the dream or the precise images used (the natural family, the city of Athens, early Christianity, communes or fraternity), it is always a matter of a lost age in which the community was enveloped in tight, harmonious and unbreakable bonds and in which, above all, it limited itself, through its institutions, rituals and symbols, the representation of its immanent unity, intimacy and autonomy. Distinguished from society (which is a mere association and division of forces and needs) the community was not only intimate communication among its members, but also organic communion with its existence. Conversely, in Nancy's view, "So that community, far from being what society has crushed or lost, is what happens to us—question, waiting, event, imperative—in the woke of society. Nothing, therefore, has been lost, and for this reason nothing is lost. We alone are lost, we upon whom the 'social bond' (relations, communication), our own invention, now descends heavily like the net of an economic, technical, political, and cultural snare. Entangled in its meshes, we have wrung for ourselves the phantasms of the lost community. What this community has 'lost' -the immanence and the intimacy of a communion—is lost only in the sense that such a 'loss' is constitutive of 'community' itself." These passages are taken from The Inoperative Community, quot. and are found respectively on pp. 10 and 11–12.

[5] Therein, p. 2.

[6] Ibid. These themes were also addressed by M. Merleau-Ponty in his last course given at the Collège de France in 1961, entitled Philosophy and non-philosophy since Hegel, quot.

1 After Communism, to Think the Community

council. In a sense, all ventures adopting a communitarian opposition to "real communism" have by now run their course or been abandoned, but everything continues along its way as though, beyond these ventures, it were no longer even a question of thinking about community. Yet it is precisely the immanence of man to man, or it is man, taken absolutely, considered as the immanent being par excellence, that constitutes the stumbling block to a thinking of community. A community presupposed as having to be one of *human beings* presupposes that it effect, or that it must effect, as such and integrally, its own essence, which is itself the accomplishment of the essence of humanness. [...] Consequently, economic ties. Technological operations, and political fusion (into a *body* or under a *leader*) represent or rather present, expose, and realize this essence necessarily in themselves. Essence is set to work in them; through them, it becomes its own work. This is what we have called "totalitarianism," but it might be better named "immanentism."[7]

Other, less radical forms of community politics, which include the nonorthodox models of Hegelian Left and Marxism, equitably share the inherent flaw in communism. In all these forms, the ultimate goal is the attainment of a representable and totalizing community. Precisely in sharp contrast to such communitarian ideologies, Nancy recalls—in a short note added to the text *The Inoperative Community*—that the title with which Jean-Christophe Bailly presented the issue of the journal *Aléa, La communauté, le nombre*, had been more than an invitation in itself; "Already a text, already an act of writing, increasing in number, summoning writing":[8] summoned to "give voice to" a thought about something that, while unable to be represented, grasped or confirmed, could not be reduced to silence. What could not be represented was community. If, in fact, we read Bailly's introductory text, the reason for the nonrepresentability of community becomes immediately clear. It is *in* the number, *of* the number, and therefore nonrepresentable, like the number, which is always indefinite with respect to the hypothesis of the infinitely numerable and like the set of numbers N that remains unimaginable. Yet, to say nonrepresentability of community means to already provide it with *sense*; it means to grasp the nonrepresentable sense of community as it is.[9] It is no coincidence that the images and visions of the everyday collected by Bailly, through *someone's* distracted and then more attentive eye, refer precisely to the uncountable and therefore always *approximate* set of *presences, gazes, spaces, bodies*.[10] At the end of the same year—1983—it was Maurice Blanchot who dealt with the theme of community in his essay *La communauté inavouable*; an essay in which the philosopher took up the theme that, in *The Inoperative Community*, Nancy had placed at the center of his own reflection. It is weird to speak of the communitarian need in the era of the end of communisms,

---

[7] Therein, pp. 2–3.
[8] Therein, p. 42.
[9] On this topic see Dell'Erba, P.: Ai margini del discorso poetico, in "Studi Filosofici" XVIII, (1995), p. 211.
[10] As Bailly writes: "A man walks down a path, two men talk on the terrace of a café, a woman leaves a hotel, a dense crowd advances, human clusters come undone, merge. These images do not represent community—that is not representable—these are scenes, views. Do we have anything else? The number can only be imagined in reduced form (yet, even an immense crowd is small), and this, in discourse, is already a policy: a quiet village, its bell tower, as if to say nothing"; Bally, J.-C.: *La communauté, le nombre*, in "Alea", 4, (1983), p. 7 (my translation).

even weirder to speak of community in an era that does not identify itself as the heir of ideologies, but works towards moderate politics from left to right and vice versa. Unquestionably, before the Western hypothesis of the global village,[11] communism was the last communitarian project, or rather represented the last community designed by an Idea of the History of Humanity and an Idea of Man. From this historical turning point, annihilating in many respects, the French philosopher begins his reflection on the inoperability of community. Seeking the reasons for the failure of the communist project, denying the scheme of the betrayal of "an originary communist purity of doctrine or intention,"[12] he proves how the very communist ideas of History and Man fail to attain the sense or *a* sense of community. Thus, by reading Bataille and in particular his text on sovereignty,[13] Nancy testifies that the failure of communism consists in its representative logic of the "progressive humanization of the world"[14] and the "enactment" of its own essence. According to the philosopher, therefore, – in line with Batallian[15] and Merleau-Pontyan analysis—the greatest

---

[11] In the volume The Creation of the World or Globalization, Jean-Luc Nancy sets the world in the balance between creation and destruction. Indeed, the philosopher poses a dramatic question: can what we call "globalization" give birth to a world or its opposite? The complexity of the question, and thus of the answer, lies entirely in the utterance and its combinatorics, because the two terms are joined by a conjunction that—as Nancy himself writes in the opening of the volume—is to be understood "must be understood simultaneously and alternatively in its disjunctive, substitutive, or conjunctive senses." (p. 29) However, in Nancy's view, the problem posed by philosophy lies in the fact that "The world has lost its capacity to "form a world" [faire monde]: it seems only to have gained that capacity of proliferating, to the extent of its means, the "unworld" [immonde], which, until now, and whatever one may think of retrospective illusions, has never in history impacted the totality of the orb to such an extent. In the end, everything takes place as if the world affected and permeated itself with a death drive that soon would have nothing else to destroy than the world itself. (…) It is as if being itself—in whatever sense one understands it, as existence or as substance—surprised us from an unnamable beyond" (pp. 34–35). In Nancy's judgment, which not surprisingly returns to Hegel, the movement of the world is somehow suspended and, along with it, the certainty of necessary historical progress as well. What has dissipated is the link-"every link"-between "knowledge, ethics, and social well-being" (p. 34). The concept of world has always been subordinate to the concept of worldview; but a world seen, a world represented, is a world hanging in the gaze of a subject-of-the-world. However, such a subject internally burdens the weight of the contradiction that he himself cannot be in the world. Thus the question of the world, as a world seen or a world represented, is—throughout the history of the West—the question of the world, the question of the necessity and sense of the world, which according to Nancy is actually the axis of self-deconstruction that runs through all onto-theology (cf. p. 4). From Descartes to Malebranche and Leibniz, "the decisive feature of the becoming-world of the world, as it were—or else, of the becoming-world of the whole that was formerly articulated and divided as the nature-world-God triad—is the feature through which the world resolutely and absolutely distances itself from any status as object in order to tend toward being itself the 'subject' of its own 'worldhood'—or 'world-forming.' But being a subject in general means having to become oneself …" (p. 41).

[12] Nancy, J.-L.: The Inoperative Community quot., p. 2.

[13] Bataille, G.: The Accoursed share, vol. II & III, Mit press, Cambridge, Massachuttes (1992).

[14] See Esposito, R.: Il comunismo e la morte, Introduction to the Italian ed. of Bataille, G.: *La Sovranità*, Il Mulino, Bologna, (1990), (my translation).

[15] A position also shared by M. Blanchot in his work dated 1995, entitled *The Unavowable Community*, quot.

obstacle to the realization of the communist project consists precisely in the idea of a man absolutely capable of producing himself, his environment and the world. In *The Compearance*,[16] a text written seven years after *The Inoperative Community*, Nancy deals once again with communist thought and program. Indeed, while it is true that we are still in the time of the maximum unfolding of individualist wretchedness, and while communism, although no longer constituting our insurmountable horizon, still remains the only thought of the "common of men," it is indeed difficult (if not impossible) to avoid its confrontation. By reconsidering the undoubtedly emblematic Marxian character or impetus which, completely missed by the real politics of communist totalitarianisms, found its physiognomy sketched out in *The German Ideology*,[17] written between the end of 1945 and the fall of 1946, Nancy tries to identify the inherent limit of the analysis of the Marxian "real" and to outline the features of its overcoming. In this regard, we should recall that the scheme of the materialist conception of man and history set the "real" individual against the abstract and monadic individual of the "robinsonnades."[18] According to Nancy, however, the Marxian program—which presented a society as the place of "mutual creation" or "mutual generation" in which "men create themselves reciprocally both physically and spiritually"[19] and in which the "real condition of a real multiplicity of real relationship"[20] is given—would fail, though the essential sense of the polis would emerge: not understood as the combinatory sum of all human activities and functions, but as the place of compearance, that is, of being-in-common.[21] Nancy writes about being-in-common by "downgrading," rather than replacing, the term community. Being-in-common has no representations; rather, it represents the absence of representation. It needs to think of being-in-common as the word that cannot own the object of its desire. The thought of being-in-common and its nonrepresentability is a thought that challenges its writing, since the word—transcribed or spoken—is the sketch, the trace, the spacing of a thought delivered to its limit: the openness to all possibilities or impossibilities of community.

This approach gives birth to Nancy's attempt to think an essential sense of the political without confusing it with the Idea of a program consisting of the theses and projects of a party:

> If politics is again to mean something, and mean something new, it will only be in touching this 'essentiality' of existence which is itself its own "essence," that is to say, which has no essence, which is "arch-essentially" exposed to that very thing. In its structure and nature, such an exposure contains at the same time the finitude of all singularity and the in-common

---

[16] Nancy, J.-L.: *La Comparution/The Compearance*. Political Theory 20 (3):371–398, quot.

[17] Marx, K. & Engels, F.: *The German Ideology*. In Science and Society. International Publishers. (1975). pp. 19–581.

[18] Nancy J.-L.: *La comparizione*. In Vv., Aa., Politica a venire. Quot. note n.24 (my translation).

[19] Id.: *La Comparution/The Compearance*. Political Theory 20 (3):371–398, quot. p. 387.

[20] Therein, p. 378.

[21] On this point Hannah Arendt has made very sharp reflections in her volume dated 1958, entitled The Human Condition. University of Chicago Press, Chicago.

of its sharing. This 'at the same time' does not imply a juxtaposition: but finitude and in-common are the same thing.[22]

To subtract the "political" from the productive and practical politics of communism means, therefore, to put oneself in the condition of rethinking its possibility as no longer dissolved in the "sociotechnical element of forces and needs,"[23] but as redefined in the ontological approach to community, in order for the political to designate (occur as) the singularity of existence. Moreover, on the one hand, it means subtracting man (who exists politically) from the Hegelian reality of an *unhappy consciousness* resolving in itself and in reason the sense of the *rational unity* of the Whole, understood as absolute knowledge—the first affirmation of which consists in the dual subjection to the fear of death and to the work of the slave. On the other hand, it also means subtracting man from the converging communist hypothesis, which glimpsed the possibility of a humanity capable of finally freeing itself through the acquisition and appropriation of all productive forces, as well as through the affirmation of *class consciousness*. Now, the juxtaposition of the two humanities, both the Hegelian and the Marxian, is by no means accidental: one is real (with the term real referring to the dialectical real) and the other is praxical-realistic. Nancy's criticism of communist humanism is therefore matched by the thematization of a direct relationship or specular compatibility between Hegel's philosophy of action and Marx's theory of praxis,[24] inspired by the Batallian denegation of both perspectives. Starting from the Hegelian conceptual acquisition according to which, in the dialectical master-slave (or lord-bondsman) opposition, the consciousness of the master is revealed as servile consciousness, Bataille elicits the consequence that the former is wholly ascribable to the category of the "'work,'" since it is determined in the "inessential working" of the slave. It follows that the movement of the *negative*, originating as the moment of the master's *enjoyment of the thing*, is also wholly absorbed in and coincident with industrious productivity. Hegel further clarifies this device, in which what is lost is independent sovereignty, ultimately made inessential with respect to the operative truth of servile consciousness:

> In this recognition the unessential consciousness is for the lord the object, which constitutes the *truth* of his certainty of himself. But it is clear that this object does not correspond to its Notion, but rather that the object in which the lord has achieved his lordship has in reality turned out to be something quite different from an independent consciousness. What now really confronts him is not an independent consciousness, but a dependent one. He is, therefore, not certain of *being-for .. self* as the truth of himself. On the contrary, his truth is in

---

[22] Id.: La Comparution/The Compearance. Political Theory 20 (3):371–398, quot., p. 390.

[23] Id.: The Inoperative Community. Quot., p. 2. For a more in-depth examination of the thought of the essence of the political, see: Nancy, J.-L. and Lacoue-Labarthe, Ph.: Ouverture, in Rejouer le politique. Galilée, Paris (1981).; on the concept of the "withdrawal of the political," it is useful here to refer to the note by Nancy placed in the writing providing an introduction to the Italian version of M. Blanchot's volume The Unavowable Community (La Comunità Inconfessabile), entitled: La comunità affrontata. Reference is to p. 14.

[24] See Esposito, R.: Il Comunismo e la morte, in La sovranità, quot. p. 17 and ff.

1 After Communism, to Think the Community

reality the unessential consciousness and its unessential action. The *truth* of the independent consciousness is accordingly the servile consciousness of the bondsman.[25]

Thus, the relationship between Hegel's philosophy of action and Mark's theory of praxis is delineated—as we have already anticipated. The Hegelian desire to encompass the totality of human experience in the system implies that man *works* primarily to achieve the realization of his own essence—on the other hand, the knowledge or self-knowledge path of consciousness merely corroborates this consideration. The idea of a man who achieves knowledge of his own essential reality through his own work meets, in a specular way, the ideal of communist humanism, according to which the essence of a man is realized through the deployment of his productive power and consists in his ability to make and produce his own essence. Bataille's understanding and experience of communism, in its drift to totalitarian state, showed him not only the degeneration or betrayal of the initial project,[26] but especially the impossibility of grasping the deepest sense of existence in communist humanism. Indeed, the communist project, by unveiling and ensuring it uniformly in the description of the totality of natural needs, informed existence exclusively upon the profit designed by a subject: man himself, "taken absolutely, considered as the immanent being par excellence."[27] This devaluation of existence, grasped and imprisoned in servile occupations and subservient to the order of things,[28] lacked the "sacrificial nature of existence itself, the desire for being outside itself, outside an existence that exists as dispersion and as generosity"[29] indicated by Bataille. This is the reason for which Nancy writes that Bataille "has gone farthest into the crucial experience of the modern destiny of community."[30] Now, to ascertain the scope of this assertion means to deal firstly with the thought of experience—"the act of existence and life "[31]—that Bataille defined as "inner." Inner experience was for Bataille the experience of the unknown—"a presence which is no longer in any way distinct from an absence"[32]—and was the experience of dialectically irretrievable negativity, bringing subjectivity to its extreme dispossession and to the extreme moment of its *désoeuvrement*. It is therefore the sovereign exposure to Nothingness—as we have already seen in the first part of this work -, for which the subject, as in Hegel, does not perform any permanent movement where negativity is reabsorbed: "in the

---

[25] Hegel, G. W. F.: Phenomenology of spirit, quot., pp. 116–117.
[26] See Nancy J.-L.: The Inoperative Community, quot., pp. 21 and ff.
[27] Therein, p. 3.
[28] On this theme see Lannou, J.-M.: Bataille: la plénitude souveraine, in "Revue de Métaphisique et de Morale," juill.-sept., (1997), pp. 431–453.
[29] Rella, F.: Lo sguardo ulteriore della bellezza, Introduction to Bataille G.: La parte maledetta. Boringhieri, Turin, (1992), p. XXXII (my translation).
[30] Nancy J.-L.: The Inoperative Community, quot., p. 16.
[31] Rella, F.: Lo sguardo ulteriore della bellezza, Introduction to G. Bataille, quot. p. XIX (my translation).
[32] Bataille, G. & Boldt-Irons, L.A.: (eds.) Inner Experience. State University of New York Press, Albany (1988) p. 5.

NOTHING [...] being is 'outside itself'; it is in an exteriority that is impossible to recapture."[33]

In being "outside itself" the subject is devoid of the dimension of "in itself" and "for itself." Exposed to this exteriority and suspended over it, the subject is no longer the subject of experience, for experience now becomes sovereign, becomes the authority:[34] "the only subject of the destitution of all subjectivity."[35] Therefore, what the subject is destined for is a dissociation from itself, the moment in which it is turned into anything other than itself, the moment in which the being singular—the being separated from others in its individuation and individuality—exceeds its limits to access sovereignty, the continuity of nonbeing in which "unrestrained communication"[36] is rendered. Therefore, it is in the sovereign experience of the loss of the self, in the denial of self and life, in the "excessive and painful leaning over the abyss of death"[37] that Bataille conceives community:

> The living being who sees his fellow die can no longer exist except outside himself [...] In that moment, each of us is driven out of the narrowness of our individual personhood and, to the greatest extent possible, we lose ourselves in the community of our fellows. That is why communal life must hold itself to the same level as death. In private, most lives are fated to be trivial. But a community cannot endure except at the same level of intensity as death. It will start to rot as soon as it does not have to face the grandeur of danger.[38]

Death is the experience of the absolutely inappropriate and inaccessible exposing the unknowable absolute, and therefore, cannot be crossed. Confronted with the "dying" other, the living one experiences the loss of his or her own self through the experience of the other's death; however, this experience is anything but "experienceable." Indeed, the living one experiences neither his or her own death nor the death of the other, just as the dying one does not fully experience his or her own death either—for he or she dies without taking possession of it, without being able to affirm or witness it. Death thus comes to constitute the elusive otherness, in the sense that what is in common is not the experience of death, but rather the impossibility of accomplishing that very experience in common. As if to say that we are made up of something inappropriable. Therefore, what is in common is this singular exposure to death, exposure to the extreme experience of the non-experienceable; this is why what is ultimately revealed is not community, but an impossible communication: the impossibility of community—the "community of the impossible community."[39]

---

[33] Nancy J.-L.: The Inoperative Community, quot., p. 18.

[34] See Bataille, G. & Boldt-Irons, L.A.: (eds.) Inner Experience. quot. pp. 7 and ff.

[35] Esposito, R.: Communitas. Origine e destino della comunità, quot. p. 133 (my translation).

[36] Lannou, J.-M.: Bataille: la plénitude souveraine, in "Revue de Métaphisique et de Morale," juill.-sept., quot., p. 442 (my translation).

[37] Esposito, R.: Communitas. Origine e destino della comunità, quot., p. 139 (my translation).

[38] Bataille, G.: The limit of the useful. Edited by Cory Austin Knudson & Tomas Elliott, The MIT Press. Cambridge, Massachusetts, (2022), pp. 89–90.

[39] Esposito, R.: Categorie dell'impolitico. Bologna: Il Mulino, p. 308 (my translation). On the concept of "impossible community,' 'see in particular R. Esposito's important Introduction to the work

1 After Communism, to Think the Community

The demystification of death and community—the one subtracted from redemption in the fullness of immanence accomplished by Christian and communist logic, and the other subtracted from the idea of an essential communion—is the extreme motif from which Nancy articulates his discourse on being-in-community:

> The death upon which community is calibrated does not operate the dead being's passage into some communal intimacy, nor Joes community, for its part, operate the transfiguration of its dead into some substance or subject - be these homeland, native soil or blood, nation, a delivered or fulfilled humanity, absolute phalanstery, family, or mystical body. Community is calibrated on death as on that of which it is precisely impossible to make a work.[40]

In the thought of death, *being-with-another* reveals its own paradox, such that the *with* absolutely loses the meaning of bonding and takes on the meaning of *partition*.[41] Here it comes to light the reason for which finitude, rigorously conceived, is the ever-singular finitude, is of the being-singular that shares the being-in-finitude with the other singular. Compearance, then, is nothing but this sharing: not an acknowledgment of either oneself or the other, but rather the original communication *in appearing to one another*. Nancy's finite community is given in the partition of being—the original partition of existences.

> A singular being *appears,* as finitude itself: at the end (or at the beginning), with the contact of the skin (or the heart) of another singular being, at the confines of the *same* singularity that is, as such, always *other,* always shared, always exposed.[42]

The inoperative community to which Nancy alludes does not arise from an act of (contractual or other type of) "intersubjective" bonding"; "It does not set itself up, it does not establish itself, it does not emerge among already given subjects (objects)."[43] Rather, by reflecting a mutuality or mutual transgression without fusion, community marks the place of the *"between* as such," which is like a hit or a mark: "you *and* I (between us)-a formula in which the *and* does not imply

---

by Cantarano, G.: La comunità impolitica. Città Aperta, Troina (2003), pp. 7–13.

[40] Nancy J.-L.: The Inoperative Community, quot., pp. 14–15.

[41] Id.: Un soggetto?, quot., p. 45 (my translation).

[42] Id.: The Inoperative Community, quot. pp. 27–28. For Nancy, it is important to emphasize how the concept of "singularity" differs profoundly from that of individuality. The individual is purely the "residue" or the "left suspended" of the dissolved community; in its atomistic "indivisibility," the individual shows itself simply as "the abstract result of a decomposition" Individualism, just as any other form of immanentism, proves to be "suffocating" and "self-annihilating." This is why Nancy rejects modern individualist and neo-liberal theories. According to the philosopher's words, the individual is what remains of the dissolution of the community: "Some see in its invention and in the culture, if not in the cult built around the individual, Europe's incontrovertible merit of having shown the world the sole path to emancipation from tyranny, and the norm by which to measure all our collective or communitarian undertakings. But the individual is merely the residue of the experience of the dissolution of community. By its nature-as its name indicates, it is the atom, the indivisible-the individual reveals that it is the abstract result of a decomposition. It is another, and symmetrical, figure of immanence: the absolutely detached for-itself, taken as origin and as certainty." The quoted passage is taken again from: The Inoperative Community, cited above, p. 3.

[43] Therein, p. 29.

juxtaposition, but exposition"[44] as indicated in the passage just quoted. Taking up the Cartesian axiom concerning the cogito, Nancy replaces it with the words "I am exposed," which means, "I am first of all exposed to the other, and exposed to the exposure of the other."[45] In the gaps of mutual exposure, in the space of comparison, community is not productive, but rather formed by a basic lack or absence: the lack of a substance or stable identity that could be fixed once and for all. The salient features of Nancy's reflection outlined through the concepts of *partage-expeausition-comparution*—the focus of this book—constitute the experience of community. This experience is always to come, to be thought of, rigorously, every time:

> The existence of the existent only takes place singularly, in this sharing of singularity, and freedom is each time at stake, for freedom is what is at stake in the "each time". There would be no "each time" if there were not birth each time, unpredictably arising and as such unassignable, the surprise of the freedom of an existence.[46]

The thought of existence is thus the turn, or rather the fold, of the thought of community in its insurmountable finitude, arising from the abandonment of being determined in the experience of freedom. It is an experience that is played out at the limits of the possible, and there finds the place of its unfolding as opening, spacing, breakthrough, and inscription of the sense of existence. Freedom is thus understood not as a right but as an experience.

However, what does Nancy precisely mean by using such a term? This is what we will try to understand in the final pages of this paper, thus rounding off the topics discussed so far. Now, however, it is useful to dwell on the sacrificial question, which has pervaded our entire Western history and represents one of the crucial nodes in Nancy's thought: the detachment from the Christian perspective and from traditional politics.

2 The Question of Sacrifice in the Contemporary Thought

In a note to the text *A finite Thinking*, at the end of the chapter on the "Unsacrificeable," Nancy, shaken by a tragic event that occurred at a church in Monrovia, writes:

> Rereading these pages while editing them for their French publication as a book (August 1, 1990), I want to add the following: yesterday, between four hundred and six hundred people were massacred in a church in Monrovia, where they were taking refuge from the fighting and executions of the civil war that is tearing Liberia apart. Among them, there were many women, children, and infants. The newspaper explains that eviscerated bodies of two young children were thrown onto the altar. I'm not passing judgement on this war, or even on this particular episode. I'm insufficiently informed to do so. I simply want to note the crushing

---

[44] Ibid.
[45] Therein, p. 31.
[46] Id.: *The experience of freedom*, quot., p. 68.

weight of this configuration of signs: in Africa, upon a Christian altar, a parody of sacrifice—yet less than a parody, more a slaughter unsupported by any sacrifice.[47]

Here, then, is the point that traverses the issue of sacrifice and that Nancy identifies at the end of this extraordinary text. A conclusion that refers back to the beginning of the text on the unsacrificeable, when, quoting Bataille, Nancy writes: "There is something like a critical, or crucial point of contemporary thought in the question of sacrifice."[48] In other words, the question of sacrifice, to some extent that we shall now examine, seems to be an open and unresolved question in all respects. Why is the West determined by its relationship with sacrifice? What is the meaning of sacrifice? How does that relationship link us to the "closure" of the West? Has not the time come for the West to leave it behind? These are Nancy's questions.[49]

Socrates and Christ represent two of the greatest historical figures related to sacrifice. In fact, as the philosopher explains, it is a "self-sacrifice," or rather a "sacrifice sought, intended, and demanded by the victims' entire being, by their life and thought and message."[50] It is "the sacrifice of the subject, in the fullest sense of the word and fullest duality of the genitive."[51] In other words, it is the "sacrifice" of the West that holds the secret of participation in the transcendent and limitless communication. In this, it is infinite and universal. The sacrifice of the self (self-sacrifice) is "an appropriation, through the transgression of the finite, of the infinite truth of this very finitude."[52] Sacrifice thus stands as the element of "union" between the finite and the infinite and, in Christian terms, as the "union" between body and soul. In such a union, the dialectic of the laceration of the flesh that "offers itself to" represents its elevation to spirit. However, here again lies the folly of the sovereignty of the cogito, and the justification of the annihilation of the self as a place of transubstantiation to ultimate truth. All horror is thus redeemed and pacified in the eyes of reason. The scream of Bataille's *eye in the vagina*[53] remains the one and only witness to our sacrificial history. In its relationship with Eros and mysticism, sacrifice is here beyond measure, limitless, excessive. The access to both is different, but the

---

[47] Id.: A finite thinking, quot., p. 329, n. 61.

[48] Ibidem, pp. 53–54.

[49] On these matters, starting from Jean-Luc Nancy, the following texts are recommended: Ariemma, T.: L'Occidente messo a nudo, Luca Sossella, Milano (2019); Arnould, E.: The impossible sacrifice of poetry. Bataille and the Nancian critique of Sacrifice, "Diatrics", 26, 2, (1996), pp. 86–96 (see infra); Badiou, A.: L'offrande réservée, in F. Guibal, J.-C- Martin (dir.), Sens en tous sens. Autour des travaux de Jean-Luc Nancy, Galilée, Paris, (2004), pp. 16–24; Cecala, P.: Guerra, sovranità, responsabilità. Una riflessione con Nancy e Derrida, in U. Perone, Intorno a Jean-Luc Nancy, quot., pp. 127–132; De Petra, F.: Comunità, comunicazione, comune. Da George Bataille a Jean-Luc Nancy, Derive Approdi, Roma (2010).

[50] Nancy, J.-L.: A finite thinking, quot., p. 56.

[51] Ibid.

[52] Therein, p. 59.

[53] See Bataille, G.: *Story of the eye* (J. Neugroschel, Trans.; First City Lights edition). City Lights Books 1987.

exit is identical: it is death. The *do ut des* of sacrifice has no return, no promised *munus*, unrepresentable as alterity.

> Sacrifice as self-sacrifice, universal sacrifice, the truth and sublation of sacrifice, is the very institution of the absolute economy of absolute subjectivity, which can only really mime the passage through negativity, in which, symmetrically, it can only reappropriate or transappropriate itself infinitely. [...] Ultimately, everything happens as if the spiritualization or dialecticization of sacrifice could proceed only by way of a tremendous act of self-denial. It denies itself under the figure of an "early" sacrifice, one that it claims to know but actually constructs for its own ends and itself ratifies in the form of an infinite process of negativity, which it passes off under the "sacred" or 'sacralizing' label 'sacrifice.' In this way, however, the sacrificial destruction that it makes such a show of abandoning co "early" sacrifice is installed at the heart of the process. At its center, this double operation simultaneously combines, in an onerous ambiguity, the infinite efficacy Of dialectical negativity and the bloody heart of sacrifice.[54]

Then, Nancy wonders: how to deal with such denial? Bataille followed the logic of the dialectical overcoming of sacrifice by offering torn out and tortured bodies, ecstatic at the same time. He also did so throughout his reflection on the Nazi death camps. What was at stake there, according to Bataille, was given by the senselessness of the very existence of the camps on the one hand, and on the other, by the will that does not refuse to face horror for it is characterized as "the possible" of man. In Bataille's words echoed by Nancy: "In a universe of suffering, of baseness and stench, we still have the luxury [*le loisir*] of measuring the abyss, its absence of limits and this truth that obsesses and fascinates."[55] The death camp is thus the place that—by means of horror—grants us access to such truth. The senselessness of the camps, which on the one hand would take us outside the logic of sacrifice, actually originated under the government of reason: as Nancy further writes, it "appropriates the abyss of its own subjecthood."[56] However, insofar as the camps represent the reason for the sacrificial horror and the Jews the victims of that atrocious sacrifice, it is necessary to reflect on the equally "rationally sacrificial" role of the executioner (the Aryan race). This is what, for example, emerges from Himmler's speech[57] on October 4, 1943: according to the latter, it is a matter of acknowledging the intolerable by the victims and, at the same time, of the quieter and more interior sacrifice by the executioners. On closer inspection, then, the German people here entirely

---

[54] Nancy, J.-L.: A finite thinking, quot., pp. 62–63.

[55] Therein, p. 68. Here, J.-L. Nancy echoes the text by Bataille, G., & Rottenberg, E.: Reflections on the Executioner and the Victim. Yale French Studies, 79, (1991), pp. 15–19.

[56] Therein, p. 69.

[57] Therein, p. 70. Nancy reports, in this regard, part of Himmler's speech published Hilberg, R.: The Destruction of the European Jews. Yale University Press. Yale, (2003). We consider it useful to write it here below, in order to better understand the meaning of the reason that "appropriates the abyss of its own subjecthood"—in Nancy's words quoted earlier: "We have the moral right, we had the duty to our people to do it, to kill this people who would kill us [...] All in all, however, we can say that we have carried out this most difficult of tasks in a spirit of love for our people [... .] Most of you know what it is like to see 100 corpses side by side, or 500 or 1000. To have stood fast through this and [...] — to have stayed decent that has made us hard. This is an unwritten and never-to-be-written page of glory in our history."

2 The Question of Sacrifice in the Contemporary Thought

absorb the tragic power of sacrifice and tacitly hold its secret. Indeed, there is no "ancient" sacrifice in what lies on the outside (the devastation of the human and the fumes of the crematoria rising to the sky). In what is on the inside (the appropriation of this "sacrifice of duty" by the SS or the Aryans) there is nothing but "technique." In either case, the ancient sacrificial economy is gone, its device annihilated and the experience of the "sacrifice of the West" ended. At this point, writes Nancy:

> it will fall to us to say that there is no 'true' sacrifice, that real existence is unsacrificeable, that the truth of existence is to *be* unsacrificeable. Existence isn't to be sacrificed, and can't be sacrificed. It can only be destroyed or shared. This is the unsacrificeable and finite existence that is offered up to be shared: *methexis* is henceforth offered as the sharing out of the very thing that it shares: both the limit of finitude *and* respect for the unsacrificeable. The effacement of sacrifice, the effacement of communion, the effacement of the West: this doesn't mean that the West could be reduced to what came before it, or that Western sacrifice could be reduced to the rites that it was supposed to have spiritualized. Rather, it means that we are on the verge of another community, another *methexis*, one in which the *mimesis* of sharing would efface the sacrificial mimicry of an appropriation of the Other.[58]

In Nancy's view, this is what remains to be understood: the unsacrificable end at the bottom of the speculative operation of the West lies precisely in its being without any possible end, without meaning or redemption. We can certainly say that *The Unsacrificable* is the most radical attempt made by Nancy to move away from Bataille.[59] However, before considering what, about Bataille, relates to the question of sacrifice and in order to draw together the movements leading to the opening statements of *The Unsacrificable*, it is useful to focus on Nancy's description of the history of sacrifice. Although concise and elliptical, Nancy's sketch offers an original reading of ancient religious rituals, even if he seems to borrow some features of evolutionary sociological theories that, from Taylor to Girard and from Hubert and Mauss to Durkheim, aim to show a continuity between ancient pagan ritual sacrifice and Christian "moral" sacrifice. The originality of Nancy's reading consists in presenting the West as the place of the dialectical denegation of sacrifice itself, subtracting it from the onto-theological vision within which Christianity has accustomed us to think of it. In fact, it is not possible for us to experience or know anything about real or ancient sacrifice, because any access to its truth is historically, or rather, metaphysically forbidden. Nancy envisions the establishment of a mimetic logic at the heart of the relationship between the West and sacrifice. The onto-theological truth of Western sacrifice is represented, as we have already mentioned, by the figures of Socrates and Christ. These two figures lead back to the ancient sacrifice, repeating and structurally modifying it at the moment of dialectical overcoming (i.e., there where it reaches its completion and/or end, realizing itself). Western sacrifice is self-sacrifice; it is unique, is the embodied truth of all sacrifice,

---

[58] Therein, p. 77.
[59] See, in this regard, the contribution by Arnould, E. The Impossible Sacrifice of Poetry: Bataille and the Nancian Critique of Sacrifice. Diacritics 26 (2) (1996) pp. 86–96, in which it is emphasized that sacrifice remains a model of lack and finitude in Bataille, and therefore, still depends on the Christian interpretation of it.

or rather, is its constitutive essence. This is why self-sacrifice stands as the surplus of sacrifice, the last of sacrifices. In other words, sacrifice is sublimated because it is wholly infinitized, insofar as it is inscribed once and for all. Everything that happens is thus sublimated and overcome thanks to the sacrificial logic underlying it. And it is precisely such logic that, nevertheless, continues to exert its power of fascination. In this economy of sacrifice, then, the whole of religious anthropology would have to be rethought, if it is true that, in ritual sacrifice, the sacrificer sacrifices to God what "*lui re-vient*" and which is, so to speak, what originally comes ("*vient de*") from him and never really leaves him. In other words, Western sacrifice—and its supposed "moral" legitimacy—is based on the onto-theological truth of Christian self-sacrifice and on the closure of its history. It is a phantomic "morality," which never ceases to haunt us especially because of the sense it attaches to its end. This is why the end of the sacrifice of history would mean something quite different from its telos or completion as well. Therefore, according to Nancy, such sacrifice should rather be thought of as the revelation and exposition of its horizon or spectral essence, defying any logic of the end and freeing itself beyond an economy of spiritual return (*de la revenance*). Hence, it is not so much a matter of declaring the disappearance of sacrifice, nor of affirming the recognition that the symbolic order of history, to which it has been referred, is henceforth concealed and inoperative; rather, it is a matter of following its track that continues to obsess our minds as an inexplicable and absolutely intolerable fascination. Herein lies the whole difficulty underlying the question of sacrifice on which Bataille himself insisted so much. Sacrifice takes on the fascinating character of intolerability and inevitability. But what in sacrifice can be declared fascinating? Bataille sought to explore precisely the climax of such fascination in the erotic relationship—which, indeed, can be seen in the majority of his works, from *My Mother* to *Story of the Eye*, from *Eroticism* to *L'Abbé C*. However, it is important first to understand why the fascination of sacrifice is inevitable and why it is so seductive to us. To not allow sacrifice being fascinating means to expose it somehow to its own end, to suspend the cruelty of the sacrificial operation and its phantom. Given that sacrifice brings into play the horror of devastation, it is necessary to denounce its fascination and resist its attraction: it needs to close our eyes before the fascinating phantom passes by. Thus, on closer examination and by reading the inevitable character of the fascination "by and for" sacrifice in conjunction with its intolerable character, it is sacrifice itself that falls under a new light. In Nancy's view, Bataille went to the limits of this sublime fascination just as he experienced the impossible satisfaction of the need for sacrifice. If the latter leads us not to nothing but to simulacrum and comedy (as, for example, Bataille saw in Hegel's work), the non-comedy of bloody horror is, in turn, intolerable to the Western spirit. Therefore, for the West, sacrifice remains, in its very necessity, as if suspended between the impossibility of its full actuality and the temptation of its pure simulation. This would seem to be the impasse of Western sacrifice; an impasse with which, Bataille would have basically struggled all his life. It is a matter of understanding the relationship between sacrifice and death. It is a matter of understanding the twofold work of sacrifice: being death on the one hand, and revealing the existing in its finitude on the other, assuming death

2 The Question of Sacrifice in the Contemporary Thought

as the horizon of all existence. In *Theory of Religion*[60] Bataille states that to sacrifice means not to kill, but to abandon and give. From this short statement we can identify a form of sacrifice that is absolutely irreducible to all traditional interpretations, namely, a form of sacrifice which leads to nothing more than the unveiling of a community that, through the death of the individual person, experiences its own effacement.

Indeed, as Blanchot repeatedly points out, isn't it true that death is constitutively present in the Bataillean project, as the extreme experience of *Acéphale* well indicates?

> 'Acephale' is still bound to its mystery. Those who participated in it are not certain they had a part in it. They have not spoken, or else the inheritors of their words are tied to a still firmly maintained reserve. The texts published under that title do not reveal its scope, except for a few sentences which much later still stun those who wrote them. Each member of the community is not only the whole community, but the violent, disparate, exploded, powerless incarnation of the totality of beings who, tending to exist integrally, have as corollary the nothingness they have already, and in advance, fallen into. Each member makes a group only through the absoluteness of the separation that needs to affirm itself in order to break off so as to become relation, a paradoxical, even senseless relation, if it is an absolute relation with other absolutes that exclude all relation. Finally, the "secret" - which signifies this separation - is not to be looked for directly in the forest where the sacrifice of a consenting victim should have occurred, a victim ready to receive death from the one who could give it to him only by dying.[61]

From this moment on, sacrifice is pushed in a totally different direction that may lead to the literal meaning of Acéphale, namely its own decapitation and the convulsive role of its own members belonging to the only possible community: the community of death.

> The Acéphale community, insofar as each member of the group was no longer only responsible for the group but for the total existence of humanity, could not accomplish itself in only two of its members, given that all had in it an equal and total share and felt obliged, as at Massada, to throw themselves into the nothingness that was no less incarnated by the community. Was it absurd? Yes, but not only absurd, for it meant breaking with the law of the group, the law that had constituted it by exposing it to that which transcended it without that transcendence being other than the group's, i. e., to the outside which was the intimacy of the group's singularity. In other words, the community, by organizing and by giving itself as project the execution of a sacrificial death, would have renounced its renunciation of creating a work, be it a work of death, or even the simulation of death. The impossibility of death in its most naked possibility (the knife meant to cut the victim's throat and which, with the same movement, would cut off the head of the "executioner"), suspended until the end of time the illicit action in which the exaltation of the most passive passivity would have been affirmed.[62]

Sacrifice and abandonment: these are the key words of the experience of community, as understood by Bataille, in which the existence of Acéphale is inscribed. Although short-lived, it designated the resolutely "aneconomic" and genuinely

---

[60] Bataille, G.: *Theory of Religion*. Zone Books, Princeton (1989).
[61] Blanchot, M.: *The Unavowable Community*. Station Hill Press, (1988), pp. 13–14.
[62] Therein, p. 14.

"inoperative" experience of a loss "without thought of return, without calculation and without safeguard." There can only be community in the endless, repeated movement of its abandonment and retreat: in other words, in its sacrifice. It follows, then, that such a community of sacrifice gives itself only in its self-effacement, experiences itself only in the very movement of its dissolution. Its presence is always that of an absence. The very time of sacrifice is thus the sacrifice of time, time exposed to its worklessness: this time does not act in sacrifice, but exposes singularities outside the insurmountable horizon of their constitutive finitude; this is perhaps what can be understood as the limit, and even the essence, of all community.

That is why—as Bataille continuously experienced—existence constitutes itself only in exceeding and exposing itself to itself precisely in the sacrificial condition. However, what is in the abandonment of sacrifice is precisely Nothing. And here, once again, the concept of sovereignty reappears. Following Nancy's words, sovereignty is the sovereign exposure to an excess or transcendence that does not present itself, but inoperatively surrenders itself. Therefore, isn't this openness of existence to its abandonment, in which Nothingness sovereignly works, the real movement of sacrifice? Let us go back again to Blanchot's words:

> Sacrifice: an obsessive notion for Georges Bataille, but whose meaning would be deceptive· if it did not glide continuously from the historical and religious interpretation to the infinite exigency it exposes itself to in what opens it to the others and separates it violently from itself. Sacrifice traverses Madame Edwarda, but does not express itself there. In *Theorie de la Religion*, it is stated: 'to sacrifice ·is not to kill, but to abandon and to give.' To link oneself with *Acéphale* is to abandon and to give oneself: *to give oneself wholly to limitless abandonment.* […] There is the gilt by which one forces the one who receives it to give back a surplus of power or prestige to the one who gives - thus, one never gives. The gift that is abandonment commits the abandoned being to giving without any return in mind, without any calculation and without any safeguard even for his own giving being: thus the exigency of the infinite that resides in the silence of abandonment. […] That is the sacrifice that founds the community by undoing it, by handing it over to time the dispenser, time that does not allow the community nor those who give themselves to it, any form of presence, thereby sending them back to a solitude which, far from protecting them, disperses them or dissipates itself without their finding themselves again or together. The gift or the abandonment is such that, ultimately, there is nothing to give or to give up and that time itself is only one of the ways in which this nothing to give offers and withdraws itself like the whim of the absolute which goes out of itself by giving rise to something other than itself, in the shape of an absence. An absence which, in a limited way, applies to the community whose only clearly ungraspable secret it would be. The absence of community is not the failure of community: absence belongs to community as its extreme moment or as the ordeal that exposes it to its necessary disappearance. Acéphale was the shared experience of that which could' not be shared, nor kept as one's own, nor kept back for an ulterior abandonment. […] The Acéphale community could not exist as such, but only as imminence and withdrawal: imminence of a death closer than any proximity; prior withdrawal of that which did not permit one to withdraw from it. Privation of the Head thus did exclude not only the primacy of what the head symbolized, the leader, reasonable reason, reckoning, measure and power, including the power of the symbolic, but exclusion itself understood as a deliberate and sovereign act which would have restored the primacy under the form of its downfall. The beheading, which should have made possible the 'endless (lawless) unfettering of the

2 The Question of Sacrifice in the Contemporary Thought

passions,' could be accomplished only through passions already unfettered, the passions affirming themselves in the unavowable community that its own dissolution sanctioned.[63]

The impossible community of Acéphale will be lacerated and lacerating, will dissolve the sovereign claim of the subject of knowledge; it will escape from all sorts of effectuality to which the subject constantly attempts to constrain it in order to reduce its expropriating scope, to eradicate, in other words, that undecidability of the other with which communitary experience continuously confronts it. As Esposito points out:

> The metaphor of acephality alludes to the non-humanity nested in man as his constitutive otherness: in the sense that man, instead of his own identity - the identity of "his own" - is constituted by what does not belong to him, by an absolutely inappropriate impropriety. This does not mean that the subject disappears altogether; it means that it remains devoid of that foundation - precisely the head as the place par excellence of knowledge - that makes it a subjectum suppositum, a presupposed subject. It is as if the metaphysics of presupposition is pierced, interrupted, shattered by a wound that recalls both passion and passivity: as if the 'being under' of subjectivity should turn from supposition into subjection. As if the 'subject of' - of thought, will, representation - had to, or could, in a final self-destructive impulse, become 'subject to': no longer presupposed, but simply exposed to an inessential existence precisely because it is not defined by any essence other than existence itself. And - what is most interesting - a common existence. This community, in which subjects do not find themselves but are lost - or find themselves in their own and others' loss, in the loss of any proprium - is the specific object of Bataille's reflection in the years immediately preceding the war.[64]

Therefore, it is not enough to stand up to death in order for community to exist; it is not enough to look into the face of the extreme power of the negative: it will always be possible for the subject to make use of it, to bend death to the order of sense, to make it operative. Rather, it is a matter of having access the expropriating nature of dying, i.e., to the fact that death is what externalizes the subject, without the latter being able to return to itself from that "absolute devastation" to which the knowledge of the other destines it. We can certainly say that, in the time span from the Notion of dépense to the inner experience, i.e., from 1933 to 1943, and culminating in the experience of the failure of Acéphale and the staging of Numantia,[65] the centrality of sacrifice definitely comes to an end in Bataille. What in fact Numantia puts on stage is the opposite of a sacrifice: there, an entire people agonizes, and thus not just an individual on whose sacrifice, around whose death, a community is founded and endures. Community is not the result of individual or even group sacrifice;

---

[63] Therein, pp. 15,16, 57.

[64] Esposito, R.: La comunità della perdita, Introduction to Bataille, G.: La congiura sacra. Bollati Boringhieri, Turin (1997), p. XXXI (my translation).

[65] Numantia is the city that, besieged by the Romans in 133 B.C., decided to self-destruct rather than surrender to the victors. For the Spanish people, this episode became a symbol of freedom and independence, even to the point of prompting Cervantes to stage its tragic story. For the Spanish text, see: De Cervantes, M.: El cerco de Numancia. Comunidad Madrid, Madrid (1997). The story of Numancia was effectively taken up by Moroncini B.—who traced its theoretical implications in a dialogue with Bataille, Blanchot, Nancy—in his text La comunità e l'invenzione. Cronopio, Naples (2001).

community exists in the moment when the people of Numantia stop existing by dying. The community of Numantia exists at the moment it becomes nothing. Acephalous, headless, is thus the death of the community of Numantia, for it neither builds nor edifies, does not transmute into being,[66] represents the disproportion of being. On closer inspection, then, "the staging of the collectivist self-decapitation practiced by the citizens of Numantia, besieged by the Romans, refers not simply to an extreme claim to freedom, but also to a need for a community recognizable only by the elimination of that 'interdiction' locking the individual into its uniqueness and keeping it away from any 'othering.' The fact that this possibility must pass through a sacrifice, a wounding, or even the death of the subject, means that not only Bataille's community has nothing to do with the small countries, the sense of rootedness and belonging to which old and new communitarianisms look, but that it is defined by an irrepressible subtraction from itself. A community that is unavowable, inoperative, impossible—or of those who have no community—since the only thing its members can share is not a presence, but rather a lack: *Communication* takes place only *between two beings brought into play*—torn, suspended, both bending over their nothingness."[67] Therefore, it is necessary to "access the otherness of the other, the othering of the other; it is necessary to know—with an excess of knowledge, a non-knowledge—that the other escapes measurement, all measurement, even that which, in the order of the measurable, leaves an empty box for disproportionality. The subject must suffer the innumerable death of the 'other.'"[68] In *Acéphale,* what could not be put in common was death, the death of the other, because such death could not become a "common measure." It is the community itself, then, that suffers this sort of *essential* implosion or annihilation; it is the community itself—to borrow Blanchot's words again—that cannot be put in common. This, therefore, is the reason why *Acéphale,* which is "abandonment and gift," according to Bataille's words, is:

> [...] integral sacrifice, i.e., that of the communitary illusion: that community is possible in presence, as presence, even and especially when the presence of community ultimately is given in the death of all. [...] The illusion of common death, which corresponds to that of a community of sovereigns alone, represents the ultimate resistance of the subject of knowledge to the experience of the death of the other: by dying, in the illusion of seeing himself die, he wants to make the death of the other an object of his knowledge, to conform it to him. But the death of the other is of the other: community is its absence. Yet the absence of community is not the failure of community: it belongs to it just as to its ultimate moment; or as to the test that exposes it to its necessary disappearance.[69]

In the dialogue between Blanchot and Nancy, which exemplarily takes place in *The Unavowable Community,* what emerges is a concept of community that does not refer back to anything immortal or transcendental, nor even to something

---

[66] Moroncini, B.: La comunità e l'invenzione, quot. See, in particular, pp. 106–108.

[67] Esposito, R.: Termini della politica, Introduction to Vv. Aa. Oltre la politica. Antologia del pensiero "impolitico". Mondadori, Milan (1996), pp. 24–25 (my translation).

[68] Moroncini, B.: Community and Invention, quot. pp. 195–196 (my translation).

[69] Therein, p. 196 (my translation)

(blood-relatedness, race or ethnicity) that would a priori determine its characteristics. It rather refers to a concept of community that takes upon itself "the impossibility of its own immanence, the impossibility of a communitarian being as subject. In a way the community takes upon itself and inscribes in itself the impossibility of the community ... A community is the presentation to its members of their mortal truth [...]. It is the presentation of finitude and of excess without possibility of return that founds the finite-being."[70] As Blanchot also states, taking up Nancy's words:

> community [...] maintains itself only as ·the place - the non-place - where nothing is owned, its secret being that it has no secret, working only at the unworking that traverses even writing, or that, in every public or private exchange of words, makes the final silence resound, the silence where, however, it is never certain that everything comes, finally, to an end. No end there where finitude reigns.[71]

But if there is no possible end—and thus no possibility of death—there, where finitude is sovereign, then the sacrificial experience—understood as an annihilating path to salvation—can also be said to have ended. Our century has seen—with the holocaust—the end of sacrifice. The existence of the camps determined the limit of sacrificial thinking, caused its self-exhaustion. In other words, it sanctioned its intolerability. In the death camps lies the last, ultimate horizon of modern thinking about sacrifice. Sacrifice, there, exposed itself and abandoned itself to the unsacrificeable. Something in the existence of the camps eludes sacrifice itself; an excess, we might say, which actually announces the end of the sacrificial operation as the work of death. The camp is the no-longer-spatial (a-spatial) place of the human. In the lagers, "human beings, reduced to bare biological life, have *really* become mere interchangeable specimens of the species. This is achieved primarily by means of terror, which, in pushing humans against each other, destroying the space that separates them, replaces the limits and channels of communication between individuals with an iron bond holding them so tightly together that their plurality fades into one giant-sized Man."[72] What exceeds the sacrifice and thus makes it intolerable is therefore not the death to which the sacrifice apparently leads, but the non-life, as in to say the inhumanity of existence.[73] The rising of the fumes from the crematoria into the sky is not the actual symbol of extermination. Rather, it consisted in the

---

[70] Blanchot, M.: The Unavowable Community. Station Hill Press, (1988), p. 11. See at this regards: Bernasconi R.: On deconstructing nostalgia for community within the West: the debate between Nancy and Blanchot, "Research in Phenomenology", 23, (1993), pp. 3–21; Hill L.: Nancy, Blanchot. A Serious Controversy, Rowman & Littlefield International, London (2018); Resta, C.: La comunità degli amanti e la passione politica. Il dissidio tra Nancy e Blanchot, in "Shift. International Journal of Philosophical Studies", 2/2021–1/2022, pp. 147–166; Rogozinski, J.: L'impossibile comunità della comunità, in "Shift. International Journal of Philosophical Studies", 2/2021–1/2022, pp. 167–176.

[71] Therein, pp. 19–20.

[72] Forti, S.: *Il totalitarismo*. Laterza, Bari (2001). p. 87 (my translation).

[73] See, in this regard, chapter four on tanatopolitics in the volume by Esposito, R.: (2004). Bios. Biopolitics and Philosophy, quot., pp. 115–157; Agamben, G.: Homo sacer. Il potere sovrano e la nuda vita. Einaudi, Turin (1995).; and Id.: Quel che resta di Auschwitz . L'archivio e il testimone. Bollati Boringhieri Turin (1998).

devastating power of depersonalization of the human, from the bodily incision of numbers to the total reduction of any reasons for physical differentiation. No longer human bodies, but indistinct bodily masses. The immolation of the human, of which the holocaust was an expression, is the ultimate marker of the "sacrifice of the West." The West self-sacrifices itself in the horror of the Holocaust and opens itself to the process of globalization. However, for the sake of existence, Nancy refuses to embrace the possibility of sacrificial experience. The impossibility of infinitizing existence through sacrificial experience releases existence itself from any form of transcendence and places it in the space of finitude. It is precisely the finite character of existence that makes it unsacrificeable: as Nancy writes, "thought rigorously and in accordance with its *Ereignis*, 'finitude' means that existence can't be sacrificed. It can't be sacrificed because it's already, not sacrificed, but offered to the world."[74] "Offered" and not "sacrificed." These words are strangely similar, but Nancy points out that "nothing is more dissimilar." What is that radically separates offering from sacrifice? This question presupposes a reference to another text by Nancy—*The Sublime Offering*—in which "offering" still remains somehow linked to the concept of sacrifice. However, the question is also present (and quite remarkably) in Nancy's texts on existence: from *The Experience of Freedom* to *The Sense of the World*. Thus, if we read these works, we will be able to identify what the philosopher means by the term "world" and, based on this, what being "offered" to the world would mean. Finite existence offers itself to the world as a "proposition" that never settles into presence, like a gift that implies nothing in exchange, for it is abandonment without any change: the only law of abandonment, such as of love, is to be without nothing in return and without any appeal; something like an abundance, perhaps, or an excess. However, in envisaging existence as abandonment, are we not led back once again to the sacrificial concept thematized by Bataille? To say that existence is *offered* means undoubtedly to make use of a word that belongs to the sacrificial vocabulary (Nancy himself admits this by referring back to the German terms, which, as we can well see, come from the same lexical origin: *Opfer, Au sopferung*). However, this serves the purpose of attempting to emphasize the fact that, if we were to say that existence is sacrificed, we should point out that "it is sacrificed *by* no one and *to* nothing."[75] "Existence is offered" *means* the finitude of existence. "Finitude expresses what Bataille means when he says that sovereignty is NOTHING."[76] It is necessary to dwell on this statement and on what Nancy writes in the following pages, because there we can see his attempt to move away definitively from those conceptions of sacrifice, which the French philosopher still sees in Bataille and Heidegger.

> A being that exists happens. It takes place. And this happening or this taking place is merely a being-thrown into the world. In this throw it is offered. And yet, it is not offered by anyone or to anyone. Nor is it self-sacrificed, since nothing, no being, no subject, precedes its

---

[74] Nancy, J.-L.: A finite thinking, quot., p. 74.
[75] Ibid.
[76] Ibid.

being-thrown. In fact, *it isn't even offered or sacrificed to a Nothingness, to a Nothing or to an Other. in whose abyss it could still impossibly enjoy its own impossibility of being.*[77]

Here is the point where—according to Nancy—Bataille and Heidegger must be corrected. Corrected and withdrawn from the fascination of sacrifice. Such fascination is in fact linked to an ecstasy toward an absolute Outside or Other:

> Western sacrifice corresponds to an obsessive fear of the "Outside" of finitude, however obscure and groundless this "outside" may be. "Fascination" already indicates something of this obscure desire to commune with this outside. Western sacrifice seems to reveal the secret of *mimesis* as the secret of an infinite, trans-appropriating *methexis* (the Subject's participation in its own subjectivicy, so to speak). *This is the appropriation of an Outside that, by being appropriated, abolishes the very idea of a "methexis," and of a "mimesis."* Ultimately, no secret is actually revealed. Or, rather, all that's revealed is the fact that there is nothing *but* this secret: the infinite sacrificial secret.[78]

In Nancy's view, the fascination of the Outside becomes—with the sacrificial experience—the place of the absolute appropriation of the Other, the place where the illusion of an infinite existence can do nothing but generate horror. Instead, the finitude offered to the world, or rather, between the folds of the world, is the only unsacrificable and possible existence. And here, the effacement of sacrifice would become one with the effacement of the West.

> One really should retrace the striking history of political sacrifice, of sacrificial politics – politics *in truth,* that is to say, the "theologicopolitical": from expressly religious sacrifice to the diverse Reigns of Terror, and to all the national, militant, and partisan sacrifices. The politics of the *Cause* to which sacrifice is due. In this sense, all theologicopolitics, including its "secularization," is and can be nothing other than sacrificial. And the sacrifice represents the access to truth, in the appropriating negation of the *finite* negativity of sense. To have to do with the *world,* which is not a "Cause" - and which is itself without any Cause - is to have to do with sacrifice no longer.[79]

Starting from here, according to Nancy, the possibility of our "politics to come" is at stake, as we shall see in the next chapter.

---

[77] Therein, p. 75.
[78] Ibid.
[79] Id.: The Sense of the World, quot., p. 89.

Chapter 6
The Restlessness of the World

The world has lost its capacity to "form a world" [faire monde]: it seems only to have gained that capacity of proliferating, to the extent of its means, the "un-world" [*immonde*], which, until now, and whatever one may think of retrospective illusions, has never in history impacted the totality of the orb to such an extent. In the end, everything takes place as if the world affected and permeated itself with a death drive that soon would have nothing else to destroy than the world itself. […] The fact that the world is destroying itself is not a hypothesis: it is in a sense the fact from which any thinking of the world follows, to the point, however, that we do not exactly know what "to destroy" means, nor which world is destroying itself. Perhaps only one thing remains, that is to say, one thought with some certainty: what is taking place is really happening, which means that it happens and happens to us in this way more than a history, even more than an event. It is as if being itself - in whatever sense one understands it, as existence or as substance - surprised us from an unnamable beyond. It is, in fact, the ambivalence of the unnamable that makes us anxious: a beyond for which no alterity can give us the slightest analogy. It is thus not only a question of being ready for the event - although this is also a necessary condition of thought, today as always. It is a question of owning up to the present, including its very withholding of the event, including its strange absence of presence: we must ask anew what the world wants of us, and what we want of it, everywhere, in all senses, *urbi et orbi*, all over the world and for the whole world, without (the) capital of the world but with the richness of the world.[1]

---

[1] Nancy, J.-L.: The Creation of the World, or, Globalization. Transl. F. Raffoul & D. Pettigrew. State University of New York, Albany (2007), pp. 34–35. Let's immediately point out some interesting studies on these themes related to globalization and the future thinking: Baptist G.: L'isola da pensare: "un mondo distinto dal mondo", Intervista con Jean-Luc Nancy, in Ead. (ed. by), Jean-Luc Nancy. Pensare il presente. Seminari cagliaritani 11–13 dicembre, Cuec, Cagliari 2010, pp. 165–170; Esposito, R.: Dialogo sulla filosofia a venire, (colloquio con J.-L. Nancy) in J.-L. Nancy, Essere singolare plurale, Einaudi, Turin (2001); Fallen, C.: Jean Luc Nancy, porté(e)s de la pensée, in Jean-Luc Nancy. Anastasis de la pensée, quot., pp. 203–210; Härle, C-C.: Sovranità, guerra e tecnica nel mondo globalizzato, in "Post-filosofie", 15, (2022), pp. 65–89; Hutchens B.C.: Jean-Luc Nancy and the Future of Philosophy, McGill-Queen's University Press, Montreal & Kingston (2005); Kakinami, R.: Re-commencement, reprise—de la pensée, in Jean-Luc Nancy. Anastasis de la pensée, quot., pp. 191–194; McQuillan, M.: Deconstruction and Globalisation: The world According to Jean-Luc Nancy, in Jean-Luc Nancy and plural thinking. Expositions of World, Ontology, Politics, and Sense, (P. Gratton and M.-E. Morin eds.), State University of New York Press, New York, (2012); pp. 57–75; Raffoul F.: The Creation of the World, in Jean-Luc Nancy and plural thinking. Expositions of World, Ontology, Politics, and Sense, quot., pp. 13–26; Rogozinski, J.: Face à l'im-monde, in Jean-Luc Nancy. Anastasis de la pensée, quot., pp. 149–156; Smerick, Ch. M.: No Other Place to Be: Globalization, Monotheism,

© The Author(s), under exclusive license to Springer Nature Switzerland AG 2024
D. Calabrò, *The Thought Awaits Us All*,
https://doi.org/10.1007/978-3-031-75401-2_6

It is from this questioning, this restlessness, that we must start.

1 Folds of the World: Community

The community, in the direction taken by Nancy, is the "withdrawal" or "subtraction of something," and this something is nothing but the Being-with: a relationship without relationship, a simultaneous exposure to the relationship and to the non-relationship. In other words, we can say that the ex-posed (posed from the outside) community that the French philosopher speaks of:

> is made up of the simultaneous immanence of the retreat and the coming of the relation, and it can be decided at any moment by the least incident—or more probably, and more secretly, it never ceases being decided at each instant—in one direction or in the other, in one direction and in the other, in "freedom" and in "necessity," in "consciousness" and in "unconsciousness," the undecided decision of stranger and neighbor, of solitude and collectivity, of attraction and repulsion. This exposure to relation/nonrelation is nothing other than the exposure of singularities to each other. (I say "singularities" because these are not only individuals that are at stake, as a facile description would lead one to believe. Entire collectivities, groups, powers, and discourses are exposed here, "within" each individual as well as among them. "Singularity" would designate precisely that which, each time, forms a point of exposure, traces an intersection of limits on which there is exposure. To be exposed is to be on the limit where, at the same time, there is both inside and outside, and neither inside nor outside. It is not yet even to be "face to face." It is anterior to entrapment by the stare that captures its prey or takes its hostage. Exposure comes before any identification, and singularity is not an identity. It is exposure itself, its punctual actuality. (But identity, whether individual or collective, is not a sum total of singularities; it is itself a singularity.) It is to be "in oneself" according to a partition of "self" (meaning both a division and a distribution), it is constitutive of "self," a generalized ectopia of all "proper" places (such as intimacy, identity, individuality, name), places that are what they are only by virtue of being exposed on their limits, by their limits, and as these very limits.[2]

Hence, from this conception of community springs a new vision of political life, or at least of the public place in which politics and political practices manifest themselves. A conception of politics that can no longer be declined according to the model of the institution—even if democratic—but rather according to that of the partition—as we shall now see more closely. Nancy makes a distinction that has become commonplace in recent continental thought, namely that between the *political* (political ideology) and *politics* (the "real" politics), where the former term designates party strategies and concrete institutional functioning, and the other term denotes the presupposed arena for these strategies.[3] Through this distinction, Nancy

---

and Salut in Nancy, in Jean-Luc Nancy and plural thinking. Expositions of World, Ontology, Politics, and Sense, quot., pp. 27–42.

[2] Nancy, J.-L.: Of Being in common. In Miami Collective (ed.) transl. J. Creech. University of Minnesota Press, Minneapolis (1991). p. 8.

[3] In this regard we also recall Hannah Arendt's position, who, in The Promise of Politics, quot., designates the agora—the one that Nancy here refers to as the arena—as the eminent place of the

suggests that the term "political" can be used to denote "not the organization of society but the disposition of community as such"; just as a public life is not entirely dissolved in the "sociotechnical element of forces and needs," the term can be a synonym for "the sharing of the community".[4] By proceeding to reflect on the difference between "operative" and "inoperative" politics (the operative politics of parties and the inoperative politics aimed at becoming ecstatic, that is, at going out of itself), we can read:

> The outline of singularity would be "political" - as would be the outline of its communication and its ecstasy. "Political" would mean a community ordering itself to the unworking of its communication, or destined to this unworking: a community consciously undergoing the experience of its sharing.[5]

Such meaning of "political" does not depend on, or at least does not simply result from, what we might call a "political will." As it is already introduced into the community, it somehow implies its very submission to the experience of community as communication. However, how does such politics of communication arise? Actually, it arises in the original violence of partition—as we will explain shortly. Indeed, Nancy is aware of the prevalence of the different powers and hegemonic asymmetries of world politics.[6] Although politics cannot be reduced to power (or an instrument of "will of power"), as he notes, the sphere of power relationships cannot be avoided. Likewise, the violence associated with it cannot be underestimated as well. Therefore, without making himself the bearer of a Christian or pseudo-Christian ideal of nonviolence, the French philosopher penetrates into the concept of violence in order to escape its common usage, which is now largely trivialized:[7]

> If we are to attempt a critical analysis of violence, without masking the inherent complexity or ambivalence of this topic, the following will have to be considered: nowadays, we are confronted with the question of violence not only understood as external violence (which leads to questions about ethical and political resistance to actual violence - without raising real questions, after all, since the consensus on this is completely unanimous, just as powerlessness is unanimous), but also as internal violence. In other words, beyond a default conviction, something remains to be thought about violence, or what is too hastily categorized under the term "violence." The "essence" of "violence" is certainly not resolved in its reprobation, and to address the problem of its "essence" (and/or its concept, and/or the history of concepts and essences themselves) may require a rearrangement of the ethical and political definitions to which we must appeal. Something remains to be thought of - or

---

"space of freedom the political", precisely where there is political freedom and there is no government nor political institution. Cf. p. 131. In addition, refer to M. Villani's volume on this matter: On extension. Jean-Luc Nancy in the wake of Hannah Arendt, Inschibboleth, Rome 2022; Time and History. Researches on the Ontology of the Present, Inschibboleth, Rome 2022, pp. 1–112.

[4] Nancy, J.-L.: The Inoperative Community, quot., p. 40.

[5] Therein.

[6] In this regard, see the major volume by Bazzicalupo L.: Politica, identità, potere. Il lessico politico alla prova della globalizzazione. Giappichelli, Turin (2004).

[7] A radical reflection on the concept of violence was carried out by Derrida in the volume entitled, Force of Law: The "Mystical Foundation of Authority", in D. Cornell, M. Rosenfeld & D. Carlson eds., Deconstruction and the Possibility of Justice. Routledge, New York (1992).

manages, today, to be thought of - which has to do with the diversity of "violence" and with an internal "bend" in "violence". This is the reason why I have given these notes the title "violence and violence" - without therefore referring to the commonplace "there is violence and violence" (= the legitimate and the illegitimate one, the good and the bad one, the revolutionary and the reactionary one, and so on); a commonplace that has also lost all credibility (with the problems that consequently arise, of State violence and revolutionary violence to "self-defense", the frenzy of "righteous" wars, death penalty, and so on). Moreover, there is yet another element that highlights a specific trait of the era, namely the fact that upstream of the various theses on violence there are clearly different modern philosophical traditions, which have complicated or deconstructed the concept or concepts of "violence".[8]

According to the analysis carried out in the following pages by Nancy, a conception of violence emerges, which, along with modernity, "has penetrated into being itself." What does this mean? It means recognizing that there is not simply *an* instrumental "use" of violence or *different* "uses" of it, but rather it is a matter of recognizing and addressing the fact that it can no longer be represented as something that lies in an external "nature" or as something that, for that very reason, can be encompassed and cushioned by culture. On the contrary, "culture itself (and/or the "subject") has had to rethink itself in violence, as *a* violence or as a "bend" *of* violence. This therefore means thinking of "violence" as constituting "subjectivity itself."[9] This implies, therefore, an ontological rethinking of the relationship between the concept of violence and the self/other relationship. The path followed by Nancy goes far beyond the stereotype whereby violence arises from the self/other relationship; instead, it is precisely the opposite: violence is the relationship itself; it is what gives rise to the origin of the self and the other; it is the *in-common* that "tears apart the integrity of the homogeneous." The relationship is thus the "arch-original withdrawal of the homogeneous, the continuous, and the substantial (or of being: the *being-in-common* is the tearing of being). There is thus an arch-violence or an absolute transcendental violence of the relationship, a violence that lies precisely in the non-substantiality and nonessentiality of the relationship, or even better, in the essentiality of its nonessentiality".[10] Therefore, reflecting on the "original violence" of the relationship, that is, on the "tearing" of the homogeneous, thanks to which *self* and *other* are given, means:

> Being able to think the event - being it differential, temporal, historical, finite, the event as such, an "as such" that results precisely in a disruptive force - disruptive of nothing, but actually disruptive (or indeed, actuality itself). Therefore, neither violence nor non-violence, but perhaps [...] what we might call the glow, the glow and the explosion of the relationship thanks to which the self and the other are given, standing at insurmountable distance from each other. We might also say that the glow is the interiority of the exteriority as such, not yet withdrawn "into" itself, but exposed as such, as an "outside" that has no "inside," the

---

[8] Nancy, J.-L.: Tre frammenti su nichilismo e politica, in VV.AA, Nichilismo e politica (edited by R. Esposito, C. Galli, V. Vitello). Laterza, Rome-Bari (2000), pp. 12–13 (my translation).

[9] Ibid, p. 15 (my translation). See, in this regard, also Freud S.: Civilization and Its Discontents. London: Hogarth Press and Institute of Psycho-Analysis (1930).

[10] Ibid, p. 16 (my translation).

outside of the relationship which creates the relationship, including - and perhaps first and foremost - the relationship with oneself. Thus violence, or better "real" violence, would be something that arises when one cannot bear the glow or the explosion in the origin. Violence would turn out to be really violent when it cannot bear the violent partition (partage) of the origin. Nor can it withstand it since it adheres to the representation of an antecedent subject, a homogeneous one, to which the glow surges. Violence: a rage against the glow.[11]

We are thus coming to a nodal point in the relationship between violence and the *self/other* relationship: the partition—the original violence—is what must be endured; it is the task imposed by the *finite sense* of existence. Therefore, it is inhomogeneity, seen by modernity as violence to be annihilated and suppressed with equal violence in order to recompose or reconstitute—so to speak—the unitary order, the one-all within which, however, on closer inspection, the worst misdeeds are concealed (see totalitarian experiences),[12] and that needs to be profoundly rethought. Thus, it needs to preserve an "inoperative" dimension within the strategic aims, so that they do not become "totalizing" and thus oppressive. In other words, strategic affairs must always retain the memory of an inoperative domain: that of a distributed public space, which gives politics its meaning and measure. Therefore, what are the implications, especially in terms of politics and morality, of an "inoperative community" within our "conflicting civilizations"? The emphasis on "inoperativeness" does not make the course toward apathetic inactivity necessary, just as the absence of community substance.[13] It does not mean a lack of bond. Precisely, the splitting or "disruption" of total structures entails not only political and moral engagement, but also the explication of and the attention to cultural differences. As Nancy writes in the chapter of *The Inoperative Community* entitled "Myth Interrupted":

> [...] the passion of and for community propagates itself, unworked, appealing, demanding to pass beyond every limit and every fulfillment enclosed in the form of an individual. It is thus not an absence, but a movement, it is unworking in its singular "activity," it is the propagation, even the contagion, or again the communication of community itself that propagates itself or communicates its contagion by its very interruption.[14]

---

[11] Ibid, p. 17 (my translation).

[12] It is precisely within this context that R. Esposito's critical reflection on "legitimate violence" exercised against ethnic, religious, and social inhomogeneities lies. Inhomogeneities that are systematically let out by the force of the law "into a sort of "invisible community." Cf. Esposito, R.: Comunità del profondo. Esodo e diaspora alla ricerca del comune, in "Communitas" 1, (2005), pp. 229–236.

[13] On the issue of the absence of community see May T.: The community's absence in Lyotard, Nancy, and Lacoue-Labarthe, in "Philosophy Today", (1993), pp. 275–284. For what concerns the aporetic character of community, see the careful analyses carried out by Garritano F.: Aporie comunitarie. Sino alla fine del mondo. Jaca Book, Milan: (1999).; Meazza C.: La comunità svelata. Questioni per Jean-Luc Nancy, Guida, Neaples 2010; Mascia, G.: Singolare Plurale: la spaziatura dell'essere. Riflessioni sul senso dell'ontologia per una filosofia politica, in AA. VV., Ricerca in Vetrina, Franco Angeli, Milan (2015), pp. 187–191; Villani, M.: Arte della fuga. Estetica e democrazia nel pensiero di Jean-Luc Nancy, quot.; Nasone, A.: Il problema Occidente. Mito, sacrificio, comunità nel pensiero di Jean-Luc Nancy, Inschibboleth, Roma 2023.

[14] Nancy, J.-L.: The Inoperative Community, quot., p. 103.

Consequently, traditional cultures and civilizations play an important role, which is maintaining global and cultural differences and concretely realizing partition. In this sense, cultural movements entail a broader political significance, namely that of preventing the monopolization of "politics" seen as a totalizing global public place. This monopolization is one of Nancy's central issues. With the prevalence of economic, military, and technological power, changes in political democracy on a global scale are put at risk. In Nancy's view, today's democracy serves only to secure a "role" for technical and economic forces rather than to pursue its own expansion[15] in the political arena; in fact, a significant part of humanity is paying the price for this. Therefore, the notion of "inoperative community" serves as a bulwark against totalizing globalism (dominated by hegemonic powers) and against the surrender of political ideology to the inexorable interests of atomistic factors (be they States, corporations, or private individuals).[16]

---

[15] A renewed concept of democracy—not only and not so much as a form of government, but as "a form of life whose political and symbolic stakes can be grasped only if we go beyond the determinism of the philosophies of history and economism"—is emphasized by F. Ciaramelli in his work dated 2003, Lo spazio simbolico della democrazia. Città Aperta, Troina, p. 32.

[16] On these fundamental themes in Nancy's thought related to the concept of community, politics, and democracy, see in particular, the following texts: Bensussan, G.: L'existence démocratique: une dette, in Jean-Luc Nancy. Anastasis de la pensée, cit., pp. 131–142; Bird G.: Containing Community. From Political Economy to Ontology in Agamben, Esposito, and Nancy, Suny Press, New York (2016); Dadà S.: Dall'essere-con alla democrazia. Evoluzione dell'idea di "politico" in Jean-Luc Nancy, in M. Di Pierro, F. Marchesi (eds.), Crisi dell'immanenza. Potere, conflitto, istituzione, Quodlibet, Macerata (2019), pp. 189–202; Devisch, I.: A trembling voice in the desert. Jean-Luc Nancy's re-thinking of the space of the political, "Cultural Values", 4, 2, (2000), pp. 239–255; Devisch, I.: La «négativité sans emploi», "Symposium", IV, 2, (2000), pp. 167–187; Devisch I.: Jean-Luc Nancy and the Question of Community, Bloomsbury Publishing Plc, London, New York (2013); Devisch, I., Vandeputte, K.: Sense, Existence and Justice; or How are We to Live in a Secular World ? in Re-treating Religion. Deconstructing Christianity with Jean-Luc Nancy, quot., pp. 80–91; Gentili D.: Creazione Politica, In «B@Belonline/Print», 10–11, (2011), pp. 133–138; Harman, G.: On Interface: Nancy's Weights and Masses, in Jean-Luc Nancy and plural thinking. Expositions of World, Ontology, Politics, and Sense, quot., pp. 95–108; Ichikawa, T.: (2023), La foi et la démocratie, in Jean-Luc Nancy. Anastasis de la pensée, quot., pp. 143–148; Lèbre J.: Point de fuite. Art et politique chez Jean-Luc Nancy, in «B@belonline/print», 10–11, (2011), pp. 139–149; Lingis A.: The community of those who have nothing in common, Indiana University Press, Bloomington and Indianapolis (1994); Marchart O.: Post-Foundational Political Thought. Political Difference in Nancy, Lefort, Badiou and Laclau, Edinburgh University Press, Edinburgh (2007); Mascia V.: Jean-Luc Nancy: la chance comunitaria e l'esposizione del "senza progetto", in "Epekeina. International Journal of Ontology, History and Critics", vol. 6, 2, (2015), pp. 1–19; May, T.: The community's absence in Lyotard, Nancy and Lacoue-Labarthe, "Philosophy Today", 37, 3, (1993), pp. 275–284; Meazza, C.: Il nichilismo della forma politica. Nell'eredità del comunismo im-possibile di Jean-Luc Nancy, Orthotes, Salerno-Napoli (2024); Meazza, C.: L'ateismo del politico in Jean-Luc Nancy, in "Shift. International Journal of Philosophical Studies", (2022), pp. 105–114; Norris, A.: Jean-Luc Nancy on the Political after Heidegger and Schmitt, in Jean-Luc Nancy and plural thinking. Expositions of World, Ontology, Politics, and Sense, quot., pp. 143–158; Serafini L.: Decisione e inoperosità. Jean-Luc Nancy interprete di Heidegger, in «B@belonline/print», 10–11, (2011) pp. 271–278; Serafini L.: Inoperosità. Heidegger nel dibattito francese contemporaneo, Mimesis, Milan (2013); Vaysse J.M.: De la catégorie de communauté, in Communauté et modernité, Raulet G. and Vaysse J.M.(eds.), L'Harmattan, Paris (1995), pp. 30–61;

One thing at least is clear: if we do not face up to such questions, the political will soon desert us completely, if it has not already done so. It will abandon us to political and technological economies, if it has not already done so. And this will be the end of our communities, if this has not yet come about. Being-in-common will nonetheless never cease to resist, but its resistance will belong decidedly to another world entirely. Our world, as far as politics is concerned, will be a desert, and we will wither away without a tomb-which is to say, without community, deprived of our finite existence.[17]

Nancy analyzes the reasons and forms of the lack of recognition of Being-in-common in Western political practice and theory. Politics has consistently taken away from us the reality of coexistence, which is instead the very place of the political. This stems from the fact that community is thought of not as a problem, but as a unity, as a subject already given in its generic and not partitioned (*partagée*) identity. The origin of this conception of the political is religious and has a theological-political purpose. It remains anchored in modernity under a secularized form that makes the nation-state a unique and sovereign Subject. Nevertheless, this picture recalls a complementary one to that of democracy. In modernity, the social is taken away from us by a politics that presents itself under the double security of the sovereign State and the democratic Community (in other words, of the Subject and the Citizen). Politics starts from Being-in-common; subjects are there *with* each other, are *close to* each other, are there *for* each other. Thus, there is an immediate sense in all this. Being-in-common is pure sense, the sense among us. However, Being-in-common is undifferentiated from the very beginning and must determine itself into truth. By starting from sense, the fundamental orientation of the political is a becoming-truth. Moreover, if by this becoming-truth the political claims to ground sense, to entirely determine it in truth, then the sense is reabsorbed, the social is subtracted, the political is enclosed in a self-sufficient space of sense. The political is then shown as responding to a destiny, just as what lives history, as what sovereignty exercises, and as what sacrifice demands. These are the main components of a theological-political view of the political. Eventually, when the sense is reabsorbed into the truth, it leads to totalitarianism.[18]

The idea that politics constitutes a self-sufficient space of meaning is a hallmark of modern political forms. The theological-political factor persists in secularized politics in the form of self-sufficiency, that is, under the idea that the bond between

---

Villani, M.: Arte della fuga. Estetica e democrazia nel pensiero di Jean-Luc Nancy, quot.; de WIT, T.W.A.: Between All and Nothing: the Affective Dimension of Political Bonds, in Re-treating Religion. Deconstructing Christianity with Jean-Luc Nancy, quot., pp. 92–108.

[17] Nancy, J.-L.: The Inoperative Community, quot., p. 42.

[18] On the question of totalitarianism as a historically destinal outcome of the political, see the following works: Arendt, H. The Origins of Totalitarianism. Harcourt, Brace and Company, New York (1951); Ead.: Truth and Politics, in The New Yorker (1967); Ead.: Lying in Politics. Reflections on the Pentagon Papers. Harcourt Brace Jovanovich, New York (1972); Ead., Diario filosofico. Frammenti (1950–1964) edited by L. Savarino, in "MicroMega", (2003), pp. 28–38; Forti, S.: Il Totalitarismo, quot. Laterza Rome-Bari (2015); Ead.: La filosofia di fronte all'estremo. Totalitarismo e riflessione filosofica. Einaudi, Turin (2004); and Ead.: Spettri della totalità, in. "MicroMega" 5, (2003) pp. 198–209.

subjects is tight, whatever the nature of this bond (of love, of hate, of law, of force). This form of self-sufficiency of the political comes under two figures that constitute the two inseparable tendencies between which the entire modern political space is organized. One emphasizes the State and sovereignty; the other, the public space, law, and democracy. These two figures of the self-sufficient political relate to each other; one cannot be thought of as separated from the other. The originality of this analysis of the political illusion is to show that there is a denial of the communitarian and substantialist conception of the political, which remains captive to the illusion of the self-sufficiency of the political and locked within the very machinery of modern politics. Even if not expressed in this sense, it is possible to assume that, according to Nancy, the Arendtian conception of public space is a radical expression of it. This expression is so extreme that it is expressed not in the terms of right and law, but in those of action and power. According to Arendt, democracy is not formal; there is no sovereignty of law. Democracy rests entirely on the initiative of individuals. In this sense, it certainly consists in the negation of community with the illusion of believing that this negation provides the political space of self-sufficiency. According to Arendt—as Sontheimer rightly notes in the Introduction to the posthumous fragments collected in the volume *Was ist Politik? (The Promise of Politics)*— the question of the positive sense of the political starts from two fundamental experiences of our century overshadowed, or rather overturned, by that very sense; the rise of totalitarian systems, such as National Socialism and Communism, and the fact that nowadays, with the atomic bomb, politics has the technical means to extinguish humanity and all sorts of politics with it. Our experiences with politics in our time have been and are so dire as to make us doubt and despair of the existence of any sense of politics. Wars and revolutions, and not the functioning of parliamentary governments and party systems, constitute the fundamental political experiences of our century. Totalitarian systems, the emergence of which was analyzed by Hannah Arendt in her book on totalitarianism, are the extreme form of the distortion of the political, in that they totally eliminate human freedom and subject it to the flux of a historical determination founded on ideological bases, against which, by means of terror and the domination of ideology, all free and individual resistance becomes impossible. Based on this, Arendt insistently evokes the idea asserted for the first time in history in the Greek *polis* that identifies the political with freedom. She also notes that politics is based on the de facto plurality of men, and thus on the fact that it must organize and regulate diversities, not equalities. Contrary to the usual Aristotelian interpretation of man as *zoòn politikòn*, according to which the political is inherent in man, Arendt emphasizes that politics is not born *in* men but *among* men, and that the freedom and spontaneity of different individuals are necessary prerequisites for a space to be created among men, the only space in which politics, the real politics, becomes possible. Freedom is the sense of politics.[19] Hannah Arendt's philosophical-political conception is thus aimed at dismissing

---

[19] Sontheimer, K.: Preface to H. Arendt, Che cos'è la politica, edited by U. Ludz, transl. M. Bistolfi. Edizioni di Comunità, Milan (1995), pp. 7–8.

historical and biopolitical determinism based on ideological foundations, in order to recognize the knot that binds together life, politics, and freedom in the human condition of plurality.[20]

2 Politics to Come

Following this Arendtian direction, Nancy aims to propose a *politics to come* that no longer subtracts the sense of being-in-common and that escapes the secularized theological-political condition. Such a politics would be then based not on an already given central unity (positively in the sovereign Subject or negatively in democratic form), but on the issue of social bonding. In other words, it does not seek to produce the sense nor to determine it globally, but is rather aimed at tightening the bonds that allow the sense to flow, thus producing sense. Such a politics is only possible when the Being-in-common is acknowledged. This presupposes not only another political philosophy but also another fundamental ontology. There is no way to think about Being-in-common and challenge the assumptions of political philosophy and its conception of community outside the realm of ontology itself, thus proposing a radically new ontology: a plural ontology. We cannot understand what happens to sociality if we remain within the limits of political philosophy or of a merely regional ontology, because this would just involve thinking of the social back as a particular kind of being, aiming at an essence of the social. Sociality is not a kind of being whose essence would be the community, but a fundamental disposition or state of being that makes it impossible to have a "being" without a "*with*."

By defining the characteristics of coexistence, Nancy's essential contribution is to have recognized that what is at stake is not only anthropological but also concerns *Being* as a whole. That is not all. The French philosopher repeatedly asserts, throughout his work, that plurality is not only the condition of political existence, but also the condition of social existence in general. By social, he means—as we have tried to explain so far—the place of existence of every man: for him, therefore, the social condition in which all men find themselves consists primarily in being with others, no matter who they are. Hence, a condition that does not ascribe man to a class, a rank, a religion, and so on, but puts him in an original relationship with the whole world. Indeed, ultimately, this is because we exist in the condition of the *with*. While it is possible to determine the fundamental characteristics of sociality quite convincingly, determining its statute turns out to be much more problematic. The difficulty is felt both at the level of political philosophy and at that of ontology. A priori, the assumption of sociality as a condition of human existence implies a substantial renewal and reworking of political philosophy, which can no longer simply

---

[20] A complete reconstruction of Hannah Arendt's political thought can be found in the volume edited by Esposito, R.: La pluralità irrappresentabile. Il pensiero politico di Hannah Arendt. QuattroVenti Editor, Urbino (1987).—and in the volume by Bazzicalupo, L.: Hannah Arendt. La storia della politica. ESI Editor, Naples (1996).

pose the problem of the constitution of the political community, but must question the relationship between sociality and community. In other words, it must question how community can constitute itself in the condition of sociality, which is its own condition. Contemporary political philosophy is undoubtedly troubled by the need to take account of sociality, but it seems to waver between reaffirming the needs of community remotely from the social and the defense of an open society. All this without taking into consideration the question of the articulation between sociality and community, namely the question regarding how it is possible to understand community, since it is acknowledged as a precondition of sociality. The differences between the philosophers seem obvious here. In some respects, Heidegger ignores the problem of community. By contrast, Hannah Arendt argues that only the political can and should realize a real society against all forms of a traditionally understood community life. Man cannot exist in the condition of plurality unless through political action, and the very content of such action is precisely this condition, and not community. For his part, Nancy—as we have tried to show so far—seeks to release the political from the communitarian illusion. However, this cannot be achieved through the political affirmation of plurality against the presupposed social community. On the contrary, it is achieved by recognizing a presupposed sociality against the tendency of the political to confine itself within the idea of community self-sufficiency. Isn't it necessary that, on the one hand, sociality should be recognized as the presupposed condition of political existence in general, and of community in particular? On the other hand, should communities be recognized as a necessary mediation of sociality? Politics would have the knot of social bonds as its purpose—as Nancy argues; however, how could it achieve its purpose without constituting communities? In the network of relationships, the knots cannot simply be individuals themselves; such knots are also the communities, whether political or not, which must allow them to be-with not only within these communities, but also beyond them.

> Can one think through a politics of non-self-sufficiency? That is, as one will want to say, a politics of dependence or interdependence, of heteronomy or heterology? In the different figures of self-sufficiency, sometimes it is the social tie itself that is self-sufficient, sometimes it is the terms or units between which the social tie passes. In both cases, ultimately the tie no longer makes up a tie, it comes undone, sometimes by fusion, sometimes by atomization. All of our politics are politics of the undoing into self-sufficiency. It is therefore a matter of going toward a thought (that means indiscernibly toward a *praxis*) of the (k)not as such. It is the *tying* of the (k)not that must come to the crucial point, the place of democracy's empty truth and subjectivity's excessive sense. The (k)not: that which involves neither interiority nor exteriority but which, in being tied, ceaselessly makes the inside pass outside, each into (or by way of) the other, the outside inside, turning endlessly back on itself without returning *to* itself [...] The tying of the (k)not is nothing, no *res*, nothing but the placing-intorelation that presupposes at once proximity and distance, attachment and detachment, intricacy, intrigue, and ambivalence. In truth, it is this heterogeneous *realitas*, this disjunctive conjunction, that the motif of the contract at once alludes to and dissimulates. The whole question is whether or not we can finally manage to think the "contract" — the tying of the (k)not —according to a model other than the juridico-commercial model (which in fact supposes the bond to have been already established, *already presupposed as its own subject*: this is the founding abyss or decisive aporia of the *Social Contract*). To

think the social bond according to another model or perhaps without a model. To think its act, establishment, and binding. One would thus demand a politics without dénouement—which perhaps also implies a politics without theatrical model, or a theater that would be neither tragic nor comic nor a dramatization of foundation — a politics of the incessant tying up of singularities with each other, over each other, and through each other, without any end other than the enchainment of (k)nots, without any structure other than their interconnection or interdependence, and without any possibility of calling any single (k)not or the totality of (k)nots self-sufficient (for there would be "totality" only in the enchainment itself). Such a politics consists, first of all, in testifying that there is singularity only where a singularity ties itself up with other singularities, but that there is no tie except where the tie is taken up again, recast, and retied without end, nowhere purely tied or untied. Nowhere founded and nowhere destined, always older than the law and younger than sense. Politics would henceforth be neither a substance nor a form but, first of all, a gesture: the very gesture of the tying and enchainment of each to each, tying each time unicities (individuals, groups, nations, or peoples) that have no unity other than the unity of the (k)not, unity enchained to the other, the enchainment always worldwide and the world having no unity other than that of its enchainment. This politics requires an entire ontology of being as tying, that is, precisely perhaps this extremity where all ontology, as such, gets tied up with something other than itself. As long as we do not arrive at this extremity, we will not have displaced the theologico-political sphere.[21]

It is then a matter of thinking of the in-common as the very knot of existence, as the very act of knotting, or "the act of the tying, the act of the enchainment of singular sense to every other singular sense, the act of apportioning and interweaving that, as such, has no sense but gives a place to every event of sense."[22] Therefore, the upcoming political need can only be configured as a knotting, or as what has no identifiable sense; as "nouages"—like Nancy writes, and this term is echoed by the one suggested to him by Agamben, Hamacher, and Lacoue-Labarthe: "nuages."[23] Thus, the political problem now is to think community in its necessarily relational and "tying" condition. Here,—in the knot—lies the paradoxical condition of real freedom.

3 The Freedom in Question

Experience and freedom—these two words are perhaps the most powerful *slogans* of Anglo-American thought. On closer inspection, they constitute the fulcrum from which modern political thought originated, which has never stopped employing them *actively* in order to define its own foundations, methods, and purposes. In this sense, on the one hand, empiricism as the doctrine of experience, and civil liberties as the political content of liberalism, on the other, have come together in the common effort to remove unjustified authorities, mainly theological and political ones. However, the latter are not the only ones against which the words "experience" and

---

[21] Nancy, J.-L.: The Sense of the World, quot., pp. 111–112.
[22] Ibid, p. 115.
[23] Cf. ibid, p. 122.

"freedom" have been adopted.[24] Even philosophy has sometimes been deemed dogmatic, and has therefore been fought with appeals to experience and freedom. In short, the appeal to experience is an appeal for release from dogmas, doctrines, and *prejudgments*. Therefore, instead of "innate ideas" and pure concepts, Anglo-American thought has been shaped as a continuous elaboration of the concept of experience as freedom. Such a set of beliefs and precepts is the basis of the so-called liberal tradition. A tradition that seems to be definitively self-legitimized today, and actually constitutes the political "vulgate" of our time. However, precisely in this self-legitimization—which becomes, so to speak, the incontestable paradigm on which the liberal democratic political model is based—Nancy perceives a hidden violence that once again conceals the logical-rational recourse to a self-founding truth. Indeed, who would dare to argue that today's democracy is not liberal? Who would say that it is not founded on freedom? Indeed, there is no doubt that the defense of civil liberties is the categorical imperative of the so-called democratic policies of our States. Yet, as Nancy wonders: is this true? On what kind of theoretical framework, for example, are "just" wars organized and continue to be organized? Here the "political" problem of our time, identified and analyzed in all its aspects by the French philosopher, presents itself in all its cogency. This is precisely why Nancy, in posing such questions, cannot help but return to the origins of modern political thought and, in particular, to liberal tradition. Born initially out of opposition to Hobbes' authoritarian line, it seems to be the only tradition of thought that we can stick to in order to speak of freedom today (that is, at the end or sunset of the great totalitarianisms which occlude freedoms). In other words, the basic question is: at the end of totalitarianisms and strong regimes, how can we speak of freedom? Does the tradition of liberalism come to our aid and is it useful? Would it not be more useful and necessary to take up the question again from another perspective, namely by going back to the root question of what freedom is? These three questions outline the challenging trajectory on which Nancy's analysis unfolds.

In *The Experience of Freedom*—a work of extraordinary complexity—the French philosopher examines precisely the Anglo-American tradition in an attempt to understand the main issues that run through the thought of freedom: the question of experience and that of necessity. Nancy's main intent is to take freedom out of its—so to speak "classical"—submission to necessity. In other words, it is about subtracting freedom from a necessitating grounding. Of course, this is a subtraction that—already started by Heidegger in *Being and Time*[25]—does not seek to make freedom a pure indeterminacy, indifference or arbitrariness, which is negatively opposed to the necessitating determination of the existential process; instead, it intends to rethink it precisely from the concept of *Dasein*, or rather from the condition of existential "thrownness" that is precisely the *being-there* without grounds. Therefore, in the analysis of existence undertaken by Heidegger, the space for such

---

[24] On this topic, see Wallach, J.R.: Liberals, Communitarians and the Tasks of Political Theory, in "Political Theory", 15, 4, (1987). pp. 581–611.
[25] Heidegger, M.: Being and Time, quot.—see, in particular pp. 225–267.

a rethinking of freedom emerges in all its radicality. Nancy then aims to make the dimensions of this space more accurate: on the one hand, by turning his attention to the legacy of freedom as understood precisely in Heidegger's writings; on the other, by going back to the phrase with which Sartre launched existentialism ("we are condemned to be free"[26]), which still expresses the great subjection of freedom to necessity and well echoes the formula common to classical metaphysics, according to which freedom is the recognition of a necessity.

The experience of freedom then arises against the background of—and from the comparison with—these conceptions, which Nancy wishes on the one hand to pursue and, on the other, to overcome. Nevertheless, precisely in order to focus his discourse on this crucial issue, he first rightly widens the horizon to our tradition and addresses the *unfolding* of the concept of freedom throughout our modern history. In particular, in the *dialogue* established with Hobbes on the one hand, and with Stuart Mill on the other—the two opposing poles of English political thought, from which the respective vectors of absolutism and liberalism spring—the French philosopher finds the most significant antecedents of our age, in relation to the pivotal theme of freedom.

At the beginning of his famous treatise *On Liberty*, John Stuart Mill—as Nancy recalls—makes it clear that there would be nothing to say about the philosophical concept of freedom, since freedom itself must be understood as civil or social liberty.[27] Conversely—as Nancy again points out by focusing on the other direction—to think about freedom means, according to Hobbes, to hang freedom in "deliberation."[28] To think means "to de-liberate." However, in this way, thinking about freedom is self-limiting. Thus, both stopping the focus on the self-limiting thought of philosophical freedom by distinguishing the modes of determination and necessity, and seeking refuge for civil liberties in the limitation of systematic philosophy, results in the failure to achieve freedom, which can only be experienced ambiguously. In fact, as Hume drastically points out—who is the first to take a decisive step towards the idea of causality/necessity at the basis of Hobbesian freedom and to which Nancy precisely reaches in his genealogical retracing of our modern history -, there is no experience of the notion of cause as necessity; the latter cannot be experienced.[29] As a result, freedom cannot be experienced either. To speak of causality is simply meaningless, from this perspective. To cause, understood as an "a priori" concept applied to experience—belonging to transcendental philosophy—cannot be introduced as a legitimate way of overcoming the ambiguity within which the concept of necessary freedom stands out. Following such a path, even the ascription of a necessary connection between impressions is completely devoid of experience. Therefore, since necessity cannot be experienced, then all experience is a matter of

---

[26] Cf. in this regard Nancy's critique of Sartre in his book The Experience of Freedom, quot., see, in particular, pp. 15 and 99–101.

[27] Cf. Mill, J.S.: On Liberty. J.W. Parker and son, London (1859).

[28] Cf. Hobbes, T.: Leviathan. Ed. C. B. Macpherson. Penguin Books, Baltimore (1968).

[29] Hume, D.: A Treatise of Human Nature. Ed. P. H. Nidditch. Clarendon Press, Oxford (2009)—in particular, read section 14 of vol. I.

"probability," meaning that it becomes a matter of mere possibility. According to Hume, liberty (i.e., freedom) is not an opposition to necessity (which, in fact, does not exist), but is the movement of human faculties—a movement that is not a possession or property of man, but arises from unknown causes, such as imagination. Hence, for the philosopher, and again according to Nancy's reading, the impossibility of experiencing necessity makes the defense of the philosophical concept of freedom against the idea of its determination completely useless. Likewise, and for the same reason, it is not possible to identify the representation of freedom with an inexplicable theological doctrine: "Liberty, when opposed to necessity, not to constraint, is the same thing with chance; which is universally allowed to have no existence."[30] Thus, it is not a property of human subjectivity, nor is it a transcendent grounding. The result is a portrait of the philosophy of freedom that leaves its mark in a certain *liberality*, the main characteristic of which is to not be able to make everything possible. Liberality cannot therefore be found in simply providing impressions, since providing these "experiences" is not free, but as Hume points out from the outset, "arises in the soul originally, from unknown causes"[31]—as anticipated earlier. Rather, liberality consumes itself in the "mild force" called "imagination," which makes it possible for the soul to perceive everything. Imagination, in a generous and free way, allows the world being: it gives us (we "are" nothing but our imagination) the permanence of objects and the idea of causal connections; two ideas that Hume shows to be mutually incompatible. An independent and interconnected world dwells in a gift, a generosity, a liberality that is thus emancipated from the traditional philosophical concept of freedom as pure indeterminacy, indifference or arbitrariness. On closer inspection, this gift comes from a sense of astonishment before the world due to the imagination that produces a cohesive world constitution. At the same time, the liberality of imagination is more than the pure exemption from determination or constraint ("negative freedom" or indeterminacy), and less than the self-determination or overwhelming of inner constraints ("positive freedom"). Liberality, which always escapes this alternative—between necessity and arbitrariness -, takes place in imagination, as long as imagination names a space of simple possibility that does not defer to a necessitating constitution. This is why the thought of imagination—according to Nancy's interpretation—tears Hume away from the human. The thought of this abysmal foundation leaves the individual abandoned, without any business, without any relationship; in one word, it leaves the individual *free*. The deep abyss of the thought of imagination is freedom. The thought of imagination is the experience of freedom. The experience of the world, as Nancy points out, has the sense of a dangerous crossing of the boundary; in other words, the experience of moving in the world without any grounding:

> an experience is an attempt executed without reserve, given over to the *peril* of its own lack of foundation and security in this 'object' of which it is not the subject but instead the passion, exposed like the pirate (peirātēs) who freely tries his luck on the high seas. In a sense,

---

[30] Ibid., p. 96.
[31] Cf. ibid., p. 11.

3 The Freedom in Question

which here might be the first and last sense, freedom, to the extent that it is the thing itself of thinking, cannot be appropriated, but only "pirated": its "seizure" will always be illegitimate.[32]

The experience of thought—or, more precisely, of "meta-thought"—does not consist in "impressions" or their "reflections" but, rather, in a dangerous crossing of the boundary of thought. The boundary experience—which designates a *de-finite* experience—is the experience of freedom. Crossing this boundary is undoubtedly "imaginary" but, for that reason, is fundamental. At the boundary of thought—or, in this case, at the conclusion of the investigation into the nature of human understanding—grotesque and singular monsters come forward. When Hume conceives himself as a "grotesque monster," he envisions that this unreal entity could henceforth belong to no community. Each paragraph of *The Experience of Freedom* exposes the community of the grotesque and shows this singularly complex community as *the* community. Hume does not rely on nature and its passions to bring the unreal back to the real, nor does he attempt to discover a way back to the familiar. Likewise, Nancy does not attempt to show why the familiar world is in disorder and how it could be put in order, having become known. This is the strangeness and difficulty of the thought of freedom that Nancy pursues: the abyssal nature of freedom, its withdrawal from all foundations implies the dissolution of all relationships; but this very dissolution constitutes community. On the other hand, Hume has determined in advance—just like the metaphysical traditions to which he nevertheless refers—that community means participation in a common substance, in a common life, that is, the sharing of human nature. If, on the contrary, the experience of community were not a common substance but the dissolution of substantiality, as well as subjectivity and the abandonment of which Hume speaks, this would not mark the end of the questioning of the understanding of human nature, but rather the beginning of a free thought. Moreover, thinking would no longer mean making absolute distinctions and seeking solid grounding; it would simply be an exposure to dissolution and groundlessness. By following Hume's line of thought, Nancy does not link the theme of the experience of freedom to a certain, ineffable "lived experience." It is the experience of an exposure to groundlessness, the "experience of experience."[33] In addition, no conclusion is drawn from the subject's inability to give himself a grounding for his presence; on the contrary, this inability is exactly what constitutes the experience of freedom.

The point is that subjectivity—which defines itself as something that essentially secures its own identity—cannot stand on a supposed grounding. However, on the other hand, the sinking of subjectivity does not mean that human beings are not strong enough to realize what they desire. It is precisely through such a conception of human frailty that Sartre came to the following conclusion: "we are condemned to be free." Subjectivity is not powerless, or better, is not devoid of power; if power implies causality, then the sinking of subjectivity means that it has no power, and

---

[32] Nancy, J.-L.: The Experience of Freedom, quot., p. 20.
[33] Ibid., p. 87.

this marks altogether the end of subjectivity. Thus, freedom is defined in this very end. A freedom that, in this case, is not defined in a limited space of action, but rather leads to openness—in thought, in experience—about limit, about groundlessness, about "existence" without essence. As the only condition to which *The Experience of Freedom* is dedicated, the exclusion of self-supporting subjectivity (and here the disempowerment of the cogito discussed in the first part of this paper finds its full meaning) constitutes the realization of existence according to the terms indicated by Heidegger, whereby the essence of *Dasein* lies in existence. It is the being-there that is precisely "thrown" into existence without any grounding. Therefore, the term "existence" here means the absence of grounds and, consequently, the deprivation of the unity, the identity, and the consistency that every affirmation of essence presupposes. The inability of the subject to ground himself requires no further work; instead, it requires the abandonment of the idea of subjectivity in favor of a thought of abandonment, of existence, of freedom.[34] Hence, at this point, the line of discussion can go back to Hume's question of the imagination and connects—so to speak—to the themes of Heidegger, who—not by chance— precisely during the working out of the condition of *Dasein* in *Being and Time*— studied Kant and analyzed, in particular, the role of transcendental imagination. Indeed, according to Nancy, the question of freedom requires a rethinking of the decisive confrontation between Heidegger and Kant, grafted precisely on the fundamental character of transcendental imagination. The latter, by offering a free space in which things can be found, proves to be the original freedom[35] on the one hand, and the abyssal "grounding" of subjectivity on the other. In this sense, not only it nullifies the idea of subjectivity as a self-supporting unity, but also above all and precisely for this reason, it causes the distinction between transcendental condition and empirical evidence to collapse. One sign of this collapse—and it is what Nancy pays attention to—is Kant's invention of what he calls (in a way we might define as "oxymoronic") the "fact of reason." As a fact, it belongs to the domain of empirical evidence; as a fact *of* reason and a fact *for* reason, its exposition can only be produced in non-empirical terms.[36] By discovering this "fact," Kant opens philosophical thought to another empiricism and solves, by means of freedom, the *impasse* of the third antinomy concerning the constitution of the world. Solving this antinomy in favor of freedom lays the basis for an empiricism made not of impressions or sensations, but of free connections. Indeed, the "fact of reason" is something that eludes any founding demonstration; it cannot ground itself on anything earthly, nor

---

[34] On this major theme, Nancy finds the Heidegger of Being and Time, with whom he begins a close and illuminating confrontation that will lead him -as we shall see shortly—to take up Kant's reading of Heidegger.

[35] Cf. in this regard Heidegger, M.: Kant and the Problem of Metaphysics, quot.; Nancy, J.-L.: L'impératif catégorique. Flammarion, Paris (1983).—see, in particular, pp. 115–137; and Id.: Le discours de la syncope. Flammarion, Paris (1992), pp. 106–109.

[36] Cf. Nancy, J.-L.: L'impératif catégorique, quot., pp. 20–22.

can it suspend itself.[37] By solving the Third Antinomy in favor of freedom, Kant leads his thought to a new space: that of existence. An existence, then, without basis or rational demonstration, implying the deformation, or even the suppression, of the distinction between transcendental and empirical, already implied in the sentence "*factum rationis*."

The "fact of reason," according to Kant, consists in moral awareness: more precisely, in having to expose oneself to new, necessary, unconditional, "categorical" imperatives.[38] There, where the necessity of these imperatives lies not in a necessary connection between objects, but in their simple possibility. In other words, the exposition of open existence in the space of a *factum rationis* requires this fact to be taken to its limit, to the very limit of free possibility.

Not surprisingly, Nancy finds in Kant his truest interlocutor as well. For the French philosopher, in fact, we experience freedom only when we are exposed to groundlessness, to the finite, to *Mitdasein*. Therefore, it is not a matter of building a world out of the fragmented and disconcerting experiences, but of exposing oneself to the event that takes place in the space of existence, of groundlessness, of liberality, of generosity. It is the emergence, without any grounds, without possession, of the *sur-prise*. Thus, the empiricism Nancy alludes to can only show the experience of "surprise" as something that eludes any insistence on groundings, any demand for necessary connections, and any application of the cause-and-effect process. Surprise, then, *is* an experience, and any empiricism without surprise, any empiricism aimed entirely at the usual and the ordinary, in an effort to do justice to empiricism, fails miserably.

In the closing paragraphs of *The Experience of Freedom*, the question of decision emerges. That question, as Nancy promptly makes clear, cannot be avoided. However, the unavoidability of decision is not to be regarded as a condemnation to freedom—in a Sartrian sense; on the contrary, it is the condition of freedom, even in order to ensure freedom—or to simply defend civil liberties. Freedom cannot be safeguarded, and in this way, a decision *in favor of* or *against* freedom—in favor of or against "existence" without essence, in favor of or against community without common substance—is always necessary and is always already made. Freedom cannot be granted, and so any work of liberation implies that this work must always be willing to abandon itself in favor of liberality, generosity, and abandonment of its plans and destiny. In relation to the condition of freedom, it could be incorrectly assumed that it can have the roots of its grounds in a desire to safeguard freedom against its enemies, *but it cannot be done that way*. Even under the guise of defending civil liberties, this mistake takes away the "surprise" of freedom: its attainment, without possession.

---

[37] Cf. Kant, I. Critique of Pure Reason, ed. and trans. P. Gruyer and A.W. Wood. Cambridge University Press, Cambridge (1998); and Id.: Grounding for the metaphysics of morals, transl. J.W. Ellington. Hackett Publishing, Cambridge, MA (1993), p. 7 et seq.

[38] On this topic, see Gilbert-Walsh, J.: Broken imperatives. The ethical dimension of Nancy's thought, in "Philosophy & Social Criticism," (26) 2, (2000). pp. 29–50.

In conclusion, the theoretical framework that prevails in the writing of *The Experience of Freedom* goes, in the first instance, against the current conceptions of freedom that relate it to a faculty, a right or a good to be protected in different ways. Likewise, it banishes all that philosophical tradition that, from Spinoza to Nietzsche, ends up limiting and subordinating freedom to necessity. More originally, but also everyday more and more, to be free means simply *to decide to exist*, without any anchorage to an essence or a grounding: being withdraws, recedes, and surrenders the existing to freedom, to the mere fact of existing in the horizon of possibility. Indeed, a grounded freedom would take on the features of causal necessity, the subjection of the fact of existing to an immanent or transcendent idea: if God has historically become the name of this necessary freedom, then the death of God declared by the accomplished nihilism will be the condition of a free dissemination of existence in its irreducible singularity. When human freedom becomes free from the yoke of the grounding, restoring it to the finiteness of its singular self-producing, history appears as the "advent" and the "surprise" of a new "flowering of existence."[39] Therefore, existence has neither essence nor laws foreign to it any longer, but is the essence and law of itself, in a condition of "anarchy"—namely, of the absence of grounding principles—coinciding with the very exercise of freedom. Freed from a grounding that constrained its movements, the thought also becomes passion, freedom in action, astonishment, prodigal space without any calculation of meaning, and an experience of ontological generosity. Freedom is like a thunderbolt, a glow that overwhelms and surprises, a dizzying leap into existence, and not devoid of that intoxication released by the splinters of the possible. Thus, Nancy occupies "the space left free by Heidegger" who—although he opened up the possibility of a thought of existence—ended up attributing ontological primacy to truth and not to freedom, still assigning it to Being as an overpowering destiny, and thus limiting its role to an understanding of necessity. Moreover, this also explains his reluctance towards the Holocaust.[40] Instead, by radicalizing the experience of finiteness thrown into the world and thus going beyond Heidegger, according to Nancy, we will also rediscover the sense of our being-in-common, gripped to an existence that occurs

---

[39] On the themes related to the "Experience of Freedom" in Jean-Luc Nancy, particular attention should be given to the following textes: Argyros, S.: Noli me tangere: expérience de la liberté, in Jean-Luc Nancy. Anastasis de la pensée, quot., pp. 73–78; Bailly, J.-C.: La surprise recommencée du sens (II) (sur Jean-Luc Nancy), in Jean-Luc Nancy. Anastasis de la pensée, quot., pp. 241–244; Baptist G.: Un pensiero all'erta, in EAD. (a cura di), Jean-Luc Nancy. Pensare il presente, CUEC, Cagliari, (2010), pp. 15–20; Berto G.: La scrittura della libertà, in A. Potestà, R. Terzi (a cura di), Annuario 2000–2001. Incontro con Jean-Luc Nancy, quot., pp. 127–139; Ciccarelli R.: Jean-Luc Nancy: il potere della libertà, in «Democrazia e diritto», n. 3-4, (2000), pp. 124–137; Id.: La potenza che dunque siamo. Saggio sull'esperienza della libertà, in «B@belonline/print», 10–11, (2011), pp. 59–69; Esposito, R.: Libertà in comune, in AA.VV., Incontro con J.-L. Nancy, quot., pp. 223–230; Vitiello V.: Jean-Luc Nancy e il problema della libertà, in Annuario 2000–2001. Incontro con Jean-Luc Nancy, quot., pp. 140–150.

[40] On Heidegger's reticence after the Holocaust, Philippe Lacoue-Labarthe wrote very important pages in his work Heidegger, art, and politics: the fiction of the political, transl. C. Turner, Blackwell, Oxford (1990).

individually every time, but realized by a plurality of voices, in a partitioning that constitutes the space of every egalitarian relationship. In Nancy's work, this community, grounded in the sharing of the exposure to existence and that resists any appropriation, takes on the unexpectedly revolutionary trait of an ethics of generosity, of a perpetual openness that renews the wonder of birth. If we now go back to the idea of community as understood by the French philosopher, we will be able to understand how this community or—to put it better—this being-in-common is intrinsically linked to the idea of freedom as experience and possibility. Indeed, if community is not to be understood as a transcendental background nor as destiny, but as a mode of being of existence as such, as original, without rational agreements between individuals, then freedom is the other side of community for it is not the prerogative or preexisting right of the individual. According to Nancy, freedom does not belong to collective entities, such as class, humanity or spirit. It always relates to the singular existence, even when it sets collective processes in motion. Here is the mistake made by Hobbes—who understood freedom as sovereignty -, by Rousseau—who understood freedom as general will -, by Hegel—who understood freedom as state self-recognition—and by Sartre—who reversed the concept of freedom into its very opposite, in that he understood it as the final recognition of an ethical necessity. In the whole philosophical tradition—and this is Nancy's criticism—freedom fades away. Only at times, in the line connecting Kant with Heidegger, freedom reemerges as unresolved, only to then disappear again. Therefore, it needs to start over precisely from those gaps, from the gaps in that line in order to rethink it. Well, upon what basis? On an ontological basis, in that freedom, as previously mentioned, has to do with existential ontology insofar as it is its common experience. Nancy's text on freedom, or rather on the experience of freedom "is neither a philosophy nor a history of freedom - we should rather say that it is a release of history and philosophy from the compulsion to re-present itself in a literally exhausted way."[41] From this point of view, "Nancy's philosophical journey traces the contours and the possibility of a general disorientation. [...] The extreme possibility of doing philosophy in the age of the end of philosophy. If philosophy can no longer be a conception of the world, if it can no longer ascribe to it its own sense or even any other sense, nevertheless, it can constitute the opening of a space of thought in which the world recognizes itself as the only sense. The world - the relationship it creates, the tangles it weaves, the encounters it releases into the grain of a finite existence because it is never coincident with itself, always overlooking the other than itself. This inclination of existence toward its outside - its compearance in the singular plurality of the world - is what characterizes Nancy's thought in a constitutively political key. If sense coincides with existence, it means that we can finally "introduce ourselves" to ourselves without any more intermediaries or mediators—to one another, in the infinite sharing of a common experience. Such an

---

[41] Esposito, R.: Libertà in comune, Introduction to J.-L. Nancy, L'esperienza della libertà, quot., p. XI (my translation).

experience is that of freedom".[42] This is why, according to the French philosopher's repeated assertions, freedom is not something we have, but is something *we are*. It is the decision of existence as such, for itself. Therefore, it is not an object to be studied or examined, but the very practice of the experience of existence, which stands beside a sphere of meaning permeated *with* and undermined *by* the subjectivist framework of Western philosophical tradition. To think about freedom requires not thinking about an idea, but about a singular fact; it requires pushing thought to the very edge of a fatality that precedes it. It is precisely for this reason that Nancy repeats Heidegger's deconstructive gesture toward the metaphysics of subjectivity and inscribes the experience (factuality) of freedom "before" and simultaneously "alongside" community: "Freedom is nothing but a withdrawal of being *without any residue*—entirely resolved in the partition of existence. There is no being separate from the existence of every existent. Existence is the nothingness of being that keeps us in common relationship, having in common nothing but this relationship. Here is the *munus* that freedom shares: the non-being or nothingness-of-being that enables and, at the same time, *constitutes* the relationship as a partition of existence."[43] Freedom is "community itself in its infinitely singular—and therefore also plural—spacing: the plural singularity of community. [...] Freedom is the interval, the limit, the difference that cuts the community in the shape of the "every time," of the "from time to time," of the "one at a time"—of the transcendence that suspends it on its own outside, or that projects that outside within it. Freedom is the *internal exteriority* of community. The beginning, the blow, the explosion that opens up in it and that it opens up each time. Community opens up to the excess of *any* existence: it is freedom."[44] This freedom assigns us a task, *the* task Nancy ascribes to the *finite thought* of existence, of *our* singular, partitioned existence:

> daring to think the unthinkable, the unattributable, the intransigent qualities of being-with, while not subjecting it to any kind of hypostasis. It is not a political or economic task; it is more serious yet than that and it commands, in the long run, both the political and the economic. We are not in a 'war of civilisations', we are in an internal tearing apart of the only civilisation that civilises and barbarises the world in the one action, since this civilisation has already come up against the extremity of its own logic: this tearing apart presses the world back entirely into its own keeping, presses the human community back entirely into its own keeping and into the keeping of its own secret, without god and without any market value. It is with these elements that work must be done: with community confronted by itself, with us confronted by us, the with confronting the with. A confrontation doubtless belongs essentially to community: it is a question simultaneously of a confrontation and of an opposition, of an encounter where one goes out to meet oneself, so as to challenge and test oneself, so as to divide oneself in one's being by a remove that is also the condition of that being.[45]

---

[42] Ibid., pp. X-XI (my translation).

[43] Ibid., p. XXIX (my translation).

[44] Therein (my translation).

[45] Nancy, J.-L.: The confronted community, transl. A. Macdonald. Postcolonial Studies, 6, 1, (2003), p. 34.

3 The Freedom in Question

There is freedom only among the folds of the world, among its discards, its excesses, and its subtracted places. Subtracted from what? From an eternal immanentism or a "too human" desire for transcendence. Only in this way can it be possible to stand between the folds of the world—for we ourselves, individually, are *unfoldings* of the world. Here, freedom has no beginning or end. It simply *is*. Just "unfolded" as well, exposed *to* and *into* the "skin" of the world and its restlessness.

Bibliography of Jean-Luc Nancy

(1963), *Un certain silence*, "Esprit", 31, pp. 555–563.
(1966a), *André Breton*, "Esprit", 34, pp. 848–849.
(1966b), *Marx et la philosophie*, "Esprit", 34, pp. 1074–1087.
(1967), *Catéchisme et persévérance*, "Esprit", 35, pp. 368–381.
(1968), *Nietzsche. Mais où sont les yeux pour le voir?*, "Esprit", 36, pp. 482–503.
(1969), *Commentaire*, "Bulletin de la Faculté des Lettres de Strasbourg", pp. 189–198.
(1971), *Friedrich Nietzsche. Rhétorique et langage*", with Philippe Lacoue-Labarthe, "*Poétique*", 5, pp. 99–142.
(1972), *La thèse de Nietzsche sur la téléologie. Nietzsche aujourd'hui, I. Intensités*, Christian Bourgois, Paris.
(1973), *La remarque spéculative (un bon mot de Hegel)*, Galilée, Paris.
(1975a), *Logodaedalus (Kant écrivain)*, "Poétique", 21, pp. 24–52.
(1975b), *Le ventriloque*, in AA.VV., *Mimesis des articulations*, pp. 271–338, Aubier-Flammarion, Paris.
(1975c), *La linguistique défaite*, "Quinzaine Littéraire", p. 202.
(1976a), *Le discours de la syncope. I. Logodaedalus*, Flammarion, Paris.
(1976b), *Note*, "Première Livraison", p 4.
(1977a), *Lapsus judicii*, "Communications", 26, pp. 82–97.
(1977b), *Entre acte*, preface to Jean-Louis Galay, *Philosophie et invention textuelle. Essai sur la poétique d'un texte kantien*, Klincksieck, Paris.
(1977c), *Larvatus pro deo*, "Glyph", 1, pp. 14–36.
(1977d), Interview with François Laruelle, in LARUELLE F., *Le déclin de l'écriture*, Aubier-Flammarion, Paris, pp. 245–252.
(1978a), *Les raisons d'écrire*, "Première Livraison. Misère de la Littérature", pp. 83–96.
(1978b), *Mundus est fabula*, "MLN", 93, 4, pp. 635–653.
(1978c), *Menstruum universale*, "Sub-Stance", 21, pp. 21–35.
(1978d), *La langue enseigne*, "Cahiers Critique de la Littérature", 5, pp. 78–84.
(1979a), *Ego sum*, Flammarion, Paris.
(1979b), *La jeune carpe*, "Première Livraison. Haine de la Poésie", pp. 93–123.
(1979c), *"Fin de la métaphysique" ou fin de l'enseignement?*, "Les Études Philosophiques", 3, pp. 303–305.
(1979d), *Monogrammes (Chronique)*, "Diagraphe", 20, pp. 129–137.
(1979e), *Monogrammes II*, "Digraphe", 21, pp. 131–138.
(1980a), *Fabrication d'un sonnet*. "Anima", 3.

(1980b), *Monogrammes III*, "Digraphe", 22–23, pp. 221–223.
(1980c), *Monogrammes IV*, "Digraphe", 24, pp. 131–137.
(1980d), *Catalogue*, "Avant-Guerre", 1, pp. 21–30.
(1981a), *La voix libre de l'homme*, in AA.VV., *Les fins de l'homme. A partir du travail de J. Derrida*, pp. 163–182, Galilée, Paris.
(1981b), *La vérité impérative*, in Marc Michel Travaux (ed. by), *Pouvoir et vérité*, C.E.R.I.T., pp. 21–43, Cerf, Paris.
(1981c), *Monogrammes V*, "Digraphe", 25, pp. 199–208.
(1981d), *L'Être abbandonné*, in "Argiles", n° 23–24.
(1982a), *Le partage des voix*, Galilée, Paris.
(1982b), *The jurisdiction of de Hegelian monarch*, "Social Research", 49, 2, pp. 481–516.
(1982c), *Das unendliche Ende der Psychoanalyse*, "Bordures", 1, pp. 5–15.
(1983a), *L'impératif catégorique*, Flammarion, Paris.
(1983b), *La joie d'Hyperion*, "Les Études Philosophiques", 2, pp. 177–194.
(1983c), *Un recours dangereux*, "L'Ane", p. 41.
(1983d), *La représentation*, (con Ph.Lacoue-Labarthe), "Théâtre Public", 52–53, pp. 13–15.
(1983e), *Il nous faut*, "Poesie", 26, pp. 93–94.
(1983f), *Les Céphéides, ces étoiles qui nous regardent*, "Le Nouvel Alsacien", 20–21, p. 7.
(1983g), *Das aufgegebene Sein*, Alphäus, Berlino.
(1984a), *La sovranità persona*, "Sapere e Potere", 1, pp. 26–41.
(1984b), *Exergues*, "Aléa", 5, pp. 23–26.
(1984c), *L'offrande sublime*, in "Po&sie", n°30, pp. 76, 104.
(1985a), *Dies irae*, in AA.VV., *La faculté de juger*, pp. 9–54, Minuit, Paris.
(1985b), *Il dit*, "Cahiers Du Grif", pp. 103–105.
(1986), *L'oubli de la philosophie*, Galilée, Paris.
(1987a), Des lieux divins, T.E.R., Mauvezin.
(1987b), *Interventions*, "Qui Parle", 1, 2, pp. 8–11.
(1988a), *L'expérience de la liberté*, Galilée.
(1988b), *Topos: who comes after the subject?* (Introduzione), "Topoi", 7, p. 2.
(1988c), *Le rire, la presence*, "Critique", XLIV, 488–489, pp. 41–60.
(1988d), *Wild laughter in the throat of death*, "MLN", 102, 4, pp. 719–736.
(1988e), *Elliptical sense*, "Research in Phenomenology", pp. 175–190.
(1988f), *L'offrande sublime*, in AA.VV., *Du sublime*, pp. 37–75, Belin, Paris.
(1988g), *Fragments de la bêtise*, "Le Temps de la Réflexion", IX, pp. 13–27.
(1988h), *Le sens en commun*, "Autrement", 102, pp. 200–208.
(1988i), *Die undarstellbare Gemeinschaft*, P. Schwartz, Stuttgart.
(1989a), *L'histoire finie*, "Revue Des Sciences Humaines", 89, 213, pp. 75–96.
(1989b), *Auftritt lettaus*, "Akzente. Zeitschrift Fur Literatur", 36, 5, pp. 388–390.
(1989c), *Beheaded sun*, "Qui Parle", 3, 2, pp. 41–53.
(1989d), *Abrégé philosophique de la révolution française*, "Poesie", 48, pp. 211–218.
(1990a), *La communauté désœuvrée*, Christian Bourgois. Paris.
(1990b), *Une pensée finie*, Galilée, Paris.
(1990c), *Sens elliptique*, "Revue Philosophique", 2, pp. 325–347.
(1990d), *Finite history*, in AA.VV., *The States of 'theory'. History, art, and critical discourse*, pp. 149–174, Columbia University Press, New York.
(1990e), *Sharing voices*, in ORMISTON G. L. e SCHRIFT A.D., *Transforming the hermeneutic context: from Nietzsche to Nancy*, pp. 211–259, State University of New York Press, New York.
(1990f), *Exscription*, "Yale French Studies" (*On Bataille*), 78, pp. 47–65.
(1990g), *Our history*, "Diacritics", 20, 3, pp. 97–115.
(1990h), *Vox clamans in deserto*, "Furor", 19–20, pp. 3–17.
(1990i), *À suivre*, "Lettre International", 24, p. 7.
(1991a), *Le poids d'une pensée*, Le griffon d'argile, Québec.
(1991b), *Manque de rien*, in AA.VV., *Lacan avec les philosophes*, pp. 201–206, Albin Michel, Paris

(1991c), *The unsacrificeable*, "Yale French Studies. Literature and the Ethical Question", 79, pp. 20–38.
(1991d), *Entretien sur le mal*, "Apertura. Collection De Recherche Psychanalytique", 5, pp. 27–31.
(1991e), *La pensée préfabriquée*, "Lettre International", 29, p. 74.
(1991f), *Der Preis des Friedens. Krieg, Recht, Souveränität-technè*, "Lettre International",14, pp. 34–45.
(1991g), *Het bestaan dat niet te offeren is*, in TEN KATE L., *Voorbij het zelfbehoud. Gemeenschap en offer bij Georges Bataille*, pp. 79–102, Garant, Leuven.
(1992a), *Corpus*, Métailié, Paris, trad. it. di A. Moscati, *Corpus*, Cronopio, Napoli, 1995.
(1992b), *La comparution/ The compearence from the existence of "communism" to the community of "existence"*, "Political Theory", 20, 3, pp. 371–398.
(1992c), *Les iris*, "Yale French Studies", 81, pp. 46–63.
(1992d), *Un sujet?*, in AA.VV., *Homme et sujet*, pp. 47–114, L'Harmattan, Paris, now in "Shift. International Journal of Philosophical Studies", n° 1, 2017, pp. 153–188.
(1992e), *Le temps partagé*, "Traverses", 1, pp. 70–79.
(1992f), *Monogrammes VI. De la figure politique à l'évènement de l'art*, "Futur Antérieur", 10, pp. 104–113.
(1992g), *L'indestructible*, "Intersignes", 2, pp. 236–249.
(1992h), *La grande loi*, "Io", 1, pp. 43–46.
(1992j), *An der Grenze: Gestalten und Farben*, "Lettre International",16, pp. 12–14.
(1992k), *À la frontière, figures et couleurs*, "Le désir de l'Europe", pp. 41–50, Editions de la Différence et Carrefour des Littératures Européennes, Paris et Strasbourg.
(1992l), *La naissance continuée d'Europe*, "Le désir de l'Europe", pp. 253–255, Editions de la Différence et Carrefour des Littératures Européennes, Paris et Strasbourg.
(1992m), *Le piège tendu à la régression*, "Le désir de l'Europe", pp. 56–59, Editions de la Différence et Carrefour des Littératures Européennes, Paris et Strasbourg.
(1992n), *Un autre «oui»*, "Le Monde des débats", p. 1.
(1993a), *Le sens du monde*, Galilée, Paris.
(1993b), *Zwischen Zerstörung und Auslöschung*, "Deutsche Zeitschrift Für Philosophie", 41, pp. 859–864.
(1993c), *On the threshold*, "Paragraph", 16, 2, pp. 111–121.
(1993d), *'You ask me what it means today…'.*, "Paragraph", 16, 2, pp. 108–110.
(1993e), *The experience of freedom*, trad. di Bridget McDonald, Stanford University Press, Stanford
(1993f), *The birth to presence*, trad. di Brian Holmes e altri, Stanford University Press, Stanford.
(1993g), *Lob der Vermischung*, "Lettre International", 21, pp. 4–7.
(1993h), *Monogrammes XI*, "Futur Antérieur", 16, 2, pp. 141–144.
(1993i), *Monogrammes XIII*, "Futur Antérieur", 18, pp. 61–66.
(1993j), *L'art: fragment*, "Lignes", 18, pp. 153–173.
(1994a), *Les muses*, Galilée, Paris.
(1994b), *De l'écriture: qu'elle ne relève rien*, "Rue Descartes", 10, pp. 104–109.
(1994c), *Démesure humaine*, "Epokhè", 5, pp. 257–261.
(1994d), *Les deux phrases de Robert Antelme*, "Lignes", 21, pp. 154–155.
(1994e), *Renouer le politique*, "Intersignes", 8–9, pp. 111–126.
(1994f), *Un entretien avec Jean-Luc Nancy*, "Le Monde".
(1994g), *L'époque de l'espace*, "Les Cahiers Philosophiques de Strasbourg", 1, pp. 149–151.
(1995a), *Violence et violence*, "Lignes", 25, pp. 293–298.
(1995b), *La douleur existe. Elle est injustifiable*, "Revue d'Éthique et de Théologie Morale", 195, pp. 91–96.
(1995c), *Critique de la raison pure*, "Lignes", 24, pp. 84–87.
(1995d), *Autour de la notion de communauté littéraire*, "Tumultes" (CSPRS), 6, pp. 23–37.
(1995e), *L'insuffisance des "valeurs" et la nécessité du "sens"*, "Interfaces", pp. 54–58.

(1995f), Nécessité du sens. *Yves Bonnefoy. Poésie, peinture, musique*, FINK M., 43–50. Strasbourg: Presses Universitaires de Strasbourg.
(1995g), De l'âme. *Le poids du corps*, RAYMOND J.-L. et KERN P., 173–204. Le Mans: Ecole des Beaux-arts.
(1996a), *Être singulier pluriel*, Galilée, Paris.
(1996b), *La naissance des seins*, Collection 222, Erba, Valence.
(1996c), *Être singulier pluriel*, "Quinzaine Littéraire", 695, pp. 17–18.
(1996d), *The Deleuzian fold of thought*, in PATTON P. (ed.), *Deleuze. A critical reader*, pp. 107–113, Basil Blackwell.
(1996e), *Lecture dérangée*, "Quinzaine Littéraire", 698, pp. 23–24.
(1996f), *Being-with*, "Centre for Theoretical Studies in the Humanities and the Social Sciences" (Unpublished Working Paper for the University of Essex), 11.
(1996g), *Euryopa: Blick in die Weite*, in SCHNEIDER U.J. e SCHÜTZE J.K., *Philosophie und Reisen*, pp. 11–21, Leipziger Universitätsverlag, Leipzig.
(1996h), *L'éthique originaire de Heidegger*.
(1997a), *Hegel. L'inquiétude du négatif*, Hachette, Paris.
(1997b), *Un souffle*, "Rue Descartes", 15, pp. 13–16.
(1997c), *Cours, Sarah!*, "Les Cahiers Du Grif", pp. 29–38.
(1997d), *The gravity of thought*, trad.di François Raffoul e Gregory Recco, Humanities Press, New Jersey.
(1997e), *Résistance de la poésie*, William Blake & Co, Bordeaux.
(1997f), *Technique du présent: essai sur On Kawara*, "Cahiers Philosophie de L'Art", 6.
(1997g), *Kalkül des Dichters. Nach Hölderlins Mass*, Legueil, Stuttgart.
(1997h), *The insufficiency of 'values' and the necessity of 'sense'*, "Cultural Values" 1, 1, pp. 127–131.
(1997i), *Violence et* vérité, "La *Mazarine*", 1, pp. 1–4.
(1997k), *"Tentative de définition..."*, "Lignes", 32, pp. 102–104.
(1997l), *Technique et nature. Entretien avec Hélène* Petrovsky, "Logos", 9, pp. 130–145.
(1998a), *La* déconstruction du christianisme, "Les Études Philosophiques", 4, pp. 503–519.
(1998b), *The inoperative community*, in MC NEILL W. e FELDMAN K.S. (a cura di), *Continental philosophy. An anthology*, pp. 429–440, Blackwell, Oxford.
(1998c), *Changement de monde*, "Lignes", 35, pp. 42–52.
(1998d), *Cosmos basileus*, "Lignes", 35, pp. 94–99.
(1998e), *The surprise of the event*, in BARNETT S., *Hegel after Derrida*, pp. 91–104, Routledge, London & New York.
(1998f), *Sens multiple. La techno. Un laboratoire artistique et politique du présent. Entretien avec Michel Gaillot*, Dis voir, Paris.
(1998g), *Pli deleuzien de la pensée*, in AA.VV., *Gilles Deleuze. Une vie philosophique*, pp. 115–123, Institut Synthélabo, Paris.
(1999a), *La ville au loin*, Mille et une nuits, département des éditions Fayard.
(1999b), *Weltenwechsel*, "Lettre International", 44, pp. 4–6.
(1999c), *Borborygmes*, in AA.VV., *L'animal autobiographique. Autour de Jacques Derrida*, (a cura di Marie-Louise Mallet), pp. 161–179, Galilée, Paris.
(1999d), *Vaille que vaille*, in SOUN-GUI K., *Stock Exchange*, Maison du livre d'artiste contemporain, Domart-en-Ponthieu.
(1999e), *Responding for existence*, "Studies in Practical Philosophy", 1, 1, pp. 1–11.
(1999f), *Heideggers 'originary ethics'*, "Studies in Practical Philosophy", 1, 1, pp. 12–35.
(1999g), *Experiencing Soun-gui*, "Tympanum", 3, pp. 1–12.
(1999h), *The image — the* distinct, "Heaven", pp. 44–49, Hatje Cantz, Ostfildern-Ruit.
(1999i), *Réponse aux questions d'Alex Garcia-Dütmann*, "Basileus", 2, 1.
(1999j), *Dies illa. D'une fin à l'infini, ou de la création*, "Collège International de Philosophie", pp. 77–99, PUF., Paris.

(1999k), *Thinking better of capital. An interview*, "Studies in Practical Philosophy", 1, 2, pp. 214–232.
(1999l), *Autrement dire*, "PoeSie", 89, pp. 114–119.
(1999m), *L'immémorial*, in TALBOT P. et al., *Art, mémoire, commémoration*, pp. 43–79, École Normale Supérieure d'Art de Nancy, Voix Richard Meier.
(1999n), *Le portrait (dans le décor)*, "Cahiers-Philosophie de L'Art", 8, p. 29.
(1999o), *Poème de l'adieu au poème: Bailly*, "Poesie", 89, pp. 59–63.
(2000a), *Le regard du portrait*, Galilée, Paris.
(2000b), *L'intrus*, Galilée, Paris.
(2000c), *La pensée dérobée*, "Lignes", pp. 88–106.
(2000d) *Bild und Gewalt. Von absoluter Offenbarung und dem unendlich Bevorstehenden*, "Lettre International", 49, pp. 86–89.
(2000e), *Rien que le monde*, (Entretien avec Jean-Luc Nancy. Propos recueillis par Stany Grelet et Mathieu Potte-Bonneville), "Vacarme", 11, pp. 4–12.
(2000f), *The technique of the present*, "Tympanum. A Journal of Comparative Literary Studies", 4, p. 17.
(2000g), *Nancy, le cœur de l'autre*, (raccolta di Jean-Baptiste Marongiu), Libération Livres.
(2000h), *Entre deux*, "Magazine Littéraire", 392, pp. 54–57; anche in "Sileno", *Entre dos*, 2000, n° 9, pp. 66–68.
(2000i), *Un entretien*, (Jean-Luc Nancy/Chantal Pontbriand), "Parachute", 100, pp. 14.31.
(2000j), *Au lieu de l'utopie. Les utopies et leurs représentations*, pp. 13–24, Le Quartier, Quimper.
(2000k), *Des sens de la démocratie*, "Transeuropéennes", 17, pp. 45–48.
(2000l), *La quête du sens*, (nota di Jean-Luc Nancy), pp. 102–104, GREP Midi-Pyrénées,Toulouse.
(2001a), *La pensée dérobée*, Galilée, Paris.
(2001b), *L'idolâtrie des taliban*, Libération.
(2001c), *Réponse sur une question*, "Le Philosophoire", 12, p. 20.
(2001d), "*Un jour, les dieux se retirent*", William Blake & Co., Bordeaux.
(2001e), *L'évidence du film. Abbas Kiarostami*, Yves Gevaert, Bruxelles.
(2001f), *L'«il y a» du rapport sexuel*, Galilée, Paris.
(2001g), Entretien du 23 juin 2000. *Heidegger en France II. Entretiens*, JANICAUD D., 244–55. Paris: Albin Michel.
(2001h), *La communauté affrontée*, Galilée, Paris.
(2001i), *La représentation interdite*, in "Le Genre humain", n°1.
(2002a), *De Indringer*, Boom, Amsterdam.
(2002b), *La création du monde ou la mondialisation*, Galilée, Paris.
(2002c), *Urbi et orbi*, "De Witte Raaf", 98, pp. 7–10.
(2002d), *À l'écoute*, Galilée, Paris.
(2002e), *Image et violence. L'image – Le distinct. La représentation interdite*, Galilée.
(2003a), *Noli me tangere. Essai sur la levée du corps*, Bayard, Paris.
(2003b), *Dell'Uno e della gerarchia*, trad. it. di M. Bruzzese, in "l'espressione", n° 0, anno I, pp. 55–57, and in "Lignes", n° 8, 2002.
(2004a), *Chroniques philosophiques*, Galilée, Paris.
(2004b), *Au ciel et sur la terre*, Bayard, Paris.
(2004c), *Rives, bords, limites (de la singularité)*, in «Angelaki. Journal of theoretical Humanities», n. 9, pp. 41–53.
(2005), *La déclosion. Déconstruction du christianisme, 1*, Galilée, Paris.
(2006a) *La Naissance des seins suive de Péan pour Aphrodite*, Galilée, Paris.
(2006b) *Jacques Rancière et la métaphysique*, in L. Cornu, P. Vermeren (eds.), *La philosophie déplacée. Autour de Jacques Rancière*, Horlieu, Bourg-en-Bresse 2006.
(2006c) 'In dialogo' con Jean-Luc Nancy, in D. Calabrò, *Dis-piegamenti. Soggetto, corpo e comunità in Jean-Luc Nancy*, Milan, Mimesis.

(2007) *L'arte, oggi*, in F. Ferrari (ed.) *Del contemporaneo. Saggi su arte e tempo*, Mondadori, Milano 2007, pp. 1–20.
(2008a) *Verité de la démocratie*, Galilée, Paris.
(2008b) *Le poids d'un pensée, l'approche*, Éditions de la Phocide, Paris-Strasbourg.
(2009a) *Le Plaisir ad dessin*, Galilée, Paris.
(2009b) Démocratie finie et infinie, in É. Hazan (dir.) Démocratie, dans quel état?, La Fabrique, Paris.
(2009c) Dieu. La justice. L'amour. La beauté. Quatre petites conférences, Bayard, Montrouge.
(2009d) *On the Commerce of Thinking: Of Books and Bookstores*, Fordham University Press, New York.
(2009) *Corpus*, Fordham University Press, New York.
(2010a) L'Adoration. Déconstruction du Christianism II, Galilée, Paris.
(2010b) *Corpo teatro*, Cronopio, Napoli.
(2010c) Identité. Fragments, franchise, Galilée, Paris.
(2010d) *Die* Liebe, *übermorgen*, Salon Verlag, Köln.
(2011a) *Plus d'un*, in A. Barrau - J.-L. Nancy, *Dans quels mondes vivons-nous?*, Galilée, Paris.
(2011b) *De la struction*, in A. Barrau - J.-L. Nancy, *Dans quels mondes vivons-nous?*, Galiléc, Paris.
(2011c) Maurice Blanchot. Passion politique. Lettre-récit de 1984 suivie d'une lettre de Dionys Mascolo, Paris, Galilée.
(2012a) *Être-avec et démocratie*, in «Po&sie», n. 135.
(2012b) L'Équivalence des catastrophes, Galilée, Paris.
(2012c) *Che cos'è il collettivo*, in U. PERONE (ed.), *Intorno a Jean-Luc Nancy*, Rosengerg & Sellier, Torino, pp. 15–22.
(2012d) *Adoration: The Deconstruction of Christianity II*, Fordham University Press, New York.
(2012e) *Preamble: In the Midst of the World; or, Why Deconstruct Christianity?*, in *Re-treating Religion. Deconstructing Christianity with Jean-Luc Nancy*, (A. Alexandrova, I. Devisch, L. T. Kate, and A. van Rooden, eds.), Fordham University Press, New York, pp. 1–21.
(2013a) *Ivresse*, Payot & Rivages, Paris.
(2013b) *The Pleasure in Drawing*, Fordham University Press, New York
(2014a) *La communauté désavouée*, Galilée, Paris.
(2014b) *L'autre portrait*, Galilée, Paris.
(2014c) Passion de la communauté. Entretien avec Danielle Cohen-Levinas, in «Cahiers Maurice Blanchot», n. 2, pp. 43–47.
(2014d) *After* Fukushima: *The Equivalence of Catastrophes*, Fordham University Press, New York.
(2015a) *Banalité de* Heidegger, Paris, Galilée.
(2015b) C'est quoi penser par soi-même? Entretiens avec Émile, Éditions de l'aube, La Tour d'Aigues.
(2016a) *Que faire?*, Galilée, Paris.
(2016b) *The Disavowed Community*, Fordham University Press, New York.
(2017a) *Un sujet furtif*, in «Shift. International Journal of Philosophical Studies», n. 1, p. 15.
(2017b) Sexistence, Galilée, Paris.
(2017c) *The Possibility of a World: Conversations with Pierre-Philippe Jandin*, Forham University Press, New York.
(2019) *Animalità animata*, Mimesis, Milano.
(2020) *Excluding the Jew Within Us*, Polity, Cambridge.
(2021a) *The Fragile Skin of the World*, Polity, Cambridge.
(2021b) *Sexistence*, Fordham University Press, New York.
(2022), *La haine des Juifs. Entretiens avec Danielle Cohen-Levinas*, Les Éditions du Cerf, Paris.
(2023a) *Derrida. Supplements*, Fordham University Press, New York
(2023b) Corpus *III: Cruor and Other Writings*, Fordham University Press, New York
(2024) *On Bernard Stiegler: Philosopher of Friendship*, Bloomsbury USA Academic, London-New York.

Bibliography on Jean-Luc Nancy with Other

(1977), NANCY J.-L. E GROMER B., Philosophie en cinquième. *Qui a peur de la philosophie?* Agacinski S., pp. 207–257, Flammarion, Paris.
(1984), NANCY J.-L., BORCH-JACOBSEN M. e MICHAUD E., *Hypnoses*, Galilée, Paris.
(1989a), NANCY J.-L. (a cura di), *Qui vient après le sujet?*, "Cahiers Confrontation", 20.
(1989b), NANCY J-.L. e DERRIDA J., *«Il faut bien manger ou le calcul du sujet»*. (Entretien avec J.-L. Nancy), "Cahiers Confrontation", 20, pp. 91–114.
(1991), NANCY J.-L. e BAILLY J.C., *La comparution. Politique à venir*, Bourgois, Paris.
(1994a), NANCY J.-L. e MARTIN F., *NIUM*, Collection 222, Valence.
(1994b), ID., *Peinture dans la grotte (sur les parois de G.B.)*, "La Part de L'Oeil", 10, pp. 161–168.
(1999), ID., *Le soleil se couche, moi aussi*, Ceaac, Strasbourg.
(1999), NANCY J.-L. e CONESA J.C., *Passages (Être, c'est être perçu - Les ambassadeurs*, Editions des Cahiers Intempestifs, Saint-Etienne
(2000a), NANCY J.-L. e FRITSCHER S., *Mmmmmm*, Au figuré, Paris.
(2000b) NANCY J.-L. and ESPOSITO, R., *Conloquium*, in R. Esposito, *Communitas. Origine et destin de la communauté*, tr. fr. by N. Le Lirzin, Puf, Paris.
(2001a) NANCY J.-L. and ESPOSITO, R., *Dialogo sulla filosofia a venire*, in J.-L. Nancy, *Essere singolare plurale*, italian transl. by D. Tarizzo, Einaudi, Torino.
(2001b), NANCY J.-L. e MONNIER M., *Dehors la* danse, RROZ, Lyon.
(2003) NANCY, J.-L. and FERRARI, F. *La pelle delle immagini*, Bollati Boringhieri, Torino 2003.
(2004a), NANCY J.-L. e LALUCQ V., *Fortino Sámano. (Les débordements du poème)*, Galilée, Paris.
(2004b) NANCY J.-L. and J. DERRIDA, *Responsabilité – du sens à venir*, in F. GUIBAL, J.-C. MARTIN (dir.), *Sens en tous sens. Autour des travaux de Jean-Luc Nancy*, Galilée, Paris 2004, pp. 165–200.
(2007) NANCY, J.-L., DIDI-HUBERMAN, G., HEINICH, N., BAILLY, J.-C., *Del contemporaneo. Saggi su Arte e Tempo*, ed. by F. Ferrari, Mondadori, Milano.
(2012) NANCY, J.-L., ALEXANDROVA, A., DEVISCH, I., KATE, T., L., ROODEN VAN, A., *On Dis-enclosure and Its Gesture, Adoration: a Concluding Dialogue with Jean-Luc Nancy*, in *Re-treating Religion. Deconstructing Christianity with Jean-Luc Nancy*, (A. Alexandrova, I. Devisch, L. T. Kate, and A. van Rooden, eds.), Fordham University Press, New York, pp. 304– 344.
(2013) NANCY, J.-L., JANDIN, P.-P., *La possibilité d'un monde*, Les Petits Platon, Paris.
(2017) NANCY, J.L., LÉBRE, J., *Signaux sensibles. Entretiens à propos de l'art*, Bayard, Paris.
(2020) NANCY, J.-L., BELHAJ KACEM, M., *Immortelle finitude. Sexualité et philosophie*, Diaphanes, Zurich, Paris, Berlin.
(2022) NANCY, J-L., COHEN LEVINAS, D., *La haine des Juifs*, Cerf, Paris.

Bibliography on Jean-Luc Nancy and Lacoue-Labarthe

(1975), *Le dialogue des genres*, (Textes de Shaftesbury, Hemsterhuis, Schelling, presentati da Ph.Lacoue-Labarthe e J.-L. Nancy), "Poétique", 21, pp. 148–175.
(1978), *L'absolu littéraire. Théorie de la littérature du romantisme allemand*, Seuil, Paris.
(1979), *La panique politique*, "Cahiers Confrontation", 2, pp. 33–57.
(1980), *Genre*, "Glyph", 7, pp. 1–14.
(1981a) *Les fins de l'homme. À partir du travail de Jacques Derrida. (Colloque de Cerisy, 23 juillet – 2 août 1980)*, Galilée, Paris.
(1981b), *Le peuple juif ne rêve pas*, in *La psychanalyse est-elle une histoire juive?*, Colloque de Montpellier, 57–92, Seuil, Paris.

(1981c) R*ejouer le politique. Cahiers du Centre de recherches philosophiques sur le politique*, Éditions Galilée, Paris.
(1982a), *Noli me frangere*, "Revue Des Sciences Humaines", 185, pp. 83–92.
(1982b), *Entretien*, "Exercices De La Patience", 3–4, pp. 219–232.
(1983), Le retrait du politique, Cahiers du Centre de recherches philosophiques sur le politique, Éditions Galilée, Paris.
(1989), *The unconscious is destructured like an affect* (Parte 1 di "The Jewish people do not dream"), "Stanford Literature Review", pp. 191–209.
(1990a), *Le titre de la lettre. Une lecture de Lacan*, Galilée, Paris.
(1990b), *The nazi myth*, "Critical Inquiry", 16, pp. 291–312.
(1991a), *Le mythe nazi*, L'Aube, La tour D'Aigues.
(1991b), *"From where is psychoanalysis possible?"* (Parte II di "The Jewish people do not dream"), "Stanford Literature Review", 8, 1–2, pp. 39–55.
(1992), *Scène*, "Nouvelle Revue De Psychanalyse", 17, 46, pp. 73–98.
(1997), *Chers amis*, in *Retreating the Political*, Routledge, London-New York 1997, pp. 143–147.

Bibliography on Jean-Luc Nancy

ADAMEK P. M., (2002), *The Intimacy of Jean-Luc Nancy's "L'Intrus"*, in «CR: The New Centennial Review», n. 3, pp. 189–201.
ALEXANDOVA, A., DEVISCH, I., KATE, T.L., ROODEN v. A., (2012) *Re-opening the question of religion: Dis-enclosure of religion and modernity in the philosophy of Jean-Luc Nancy*, Preface in *Re-treating Religion. Deconstructing Christianity with Jean-Luc Nancy*, (A. Alexandrova, I. Devisch, L. T. Kate, and A. van Rooden, eds.), Fordham University Press, New York, pp. 22–42.
ALEXANDROVA, A., *Distinct Art*, in *Re-treating Religion. Deconstructing Christianity with Jean-Luc Nancy*, (A. Alexandrova, I. Devisch, L. T. Kate, and A. van Rooden, eds.), Fordham University Press, New York, pp. 275–290.
ARGYROS, S., (2023), *Noli me tangere: expérience de la liberté*, in *Jean-Luc Nancy. Anastasis de la pensée*, (D. Dwivedi, J. Lebre, M. Montevil et F. Warin eds.), Hermann, Paris, pp. 73–78.
ARIEMMA T., (2006), *Il nudo e l'animale. Filosofia dell'esposizione*, Editori Riuniti, Roma.
ARIEMMA T., (2009), *Logica della singolarità. Antiplatonismo e ortografia in Deleuze, Derrida e Nancy*, Aracne, Roma.
ARIEMMA T., (2019), *L'Occidente messo a nudo*, Luca Sossella, Milano.
ARMSTRONG P., (2009), *Reticulations. Jean-Luc Nancy and the Networks of the Political*, University of Minnesota Press, Minneapolis-London.
ARNOULD E., (1996), *The impossible sacrifice of poetry. Bataille and the Nancian critique of Sacrifice*, "Diatrics", 26, 2, pp. 86–96.
BADIOU A., (2004), *L'offrande réservée*, in F. Guibal, J.-C- Martin (dir.), *Sens en tous sens. Autour des travaux de Jean-Luc Nancy*, Galilée, Paris, pp. 16–24.
BADIOU A., (2009), *«Existe-t-il quelque chose comme une politique deleuzienne?»*, in «Cités», n. 40, pp. 15–20.
BAILLY, J.-C., (2023), *La surprise recommencée du sens (II) (sur Jean-Luc Nancy)*, in *Jean-Luc Nancy. Anastasis de la pensée*, (D. Dwivedi, J. Lebre, M. Montevil et F. Warin eds.), Hermann, Paris, pp. 241–244.
BALIBAR, É., (2023), *Incarnations*, Postface in *Jean-Luc Nancy. Anastasis de la pensée*, (D. Dwivedi, J. Lebre, M. Montevil et F. Warin eds.), Hermann, Paris, pp. 245–246.
BAPTIST G., (2007), *L'isola da pensare: "un mondo distinto dal mondo", Intervista con Jean-Luc Nancy*, in Ead. (a cura di), *Jean-Luc Nancy. Pensare il presente. Seminari cagliaritani 11–13 dicembre*, Cuec, Cagliari 2010, pp. 165–170.

BAPTIST G., (2010), *Un pensiero all'erta*, in EAD. (a cura di), *Jean-Luc Nancy. Pensare il presente*, CUEC, Cagliari, pp. 15–20.
BAPTIST G., (2011), *La fedeltà all'apertura del finito. A partire dalle* Piccole conferenze, in «B@belonline/print», n. 10–11, pp. 33–40.
BARKER, S., (2012), *De-monstration and the Sens of Art*, in *Jean-Luc Nancy and plural thinking. Expositions of World, Ontology, Politics, and Sense*, (P. Gratton and M.-E. Morin eds.), State University of New York Press, New York, pp. 175–190.
BENJAMIN, A., (2012), *Forbidding, Knowing, Continuing: On representing the Shoah*, in *Jean-Luc Nancy and plural thinking. Expositions of World, Ontology, Politics, and Sense*, (P. Gratton and M.-E. Morin eds.), State University of New York Press, New York, pp. 213–226.
BENNINGTON G., (2010), *Not half, no end. Militantly Melancholic. Essays in Memory of Jacques Derrida*, Edinburgh University Press, Edinburgh.
BENSUSSAN, G., (2023), *L'existence démocratique: une dette*, in *Jean-Luc Nancy. Anastasis de la pensée*, (D. Dwivedi, J. Lebre, M. Montevil et F. Warin eds.), Hermann, Paris, pp. 131–142.
BENVENUTO, S., (2023), *Parler à Jean-Luc Nancy*, in *Jean-Luc Nancy. Anastasis de la pensée*, (D. Dwivedi, J. Lebre, M. Montevil et F. Warin eds.), Hermann, Paris, pp. 221–224.
BERKMAN G., (2011), *L'effet Bartleby. Philosophes lecteurs*, Hermann, Paris.
BERKMAN G., (2012), *La «chose-dehors» de la pensée*, in Ead., D. Cohen-Levinas (eds.), *Figures du dehors. Autour de Jean-Luc Nancy*, Nouvelles Cécile Defaut, Nantes, pp. 441–458.
BERNASCONI R. (1993), *On deconstructing nostalgia for community within the West: the debate between Nancy and Blanchot*, "Research in Phenomenology", 23, pp. 3–21.
BERTO G., (2003), *La scrittura della libertà*, in A. Potestà, R. Terzi (a cura di), *Annuario 2000–2001. Incontro con Jean-Luc Nancy*, Raffaello Cortina, Milano, pp. 127–139.
BERTO G., (2003), *La risonanza del soggetto*, "aut aut", 316–317, pp. 77–84.
BIRD G., (2016), *Containing Community. From Political Economy to Ontology in Agamben, Esposito, and Nancy*, Suny Press, New York.
CALABRÒ D., (2005), *Mundus est fabula*, in «Ameba», n. 1, pp. 22–27.
CALABRÒ D., (2006), *Dis-piegamenti. Soggetto, corpo e comunità in Jean-Luc Nancy*, Milan, Mimesis.
CALABRÒ D., (2009), *Jean-Luc Nancy: alla frontiera di un pensiero a venire*, in J.-L. NANCY, *Il peso di un pensiero, l'approssimarsi*, Mimesis, Milano, pp. I–XXXIV.
CALABRÒ D., (2011), *Ex-peau-sition. Dal corpo alla dismisura dell'essere-con*, in «B@belonline/print», n. 10–11, pp. 41–47.
CALABRÒ D., (2012), *The Immemorial: The Deconstruction of Christianity, Starting from "Visitation: Of Christian Painting"*, in A. Alexandrova, I. Devisch, L. Ten Kate, Van Rooden, *Re-treating Religion. Deconstructing Christianity with Jean-Luc Nancy*, Fordham University Press, New York, pp. 229–239.
CALABRÒ D., (2019), *Se l'Europa fa segno. Per una fenomenologia dello straniero*, in G. PINTUS (a cura di), *Relazione e alterità*, Inschibbboleth, Roma, pp. 9–26.
CALABRÒ, D., (2023), *La peau du monde: finitude et existence*, in *Jean-Luc Nancy. Anastasis de la pensée*, (D. Dwivedi, J. Lebre, M. Montevil et F. Warin eds.), Hermann, Paris, pp. 55–64.
CALDARONE R., (2012), *Una prassi di senso. Su* L'adorazione *di Jean-Luc Nancy*, in «Giornale di Metafisica», n. 2, pp. 149–157.
CALDARONE, R., (2022), *Il toccare della filosofia. Jean-Luc Nancy*, in "Shift. International Journal of Philosophical Studies", pp. 39–48.
CARBONE M., (2003), *Il corpo improprio*, in AA.VV., *Incontro con J.-L. Nancy*, Cortina, *Milano*, pp. 180–188.
CARBONE M., LEVIN D.M., (2003) *La carne e la voce. In dialogo tra estetica ed etica*, Mimesis, Milano.
CARIOLATO A., (2003), *Posizione, messa in posizione e differenza*, in A. Potestà, R. Terzi (eds.), *Annuario 2000–2001. Incontro con Jean-Luc Nancy*, Raffaello Cortina, Milano, pp. 189–208.

CARIOLATO A., (2012), *Christianity's Other Resource: Jean-Luc Nancy and the Deconstruction of Faith*, in *Jean-Luc Nancy and plural thinking. Expositions of World, Ontology, Politics, and Sense*, (P. Gratton and M.-E. Morin eds.), State University of New York Press, New York, pp. 43–56.

CAVALCANTE SCHUBACK, M., (2023), *Exister: transitivement*, in *Jean-Luc Nancy. Anastasis de la pensée*, (D. Dwivedi, J. Lebre, M. Montevil et F. Warin eds.), Hermann, Paris, pp. 65–72.

CAVARERO A., (2003), *L'orecchio di Nancy*, in «aut aut», n. 316–317, pp. 68–76.

CECALA P., (2012), *Guerra, sovranità, responsabilità. Una riflessione con Nancy e Derrida*, in U. Perone, *Intorno a Jean-Luc Nancy*, Rosengerg & Sellier, Torino, pp. 127–132.

CHOULET, P., (2023), *Inclus Spinoza en toi*, in *Jean-Luc Nancy. Anastasis de la pensée*, (D. Dwivedi, J. Lèbre, M. Montevil et F. Warin eds.), Hermann, Paris, pp. 225–234.

CICCARELLI R., (2000), *Jean-Luc Nancy: il potere della libertà*, in «Democrazia e diritto», n. 3–4, pp. 124–137.

CICCARELLI R., (2011), *La potenza che dunque siamo. Saggio sull'esperienza della libertà*, in «B@belonline/print», n. 10–11, pp. 59–69.

COHEN-LEVINAS D., (2012), *Le neveu de Nancy. Entretien sur la musique*, in G. Berkman, D. Cohen-Levinas (eds.), *Figures du dehors. Autour de Jean-Luc Nancy*, Éditions Nouvelle Cécile Defaut, Nantes, pp. 207–226.

COHEN-LEVINAS, D., (2022) *Être en vie*, in "Shift. International Journal of Philosophical Studies", pp. 49–56.

COHEN-LEVINAS, D., (2022), *Sans salut. Être partout où est la vie*, in "Post-filosofie", n°15, pp. 15–22.

COHEN-LEVINAS, D., (2023), *Être en vie*, in *Jean-Luc Nancy. Anastasis de la pensée*, (D. Dwivedi, J. Lebre, M. Montevil et F. Warin eds.), Hermann, Paris, pp. 47–54.

CRITCHLEY S., (1999), *The Ethics of Deconstruction: Derrida and Lévinas*, Edinburgh University Press, Edinburg.

DADÀ S., (2019), *Dall'essere-con alla democrazia. Evoluzione dell'idea di "politico" in Jean-Luc Nancy*, in M. Di Pierro, F. Marchesi (eds.), *Crisi dell'immanenza. Poter, conflitto, istituzione*, Quodlibet, Macerata, pp. 189–202.

DAL LAGO, A. (1992), *Comunità. Appunti sulla permanenza di un mito*, "aut aut", 8, pp. 5–12.

DALY, M. (1994), *Communitarianism. A new public ethics*, Wadsworth, California.

DE KESEL, M., (2012), *Deconstruction or Destruction ? Comments on Jean-Luc Nancy's Theory of Christianity*, in *Re-treating Religion. Deconstructing Christianity with Jean-Luc Nancy*, (A. Alexandrova, I. Devisch, L. T. Kate, and A. van Rooden, eds.), Fordham University Press, New York, pp. 63–79.

DE PETRA F., (2010), *Comunità, comunicazione, comune. Da George Bataille a Jean-Luc Nancy*, Derive Approdi, Roma.

DE VRIES, H. (1994), *Theotopographies: Nancy, Hölderlin, Heidegger*, "*MLN*", 109, pp. 445–477.

DERRIDA, J. (1993), *Le toucher*, "Paragraph", 16, 2, pp. 122–157.

DERRIDA J., (2000), *Le toucher, Jean-Luc Nancy*, Galilée, Paris, engl. trans., (2005) *On touching, Jean-Luc Nancy,* Stanford, Calif.: Stanford University Press.

DEVISCH, I. (2000a), *A trembling voice in the desert. Jean-Luc Nancy's re-thinking of the space of the political*, "Cultural Values", 4, 2, pp. 239–255.

DEVISCH, I. (2000b), *La «négativité sans emploi»*, "Symposium", IV, 2, pp. 167–187.

DEVISCH, I. (2000c), *Geraakt zijn. Derrida's Le toucher, Jean-Luc Nancy*, "Tijdschrift Voor Filosofie", 62, pp. 733–742.

DEVISCH, I. (2003), *Jean-Luc Nancy en het vraagstuk van de gemeenschap in de hedendaagse wijsbegeerte*, Peeters, Leuven.

DEVISCH, I. (2012) *Intermezzo*, in *Re-treating Religion. Deconstructing Christianity with Jean-Luc Nancy*, (A. Alexandrova, I. Devisch, L. T. Kate, and A. van Rooden, eds.), Fordham University Press, New York, pp. 43–45.

DEVISCH I., (2013), *Jean-Luc Nancy and the Question of Community*, Bloomsbury Publishing Plc, London, New York.

DEVISCH, I., VANDEPUTTE, K., (2012), *Sense, Existence and Justice; or How are We to Live in a Secular World ?* in *Re-treating Religion. Deconstructing Christianity with Jean-Luc Nancy*, (A. Alexandrova, I. Devisch, L. T. Kate, and A. van Rooden, eds.), Fordham University Press, New York, pp. 80–91.

DOMANIN I., (2003), *Deleuze e Nancy politici*, in AA.VV., *Incontro con J.-L. Nancy*, Cortina, Milano, pp. 209–219.

DOPPELT, S., (2023), *Still Life*, in *Jean-Luc Nancy. Anastasis de la pensée*, (D. Dwivedi, J. Lebre, M. Montevil et F. Warin eds.), Hermann, Paris, pp. 175–182

DOW K., (1993), *Ex-posing identity: Derrida and Nancy on the (Im)possibility*, in «Philosophy and social criticism», n. 19, pp. 261–271.

DUTMANN, A.G. (1993), *Immanences, transcendances*, "Paragraph", 16, 2, pp. 187–191.

DUTMANN, A.G. (1998), *In correspondence with Jean-Luc Nancy*, "Basileus", 1, 2.

DWIVEDI, D., (2022), *El comienzo de Jean-luc Nancy*, in "Shift. International Journal of Philosophical Studies", pp. 57–64.

DWIVEDI, D., (2022), *L'inizio di Jean-Luc Nancy*, in "Post-filosofie", n°15, pp. 35–46.

DWIVEDI, D., (2023), *Jean-Luc Nancy: Identification et indestinance*, in *Jean-Luc Nancy. Anastasis de la pensée*, (D. Dwivedi, J. Lebre, M. Montevil et F. Warin eds.), Hermann, Paris, pp. 33–43.

ELLIOTT B., (2010), *Constructing Community. Configurations of the Social in Contemporary Philosophy and Urbanism*, Lexington Books, Lahnam.

ESPOSITO A., (2012), *Variazioni sul politico in Jean-Luc Nancy*, in U. PERONE (a cura di), *Intorno a Jean-Luc Nancy*, Rosenberg & Sellier, Torino, pp. 29–34.

ESPOSITO, R., (2001), *Dialogo sulla filosofia a venire*, (colloquio con J-.L. Nancy) in J.-L. Nancy, *Essere singolare plurale*, Einaudi, Torino.

ESPOSITO, R., (2003), *Libertà in comune*, in AA.VV., *Incontro con J.-L. Nancy*, Cortina, Milano, pp. 223–230.

ESPOSITO R., (2004), *Chair et corps dans la déconstruction du christianism*, GUIBAL, J.-C-MARTIN (dir.), *Sens en tous sens. Autour des travaux de Jean-Luc Nancy*, Galilée, Paris, pp. 153–164.

FAES H., (1999), *En découvrant l'humaine sociabilité avec M. Heidegger, H. Arendt et J-L. Nancy*, in «Revue des sciences philosophiques et théologiques», n. 8, 83, pp. 707–736.

FALLEN, C., (2023), *Jean Luc Nancy, porté(e)s de la pensée*, in *Jean-Luc Nancy. Anastasis de la pensée*, (D. Dwivedi, J. Lebre, M. Montevil et F. Warin eds.), Hermann, Paris, pp. 203–210.

FENVES, P. (1998), *Nancy, Jean-Luc*, in *Routledge Encyclopedia of Philosophy*, CRAIG E. (ed.), pp. 651–654, Routledge, London and New York.

FERRARI, F., (2012), *The Dis-enclosure of Contemporary Art: an Underpinning Work*, in *Re-treating Religion. Deconstructing Christianity with Jean-Luc Nancy*, (A. Alexandrova, I. Devisch, L. T. Kate, and A. van Rooden, eds.), Fordham University Press, New York, pp. 291–303.

FESTA F. S., (2015), *Teologia politica. Perché mai Nancy non legge Erik Peterson?*, in «Filosofia Politica», n. 1, pp. 145–162.

FILIPPI M., (2019), *Da così tanto tempo*, in J.-L. Nancy, *Animalità animata*, Mimesis, Milano, pp. 7–13.

FISCHER, F. (2000), *Des placements du sens: Jean-Luc Nancy*, "La quête du sens", pp. 75–102. GREP Midi-Pyrénées, Toulouse.

FRASER N., (1984), *French Derrideans: Politicizing Deconstruction or Deconstructing the Political?*, in «New German Critique», n. 33, pp. 127–154.

FYNSK C., (1991), *Experiences of Finitude*, in J.-L. Nancy, *The Inoperative Community*, University of Minnesota Press, Minneapolis and Oxford, pp. VII-XXXV.

FULCO, R., (2022), *Conloquium: il dialogo tra Jean-Luc Nancy e Roberto Esposito*, in "Shift. International Journal Of Philosophical Studies", pp. 239–252.

GALINDO HERVÁS A., (2003), *La soberanía. De la* Teología Política *al* Comunitarismo Impolítico, Institució Alfons el Magnánim, València.

GARELLI, G., (2022), *Umane vestigia (Nancy su Hegel e una fanciulla che segue le Muse)*, in "Post-filosofie", n°15, pp. 47–64.
GARRITANO F., (1999), *Aporie comunitarie, sino alla fine del mondo*, Jaka Book, Milano, p. 77.
GENOVESE R., (2006), *Una critica di Nancy e Agamben*, in «La società degli individui», n. 25, pp. 26–36.
GENTILI D., (2011), *Creazione politica*, in «B@belonline/print», n. 10–11, pp. 133–138.
GILBERT-WALSH J., (2000), *Broken imperatives. The ethical dimension of Nancy's thought*, in «Philosophy and Social Criticism», n.2, p. 29–50.
GIORDANO D., (2012), *A partire da Jean-Luc Nancy. Note sulla comunicazione*, in U. PERONE (ed.), *Intorno a Jean-Luc Nancy*, Rosenberg & Sellier, Torino, pp. 141–146.
GIUGLIANO, D., (2022), *« Non c'è una società senza spettacolo ». Una riflessione su Nancy, presupponendo Debord*, in "Shift. International Journal of Philosophical Studies", pp. 65–74.
GOETZ, B., (2023), *Un Maître particulièrement amical (et « exubérant »)*, in *Jean-Luc Nancy. Anastasis de la pensée*, (D. Dwivedi, J. Lebre, M. Montevil et F. Warin eds.), Hermann, Paris, pp. 195–198.
GORIA, G., (2022), *L'ellisse speculativa. Nancy, Hegel e il passo del pensiero*, in "Shift. International Journal of Philosophical Studies", pp. 253–266.
GRATTON, P., (2012), *The Speculative Challenge and Nancy's Post-Deconstructive Realism*, in *Jean-Luc Nancy and plural thinking. Expositions of World, Ontology, Politics, and Sense*, (P. Gratton and M.-E. Morin eds.), State University of New York Press, New York, pp. 109–125.
HALLER G., (2022), *Aime qu'il passe*, in "Shift. International Journal of Philosophical Studies", pp. 199–209.
HÄRLE, C-C., (2022a), *Aristoteles und Nancy über Technik*, in "Shift. International Journal of Philosophical Studies", pp. 75–88.
HÄRLE, C-C., (2022b), *Sovranità, guerra e tecnica nel mondo globalizzato*, in "Post-filosofie", n°15, pp. 65–89.
HÄRLE, C-C., (2023), *L'immémorial: Nancy et le portrait*, in *Jean-Luc Nancy. Anastasis de la pensée*, (D. Dwivedi, J. Lebre, M. Montevil et F. Warin eds.), Hermann, Paris, pp. 161–164.
HARMAN G., (2002a), *Tool-being: Heidegger and the Metaphysics*, Open Court, Chicago.
HARMAN G., (2002b), *On Interface*, in P. Gratton, M. Morin (eds.), *Jean-Luc Nancy and Plural Thinking. Expositions of World, Ontology, Politics, and Sense*, Suny Press, Albany, pp. 95–108.
HARMAN, G., (2012), *On Interface: Nancy's Weights and Masses*, in *Jean-Luc Nancy and plural thinking. Expositions of World, Ontology, Politics, and Sense*, (P. Gratton and M.-E. Morin eds.), State University of New York Press, New York, pp. 95–108.
HUTCHENS B.C., (2002), *Archi-ethics, Justice, and the Suspension of History in the Writing of Jean-Luc Nancy*, in P. Gratton, M. Morin (eds.), *Jean-Luc Nancy and Plural Thinking. Expositions of World, Ontology, Politics, and Sense*, Suny Press, Albany, pp. 129–142.
HUTCHENS B.C., (2005), *Jean-Luc Nancy and the Future of Philosophy*, McGill-Queen's University Press, Montreal & Kingston.
HILL L., (2018), *Nancy, Blanchot. A Serious Controversy*, Rowman & Littlefield International, London.
HOLE K.L., (2016), *Towards a Feminist Cinematic Ethics. Claire Denis, Emmanuel Levinas and Jean-Luc Nancy*, Edinburgh University Press, Edinburgh.
ICHIKAWA, T., (2023), *La foi et la démocratie*, in *Jean-Luc Nancy. Anastasis de la pensée*, (D. Dwivedi, J. Lebre, M. Montevil et F. Warin eds.), Hermann, Paris, pp. 143–148.
INGRAM D. (1988), *The retreat of the political in the modern age: Jean-Luc Nancy on totalitarianism and community*, "Research in Phenomenology", 18, pp. 93–124.
INTRONA, C., (2022), *Il t(r)atto tra Nancy e Derrida: come restare in contatto*, in "Post-filosofie", n°15, pp. 90–112.
IZZO V.N., (2016), *Sulle relazioni tra città contemporanea, catastrofe e diritto*, in «Lo sguardo», n. 21, pp. 237–247.
JAMES I., (2006), *The fragmentary Demand. An Introduction to the Philospfy of Jean-Luc Nancy*, Stanford University Press, Stanford.

JAMES, I., (2012), *Incarnation and Infinity*, in *Re-treating Religion. Deconstructing Christianity with Jean-Luc Nancy*, (A. Alexandrova, I. Devisch, L. T. Kate, and A. van Rooden, eds.), Fordham University Press, New York, pp. 246–250.
JANDIN, P.-P., (2023), *Une lumière crépusculaire*, in *Jean-Luc Nancy. Anastasis de la pensée*, (D. Dwivedi, J. Lebre, M. Montevil et F. Warin eds.), Hermann, Paris, pp. 183–190.
JANDIN P.P. e DAVID A.(1989), *Penser la communauté*, "Revue des Sciences Humaines", 89, p. 213
JOSEPH M., (2002), *Against the romance of community*, University of Minnesota Press, Minneapolis.
JOSEPH, L., (2023), *L'appel de l'intime: Jean-Luc Nancy*, in *Jean-Luc Nancy. Anastasis de la pensée*, (D. Dwivedi, J. Lebre, M. Montevil et F. Warin eds.), Hermann, Paris, pp. 101–108.
KAKINAMI, R., (2023), *Re-commencement, reprise – de la pensée*, in *Jean-Luc Nancy. Anastasis de la pensée*, (D. Dwivedi, J. Lebre, M. Montevil et F. Warin eds.), Hermann, Paris, pp. 191–194.
KAMUF P. (ed.) (1993), *On the Work of Jean-Luc Nancy*, "Paragraph", 16, 2.
KAMUF P., (2002), *Béance*, in «CR: The New Centennial Review», No. 3, pp. 37–56.
KATE L.TEN., (1997), *Politiek van de verijdeling. Bataille en Nancy over gemeenschap en Politiek*, in *Rondom Georges Bataille*, COPPENS G., pp. 33–55, Acco, Leuven.
KATE L.TEN., (2012), *God Passing by: Presence and Absence in Monotheism and Atheism*, in *Re- treating Religion. Deconstructing Christianity with Jean-Luc Nancy*, (A. Alexandrova, I. Devisch, L. T. Kate, and A. van Rooden, eds.), Fordham University Press, New York, pp. 132–144.
KATE L.TEN., (2022), *The impossible encounter. Creation, Incarnation, Trynity and Miracle in Nancy and Pontormo*, in "Shift. International Journal of Philosophical Studies", pp. 89–104.
KERVEGAN J.F., (2004), *Un Hégélianisme sans profondeur*, in F. Guibal, J.-C. Martin (dir.), *Sens en tous sens. Autour des travaux de Jean-Luc Nancy*, Galilée, Paris, pp. 25–37.
KESEL DE M., (2012), *Deconstruction or Destruction? Comments on Jean-Luc Nancy's Theory of Christianity*, in A. Alexandrova, I. Devisch, L. Ten Kate, A. Van Rooden, *Re-treating Religion. Deconstructing Christianity with Jean-Luc Nancy*, Fordham University Press, New York, pp. 63–79.
KESTER G.H., (2004), *Converstaion Pieces. Community and communication in modern art*, University of California Press, Bekley-Los Angeles.
LAWRENCE F., (2011), *The Art of Listening*, in L. Collins, E. Rush (eds), *Making Sense. For an Effective Aesthetics*, Peter Lang AG, Bern, pp. 77–86.
LÈBRE J., (2011), *Point de fuite. Art et politique chez Jean-Luc Nancy*, in «B@belonline/print», n. 10–11, pp. 139–149.
LÈBRE, J., (2023), *Part'âges*, in *Jean-Luc Nancy. Anastasis de la pensée*, (D. Dwivedi, J. Lebre, M. Montevil et F. Warin eds.), Hermann, Paris, pp. 19–26.
LIBRETI J.S., (1996), *The Practice of the World: Jean-Luc Nancy's Liminal Cosmology Between Theory and History*, in «International Studies in Philosophy», n. 28, pp. 29–44.
LINGIS A., (1994), *The community of those who have nothing in common*, Indiana University Press, Bloomington and Indianapolis.
LISCIANI-PETRINI E., (2003), *quella voce "che s'effonde... di selve e d'onde"*, "aut aut", n. 316–317, pp. 57–67.
LISCIANI-PETRINI E., (2004), *Noi: diapason-soggetti*, in J.-L. Nancy, *All'ascolto*, Raffaello Cortina, Milano, pp. V-XXXI.
LISSE, M., (2012), *Literary Creation, Creation ex Nihilo*, in *Re-treating Religion. Deconstructing Christianity with Jean-Luc Nancy*, (A. Alexandrova, I. Devisch, L. T. Kate, and A. van Rooden, eds.), Fordham University Press, New York, pp. 203–214.
LIVIANA MESSINA A., (2017), *Apocalypse et croyance en ce monde. Monde, finitude et christianisme chez Nancy et Blanchot*, in J. Lèbre, J. Rogozinski, *Jean- Luc Nancy. Penser la mutation*, Presses Universitaires de Strasbourg, Strasbourg, pp. 153–168.

LOOSE, D., (2012), *The excess of Reason and the returno of religion: Transcendence of Christian Monotheism in Nancy's Dis-enclosure*, in *Re-treating Religion. Deconstructing Christianity with Jean-Luc Nancy*, (A. Alexandrova, I. Devisch, L. T. Kate, and A. van Rooden, eds.), Fordham University Press, New York, pp. 163–181.

LUCCI A., (2012), *Al cuore della tecnica: Nancy e Stiegler*, in U. Perone, *Intorno a Jean-Luc Nancy*, Rosenberg & Sellier, Torino, cit., pp. 109–114.

MAIA, T., (2023), *Dieu exsangue – Le Caravage et la Résurrection*, in *Jean-Luc Nancy. Anastasis de la pensée*, (D. Dwivedi, J. Lebre, M. Montevil et F. Warin eds.), Hermann, Paris, pp. 165–174.

MANCHEV B., (2009), *La métamorphose du monde: Jean-Luc Nancy et les sorties de l'ontologie négative*, in «Europe», n. 960, pp. 254–261.

MANCHEV B., (2012), *Ontology of Creation: The Onto-aisthetics of Jean-Luc Nancy*, in A. Alexandrova, I. Devisch, L. Ten Kate, A. Van Rooden, *Re-treating Religion. Deconstructing Christianity with Jean-Luc Nancy*, Fordham University Press, New York, pp. 261–274.

MANCHEV, B., (2023), *Le surgissement de la voix, Jean-Luc Nancy*, in *Jean-Luc Nancy. Anastasis de la pensée*, (D. Dwivedi, J. Lebre, M. Montevil et F. Warin eds.), Hermann, Paris, pp. 211–220.

MARCHART O., (2007), *Post-Foundational Political Thought. Political Difference in Nancy, Lefort, Badiou and Laclau*, Edinburgh University Press, Edinburgh.

MARIANI A., (2010), *Osservazioni filosofico-educative intorno a Jean-Luc Nancy*, in G. BAPTIST (ed.), *Jean-Luc Nancy. Pensare il presente*, Cuec, Cagliari, pp. 107–112.

MASCIA V., (2012), *Scenari della corporeità in Jean-Luc Nancy*, in "Quaderni di Inschibboleth", n°0, pp. 67–84.

MASCIA V., (2015a), *Jean-Luc Nancy: la chance comunitaria e l'esposizione del "senza progetto"*, in "Epekeina. International Journal of Ontology, History and Critics", vol. 6, n° 2, pp. 1–19.

MASCIA V., (2015b), *La messinscena del vivente. A partire da alcune riflessioni su Jean-Luc Nancy*, in *Architetture del vivente. Studi e narrazioni*, D. Calabrò and V. Mascia, pp. 153–167.

MASSÒ CASTILLA, J., (2022), *El arte sin fin tras la muerte del arte*, in "Post-filosofie", n° 15, pp. 113–128.

MATASSI E., (2011), *"Esposti al suono"*, in «B@belonline/print», n. 10–11, pp. 159–167.

MAY, T., (1993), *The community's absence in Lyotard, Nancy and Lacoue-Labarthe*, "Philosophy Today", 37, 3, pp. 275–284.

MAY T., (1997), *Reconsidering Difference. Nancy, Derrida, Levinas, Deleuze*, Pennsylvania State University Press, Pennsylvania.

MCQUILLAN M., (2012a), *Deconstruction without Derrida*, Bloomsbury, London-New York.

MCQUILLAN, M., (2012b), *Deconstruction and Globalisation: The world According to Jean-Luc Nancy*, in *Jean-Luc Nancy and plural thinking. Expositions of World, Ontology, Politics, and Sense*, (P. Gratton and M.-E. Morin eds.), State University of New York Press, New York, pp. 57–75.

MEAZZA C., (2018a), *L'effetto del reale e la prossimità del tra-noi. Fenomenologia del* parergon, Guida, Napoli.

MEAZZA C., (2019), *Il tratto del tra-noi in Jean-Luc Nancy*, in G. Pintus (a cura di), *Relazione e alterità*, Inschibboleth, Roma, pp. 53–70.

MEAZZA, C., (2022), *L'ateismo del politico in Jean-Luc Nancy*, in "Shift. International Journal of Philosophical Studies", pp. 105–114.

MEAZZA, C., (2024), *Il nichilismo della forma politica. Nell'eredità del comunismo im-possibile di Jean-Luc Nancy*, Orthothes, Salrno-Napoli.

MOHAN, S., (2022), *Decostruzione e anástasis*, in "Post-filosofie", n° 15, pp. 129–135.

MOHAN, S., (2023), *Déconstruction et Anastasis*, in *Jean-Luc Nancy. Anastasis de la pensée*, (D. Dwivedi, J. Lebre, M. Montevil et F. Warin eds.), Hermann, Paris, pp. 27–32.

MONTÉVIL, M., (2023), *Remarques sur le corps*, in *Jean-Luc Nancy. Anastasis de la pensée*, (D. Dwivedi, J. Lebre, M. Montevil et F. Warin eds.), Hermann, Paris, pp. 93–100.

MORAZZONI A.M., (2003), *Nei margini musicali dell'ascolto*, "aut aut", 316–317, pp. 85–92.

MOREIRAS A., (2018), *El incidente incospicuo*, in «Soft Power. Revista euro-americana de teoría e historia de la política y del derecho», n. 2, pp. 213–220.
MORGANTI, M., (2022), *Gorgogliare*, in "Shift. International Journal of Philosophical Studies", pp. 193–198.
MORIN M.E., (2009), *Thinking Things: Heidegger, Sartre, Nancy*, in «Sartre Studies International», n. 2, pp. 35–53.
MORIN, M.-E., (2022), *Merleau-Ponty and Nancy on Sense and Being*, At the limits of Phenomenology, Edinburgh University Press, Edinburgh.
MOSCATI A., (1995), *Corpi di nessuno*, in J.-L. Nancy, Corpus, Cronopio, Napoli, pp. 101–108.
MOSCATI A., (2003), D*i alcuni motivi nel pensiero di Jean-Luc Nancy*, in A. Potestà, R. Terzi (eds.), *Annuario 2000–2001. Incontro con Jean-Luc Nancy*, Raffaello Cortina, Milano, pp 103–113.
MOSCATI A., (2022), *Tradurre Jean-Luc Nancy*, in "Shift. International Journal of Philosophical Studies", pp. 127–136.
NEYRAT F., (2013), *Le communisme existentiel de Jean-Luc Nancy*, Lignes, Paris.
NEYRAT, F., (2023), *La necessité d'infinir: le « Que Faire » de Jean-Luc Nancy*, in *Jean-Luc Nancy. Anastasis de la pensée*, (D. Dwivedi, J. Lebre, M. Montevil et F. Warin eds.), Hermann, Paris, pp. 123–130.
NISHITANI, O., (2023), *Jean-Luc Nancy, la pensée du « partage »*, in *Jean-Luc Nancy. Anastasis de la pensée*, (D. Dwivedi, J. Lebre, M. Montevil et F. Warin eds.), Hermann, Paris, pp. 199–202.
NISHIYAMA Y., (2017), *L'adresse de l'entre-nous: l'interpretation platique di Hegel chez Jean- Luc Nancy*, in in J. Lèbre, J. Rogozinski, *Jean-Luc Nancy. Penser la mutation*, Presses Universitaires de Strasbourg, Strasbourg, pp. 127–138.
NORRIS, A., (2012), *Jean-Luc Nancy on the Political after Heidegger and Schmitt*, in *Jean-Luc Nancy and plural thinking. Expositions of World, Ontology, Politics, and Sense*, (P. Gratton and M.-E. Morin eds.), Suny, Albany, New York, pp. 143–158.
O'BYRNE, A., (2012a), *Nancy's Materialist Ontology*, in *Jean-Luc Nancy and plural thinking. Expositions of World, Ontology, Politics, and Sense*, (P. Gratton and M.-E. Morin eds.), Suny, Albany, New York, pp. 79–94.
O'BYRNE, A., (2012b), *The God Between*, in *Re-treating Religion. Deconstructing Christianity with Jean-Luc Nancy*, (A. Alexandrova, I. Devisch, L. T. Kate, and A. van Rooden, eds.), Fordham University Press, New York, pp. 215–228.
PELGREFFI I., (2012), *Il corpo-teatro fra Nancy e Derrida*, in U. PERONE (ed.), *Intorno a Jean-Luc Nancy*, Rosenberg & Sellier, Torino, pp. 83–94.
PEPERSTRATEN VAN F., (2012), *Thinking Alterity – In One or Two ? Nancy's Christianity Compared With Lyotard's Judaism*, in *Re-treating Religion. Deconstructing Christianity with Jean-Luc Nancy*, (A. Alexandrova, I. Devisch, L. T. Kate, and A. van Rooden, eds.), Fordham University Press, New York, pp. 145–162.
PETTIGREW, D., (2012), *The Task of Justice*, in *Jean-Luc Nancy and plural thinking. Expositions of World, Ontology, Politics, and Sense*, (P. Gratton and M.-E. Morin eds.), State University of New York Press, New York, pp. 159–172.
PIAZZA V., (2003), *Jean-Luc Nancy e il pensiero dell'esposizione*, in A. Potestà, R. Terzi (eds.), *Annuario 2000–2001. Incontro con Jean-Luc Nancy*, Raffaello Cortina, Milano, pp. 114–126.
PIROMALLI S., (2012), *Nudità del senso, nudità del mondo. L'ontologia aperta di Jean-Luc Nancy*, Il Poligrafo, Padova.
PONZIO, J., (2022a), *Per un realismo assoluto del reale puro. Nancy e il suono a fondo perduto della scrittura di Derrida*, in "Shift. International Journal of Philosophical Studies", pp. 267–280.
PONZIO, J., (2022b), *A corpo perduto" tra Nancy e Derrida: il desiderio ellittico della filosofia*, in "Post-filosofie", n° 15, pp. 136–152.
POTESTÀ, A., (2023), *Une voix dans le désert*, in *Jean-Luc Nancy. Anastasis de la pensée*, (D. Dwivedi, J. Lebre, M. Montevil et F. Warin eds.), Hermann, Paris, pp. 235–240.

PROFUMI E., (2013), *Sulla creazione politica. Critica filosofica e rivoluzione*, Editori Riuniti, Roma.
RAFFOUL F. (1999), *The logic of the with. On Nancy's Être singulier pluriel* "Studies in Practical Philosophy", 1,1, pp. 36–52.
RAFFOUL F. (2012a), *The Creation of the World*, in *Jean-Luc Nancy and plural thinking. Expositions of World, Ontology, Politics, and Sense*, (P. Gratton and M.-E. Morin eds.), State University of New York Press, New York, pp. 13–26.
RAFFOUL F., (2012b) *The self-Deconstruction of Christianity*, in *Re-treating Religion. Deconstructing Christianity with Jean-Luc Nancy*, (A. Alexandrova, I. Devisch, L. T. Kate, and A. van Rooden, eds.), Fordham University Press, New York, pp. 46–62.
RAFFOUL F., PETTIGREW D., (2007), Introduction, in J.-L. Nancy, *The Creation of the World or Globalization*, State University of New York, New York, pp. 1–26.
RECCHIA LUCIANI F.R., (2019), *Cos'è sessistenza: filosofia dell'esistenza sessuata*, in J.-L. NANCY, *Sessistenza*, il melangolo, Genova, pp. 8–23.
RECCHIA LUCIANI, F.R., (2022), *Jean-Luc Nancy: a Philosophy of « Being-toward-life »*, in "Shift. International Journal of Philosophical Studies", pp. 137–146.
RECCHIA LUCIANI, F.R., (2022), *Jean-Luc Nancy*, Feltrinelli, Milano.
RECCHIA LUCIANI, F.R., (2022), *Potere erotico e sessistenza: Jean-Luc Nancy con Audre Lorde*, in "Post-filosofie", n° 15, pp. 153–164.
RECCHIA LUCIANI, F.R., (2023), *Pour une critique de la raison tactile: de la philosophie du corps à l'ontologie haptique avec Jean-Luc Nancy*, in *Jean-Luc Nancy. Anastasis de la pensée*, (D. Dwivedi, J. Lebre, M. Montevil et F. Warin eds.), Hermann, Paris, pp. 109–120.
RESTA, C., (2022), *La comunità degli amanti e la passione politica. Il dissidio tra Nancy e Blanchot*, in "Shift. International Journal of Philosophical Studies", pp. 147–166.
ROA HEWSTONE, C., (2022), *Jean-Luc Nancy: de la guerra a la necesidad de una nueva ontología Política*, in "Post-filosofie", n° 15, pp. 165–182.
ROGOZINSKI, J., (2022), *L'impossibile comunità della comunità*, in "Shift. International Journal of Philosophical Studies", pp. 167–176.
ROGOZINSKI, J., (2023), *Face à l'im-monde*, in *Jean-Luc Nancy. Anastasis de la pensée*, (D. Dwivedi, J. Lebre, M. Montevil et F. Warin eds.), Hermann, Paris, pp. 149–156.
ROODEN, van A., (2012), *« My God, my God, why hast Thou forsaken me ? » Demytologized Prayer; or the Poetic Invocation of God*, in *Re-treating Religion. Deconstructing Christianity with Jean-Luc Nancy*, (A. Alexandrova, I. Devisch, L. T. Kate, and A. van Rooden, eds.), Fordham University Press, New York, pp. 189–202.
ROVATTI P.A, (2003), *Cerchiamo tutti un occhio che ascolti*, "aut aut", 316–317, pp. 93–96.
RUGO D., (2013), *Jean-Luc Nancy and the Thinking of Otherness. Philosophy and Powers of Existence*, Bloomsbury, London-New York.
SAIDEL M.L., (2012), *Dis-chiusura della sovranità teologico-politica in Jean-Luc Nancy: verso la sovranità del "con"*, in U. PERONE (ed.), *Intorno a Jean-Luc Nancy*, Rosenberg & Sellier, Torino, pp. 35–40.
SCAFOGLIO, L., (2022), *La lesione dell'immanenza. Teoria critica, ontologia, etica tra Nancy Adorno*, in "Shift. International Journal of Philosophical Studies", pp. 281–294.
SERAFINI L., (2011), *Decisione e inoperosità. Jean-Luc Nancy interprete di Heidegger*, in «B@ belonline/print», n. 10–11, pp. 271–278.
SERAFINI L., (2013), *Inoperosità. Heidegger nel dibattito francese contemporaneo*, Mimesis, Milano.
SHEPPARD D. SPARKS S., THOMAS C. EDS. (1997), *On Jean-Luc Nancy. The sense of Philosophy*, Routledge, London.
SMERICK, CH.M., (2012), *No Other Place to Be: Globalization, Monotheism, and Salut in Nancy*, in *Jean-Luc Nancy and plural thinking. Expositions of World, Ontology, Politics, and Sense*, (P. Gratton and M.-E. Morin eds.), State University of New York Press, New York, pp. 27–42.
SPARKS S., (1997), *Politica ficta*, in P. Lacoue-Labarthe, J.-L. Nancy, *Retrating the Political*, Routledge, London and New York, pp. XIV-XXVIII.

STIMILLI E., (2011), *L'essere abbandonato*, in «B@belonline/print», n. 10–11, pp. 195–202.
TODARO, B., (2022), *Résister à la chute de l'Occident. Penser l'orientalisme anorexique avec Jean-Luc Nancy*, in "Post-filosofie", n°15, pp. 183–195.
TODARO, B., (2023), *La famille de la philosophie: Jean-Luc Nancy*, in *Jean-Luc Nancy. Anastasis de la pensée*, (D. Dwivedi, J. Lebre, M. Montevil et F. Warin eds.), Hermann, Paris, pp. 157–160.
TUPPINI T., (2012), *Jean-Luc Nancy. Le forme delle comunicazione*, Carocci, Roma.
TUPPINI, T., (2022a), *Essere qualunque (Nancy e Joyce)*, in "Shift. International Journal of Philosophical Studies", pp. 177–189.
TUPPINI, T., (2022b), *Nancy e l'atomismo*, in "Post-filosofie", n°15, pp. 196–213.
TUSA, G., (2022), *Somatocene. Noi corpo del mondo*, in "Post-filosofie", n°15, pp. 214–224.
VACCARO S., (2003), *Deleuze e Nancy: pieghe di prossimità*, in A. Potestà, R. Terzi (a cura di), *Annuario 2000–2001. Incontro con Jean-Luc Nancy*, Raffaello Cortina, Milano, pp. 169–179.
VANDE VEIRE F. (1988), *De 'gemeenschap'. Over twee essays van Nancy en Blanchot*, "Yang", 24, 4, pp. 110–116.
VAYSSE J.M. (1995), *De la catégorie de communauté*, in Communauté et modernité, RAULET G. e VAYSSE J.M.(eds.), pp. 30–61, L'Harmattan, Paris.
VERGANI M., (2003), *Un pensiero affermativo*, in J.-L. NANCY, *Il pensiero sottratto*, Bollati Boringhieri, Torino, pp. 7–15.
VILLANI M., (2013), *Al di là di paura e coraggio. Tre note sull'esposizione di Jean-Luc Nancy*, in «Epékeina. International Journal of Ontoloy History and Critics», n. 2, pp. 283–305.
VILLANI M., (2017), *Arte, vita, politica nel disegno filosofico di Jean-Luc Nancy*, in J.-L. Nancy, *Il disegno del Piacere*, Mimesis, Milano, pp. 8–26
VILLANI M., (2018), *Notas sobre el paradigma infrapolítico*, in «Soft Power. Revista euroamericana de teoría e historia de la política y del derecho», n. 2, pp. 231–238.
VILLANI, M., (2020), *Arte della fuga. Estetica e democrazia nel pensiero di Jean-Luc Nancy*, Mimesis, Milano.
VILLANI, M., (2022a), *Ontologia dell'attuosità. Inoperosità e corpo in Nancy alla luce dell'infinito hegeliano*, in "Shift. International Journal of Philosophical Studies", pp. 295–309.
VILLANI, M., (2022b), *Il negativo della politica. Sul lascito teoretico di Jean-Luc Nancy*, in "Post-filosofie", n°15, pp. 225–250.
VILLANI, M., (2023), *On Extension. Jean-Luc Nancy in the Wake of Hannah Arendt*, Inschibboleth, Roma.
VITIELLO V., (2003), *Jean-Luc Nancy e il problema della libertà*, in A. Potestà, R. Terzi (eds.), *Annuario 2000–2001. Incontro con Jean-Luc Nancy*, cit., pp. 140–150.
VOZZA M., (2003), *Lo spazio lasciato libero da Heidegger*, in A. POTESTÀ, R. TERZI (eds.), *Annuario 2000–2001. Incontro con Jean-Luc Nancy*, Raffaello Cortina, Milano, pp. 151–168.
VOZZA M., (2012), *Jean-Luc Nancy e la filosofia del corpo*, in U. Perone (ed.), *Intorno a Jean-Luc Nancy*, Rosenberg & Sellier, Torino, pp. 95–102.
VRIES H. DE (1994), *Theotopographies: Nancy, Hölderlin, Heidegger*, "MLN", 109, 3, pp. 445–477
VRIES H. DE, (2012), *Winke: Divine Topoi, in Nancy, Hölderlin, Heidegger*, in *Re-treating Religion. Deconstructing Christianity with Jean-Luc Nancy*, (A. Alexandrova, I. Devisch, L. T. Kate, and A. van Rooden, eds.), Fordham University Press, New York, pp. 112–131.
WARIN, F., (2023), *Jean-Luc Nancy: la grande santé*, in *Jean-Luc Nancy. Anastasis de la pensée*, (D. Dwivedi, J. Lebre, M. Montevil et F. Warin eds.), Hermann, Paris, pp. 79–92.
WATKIN C., (2009), *Phenomenology or Deconstruction? The Question of Ontology in Maurice Merleau-Ponty, Paul Ricoeur and Jean-Luc Nancy*, Edinburgh University Press, Edinburgh.
WATKIN, W., (2012), *Poetry's Promiscuous Plurality: On a part of Jean-Luc Nancy's* The Muses, in *Jean-Luc Nancy and plural thinking. Expositions of World, Ontology, Politics, and Sense*, (P. Gratton and M.-E. Morin eds.), State University of New York Press, New York, pp. 191–212.

WIT, T.W.A. de, (2012), *Between All and Nothing: the Affective Dimension of Political Bonds*, in *Re-treating Religion. Deconstructing Christianity with Jean-Luc Nancy*, (A. Alexandrova, I. Devisch, L. T. Kate, and A. van Rooden, eds.), Fordham University Press, New York, pp. 92–108.
WURZER W.S., (1997), *Nancy and the Political Imaginary After Nature*, in D. Sheppard, S.Sparks, C. Thomas (eds.), *On Jean-Luc Nancy. The sense of philosophy*, Routledge, London-New York, pp. 90–100.
ZINO A., TABACCO C., (2018), *Prefazione* a P. Lacoue-Labarthe, J.-L. Nancy, *Il panico politico*, ETS, Pisa, pp. 5–11.

General Bibliography

ADORNO T.W., *Ästetische theorie*, Suhrkamp Verlag. Frankfurt am Main
AGAMBEN G., (1990), *La comunità che viene*, Bollati Boringhieri, Torino.
AGAMBEN G., (1995), *Homo sacer. Il potere sovrano e la nuda vita, Einaudi, Torino*.
AGAMBEN G., (2018), *Homo sacer. Il potere sovrano e la nuda vita*, Einaudi, Torino 1995, now in *Homo sacer. Edizione Integrale 1995–2015*, Quodlibet, Macerata, pp. 11–168.
AGAMBEN G., (2018), *Lo stato di eccezione. Homo sacer, II, 1*, Bollati Boringhieri, Torino 2003, now with title: *Iustitium. Stato di eccezione*, in Id., *Homo sacer. Edizione Integrale 1995–2015*, Quodlibet, Macerata, pp. 169–250.
AGAMBEN G, *(2018), L'uso dei corpi. Homo sacer, IV, 2*, Neri Pozza, Vicenza 2014, now in *Homo sacer. Edizione Integrale 1995–2015*, Quodlibet, Macerata.
AGAMBEN, G., LUCCI, A., (2018), Homo Sacer. *Intervista a Giorgio Agamben*, in «doppiozero», 29 October 20, https://www.doppiozero.com/materiali/homo-sacer-intervista-giorgio-agamben.
ALDERMAN H. (1982), *By virtue of a virtue*, in "Review of Metaphysics", 36, pp. 127–153
Amendola, A., Bazzicalupo, L., Chicchi, F., Tucci, A., ((ed.), 2006, *Biopolitica, bioeconomia e processi di soggettivazione*. Macerata: Quodlibet.
AMENDOLA A., DEMITRY F., VACCA V., (2018), (ed.), *L'insorto del corpo. Il tono, l'azione, la poesia. Saggi su Antonin Artaud*, ombre corte, Verona.
ANNAS J. (1993), *The morality of happiness*, Oxford University Press, Oxford.
ANSCOMBE G.E.M. (1958), *Modern moral philosophy*, "Philosophy", 33, 124, pp. 1–19.
ARANOVITCH H. (2000), *From communitarianism to republicanism: on Sandel and his critics*, "Canadian Journal of Philosophy", 30, 4, pp. 621–647.
ARENDT H., (1951), *The Origins of Totalitarianism*, Harcourt Brace Jovanovich, New York.
ARENDT H., (1953), *Understanding and Politics*, in «Partisan Review», XX, IV, pp. 377–392
ARENDT H., (1958), *The Human Condition*, The University of Chicago Press, Chicago.
ARENDT H., (1961), *Between past and future: Six excercises in political thought*.
ARENDT H., (1963), *On revolution*, The Viking Press, New York.
ARENDT H., (1968), *Truth and Politics*, in *Between Past and Future. Eight Excercises in Political Thought*, Viking Press, New York.
ARENDT H., (1969), *On Violence*, Harcourt Brace Jovanovich, San Diego/New York/London.
ARENDT H., (1969), *Martin Heidegger zum 80. Geburstag*, «Merkur», n. 10, pp. 893–902
ARENDT H., (1978), *The Life of the Mind*, Harcourt Brace and Jovanovich, New York.
ARENDT H., (1982), *Lectures on Kant's Political Phlosophy*, © The University of Chicago
ARENDT H., (1993), *Was ist Politik?*, R. Piper GmbH & Co KG, Monaco, tr. it. di M. Bistolfi
ARENDT H., (1994), *What is Existenz Philosophy?*, in «Partisan Review», n.1, 1946, pp. 34–56, ora in *Essays in Undestranding 1930–1954*, © Harcourt Brace & Company, San Diego.
ARENDT H., (2003), *Some Questions of Moral Philosophy* (1966), in Ead., *Responsibility and Judgment*, Random House Inc, New York.

ARENDT H., (2005), *Socrates* (1954), in Ead., *The Promise of Politics*, Schocken Books, New York
ARENDT H., (2018), T*hinking without a Banister. Essays in Understanding 1953–1975*, Schocken Books, New York.
ARNSPERGER C. (2000), *Le pluralisme au-delà de la raison et du pouvoir. L'ancrage "transraisonnable" de la raison libérale*, "Revue Philosophique De Louvain", 1, pp. 83–106.
AVINERI S. E DE-SHALIT A. (EDS.) (1992), *Communitarianism and individualism*, Oxford University Press, Oxford.
BADHWAR N.K. (1996), *Moral agency, commitment and impartiality*, "Social Philosophy and Policy Foundation", 13, 1, pp. 1–26.
BADIOU A. (1992), *L'outrepassement politique du philosophème de la communauté*, in LEYENBERG G. e FORTE J.J., *Politique et modernité*, pp. 55–67, Osiris, Paris.
BADIOU A., (1997), *Deleuze. "La clameur e l'Être"*, hachette, Paris.
BADIOU A., (2009), *L'emblème démocratique*, in É. Hazan (dir.), *Démocratie, dans quel état*, La Fabrique, Paris.
BAILLY J.C. (1993), *L'adieu. Essai sur la mort des dieux*, L'aube, Paris.
BARNETT S. (ed.) (1998), *Hegel after Derrida*, Routledge, London & NewNork.
BARTHES R., HAVAS R., (1992), *Écoute* (1976), in R. Barthes, *L'obvie et l'obtus. Essais critiques III*, Seuil, Paris, pp. 217–230.
BATAILLE G., (1945), *Sur Nietzsche*, Gallimard, Paris.
BATAILLE G. (1970A), *La notion de dépense*, in Oeuvres Complètes I, pp.302–320, Gallimard, Paris.
BATAILLE G. (1970b), *Le coupable*, in Oeuvres Complètes V, Gallimard, Paris.
BATAILLE G. (1970c), *Sur Nietzsche*, in Oeuvres Complètes VI, Gallimard, Paris
BATAILLE G., (1973), *Le coupable* (1944), in *Œuvres complètes, tome 5. La Somme athéologique I*, Gallimard, Paris.
BATAILLE G., (1973), *Plans pour la somme athéologique*, in Id., *Œuvres complètes, tome 6. La Somme athéologique II*, Gallimard, Paris, pp. 360–374.
BATAILLE G., (1976), *La Souveraineté* (1954), in *Œuvres complètes, tome 8*, Gallimard, Paris.
BATAILLE G., (1978), *L'expérience intérieure*, Gallimard, Paris.
BATAILLE G., (1987), *L'Érotisme* (1957), in Id., *Œuvres complètes, tome 10*, Gallimard, Paris.
BATAILLE G., (XXXX), *L'ambiguità del piacere e del gioco*, testo di una conferenza tenuta all'ospedale *Saint'Anne* il 21 ottobre 1958 e conservato presso la *Nouvelle Bibliothéque de France*
BATAILLE G., (1997), *Choix de lettres 1917–1962. Édition établie, présenstée et annotée par Michel Surya*, Gallimard, Paris.
BAUMAN Z. (1993), M*odernity and Ambivalence*, Polity Press, Cambridge.
BAZZICALUPO L., (1996), *Hannah Arendt. La storia per la politica*, ESI, Napoli.
BAZZICALUPO L., (2000), *Mimesis e Aisthesis. Ripensando la dimensione estetica della politica*, ESI, Napoli.
BAZZICALUPO L., (2006), *Il governo delle vite. Biopolitica ed economia*. Rome: Laterza
BAZZICALUPO L., (2011), *Eroi della libertà. Storie di rivolta contro il potere*, il Mulino, Bologna
BAZZICALUPO L., (2013), *Politica. Rappresentazioni e tecniche di governo*, Carocci, Roma.
BAZZICALUPO L., (2014), *Estetica e politica nella figura dell'eroe*, in «Filosofia Politica», n. 1, pp. 77–98.
BAZZICALUPO L., (2017), *Coesistenza*, in «Filosofia politica», n. 1, pp. 47–58.
BAZZICALUPO L., (2019), *Radicalizzare le democrazia. Sulla produttività politica del vuoto o della pienezza ontologica*, in M. Di Pierro, F. Marchesi (ed.), *Almanacco di Filosofia e Politica I. Crisi dell'immanenza. Potere, conflitto, istituzione*, Quodlibet, Macerata, pp. 75– 92.
BEARDSWORTH R. (1996), *Derrida on the political*, Routledge, London and New York.
BECK U., (1986), *Risikogesellschaft. Auf dem Weg in eine andere Moderne*, Suhrkarnp Verlag, Frankfurt am Main.

BECKER L.C. (1975), *The neglect of virtue*, "Ethics", 85, 2, pp. 110–122.
BEINER R., (2005), *Il giudizio in Hannah Arendt*, in H. Arendt, *Teoria del giudizio politico. Lezioni sulla filosofia politica di Kant*, il melangolo, Genova, pp. 139–204.
BENHABIB S. (1992), *Situating the self. Gender, community and postmodernism in contemporary ethics*, Polity Press, Cambridge.
BENHABIB S., (2003), *The Reluctant Modernism of Hannah Arendt (Modernity and Political Thought)*, Rowman & Littlefield, Lanham.
BENJAMIN W., (1991), *Capitalismus als Religion*, in *Gesammelte Schriften*, Bd. VI, hrsg. von R. Tiedemann – H. Schweppenhäuser, Frankfurt a. M., Suhrkamp, pp. 100–103
BENNINGTON G. (1994), *Legislations: the politics of deconstruction*, Verso, London.
BENNINGTON G., (2010), *Not half, no end. Militantly Melancholic. Essays in Memory of Jacques Derrida*, Edinburgh University Press, Edinburgh.
BERNASCONI R. (1987), *Deconstruction and the possibility of ethics*, in *Deconstruction and philosophy. The texts of Jacques Derrida*, SALLIS J. (ed.), pp. 122–139, University of Chicago Press, Chicago and London.
BERNSTEIN R.B., (2000), *Arendt on thinking*, in D. Villa, *The Cambridge Companion to Hannah Arendt*, Cambridge University Press, Cambridge, pp. 277–292.
BERNSTEIN R.J., (1999), *Provocazione e appropriazione: la risposta a Martin Heidegger*, in S. Forti (ed.), *Hannah Arendt*, Mondadori, Milano 1999, pp. 226–248.
BERTEN A., DA SILVEIRA P. e POURTOIS H. (1997), *Libéraux et communautariens*, PUF, Paris.
BESNIER J.M. (1988), *La politique de l'impossible. L'intellectuel entre révolte et engagement*, La découverte, Paris.
BIDENT C., (1998), *Maurice Blanchot. Partenaire invisible*, Champ Vallon, Seyssel.
BIRD G., (2016), *Containing Community. From Political Economy to Ontology in Agamben, Esposito, and Nancy*, Suny Press, New York.
BIRD G., (2018), *Dwelling in the Proper: May 68, Political Economy, and Identity Politics*, in «Shift. International Journal of Philosophical Studies», n. 1.
BLANCHOT M. (1948), *L'arrêt de mort*, Gallimard, Paris.
BLANCHOT M. (1949), *La part du feu*, Gallimard, Paris.
BLANCHOT M. (1955), *L'espace littéraire*, Gallimard, Paris.
BLANCHOT M. (1969), *L'entretien infini*, Gallimard, Paris.
BLANCHOT M., (1973), *Le pas au-delà*, Gallimard, Paris.
BLANCHOT M., (1980), *L'écriture du désastre*, Gallimard, Paris.
BLANCHOT M. (1981), *La littérature et le droit à la mort. De Kafka à Kafka*, pp. 11–61, Gallimard, Paris.
BLANCHOT M., (1983), *La communauté inavouable*, Minuit, Paris.
BLANCHOT M., (2000), *Le nom de Berlin* (con due lettere di Blanchot à J.-L. Nancy), "Lignes", 3, pp. 129–141.
BOELLA L., (1990), *Hannah Arendt «fenomenologa». Smantellamento della metafisica e critica dell'ontologia*, in «aut aut», n. 239–240, pp. 83–110.
BODEI R., (1987), *Scomposizioni. Forme dell'individuo moderno*, Einaudi, Torino.
BOURDIEU P. (1988), *L'ontologie politique de Martin Heidegger*, Minuit, Paris.
BONITO OLIVA R., (2003), *Soggettività*, Guida, Napoli.
BRAIDOTTI R., (2011), *Il postumano. La vita oltre l'individuo, oltre la specie, oltre la morte*, Derive e Approdi, Roma.
BUCHANAN A.E. (1989), *Assessing the communitarian critique of liberalism*, "Ethics", 99, pp. 852–882.
CACCIARI M., (1994), Geo-filosofia dell'Europa, Adelphi, Milano.
CADAVA E., CONNOR P. NANCY J.L. (1991), *Who comes after the subject?*, Routledge, New York and London.
CALABRÒ D., (2012), *Les détours d'un pensée vivante. Transitions et chancements de paradigme dans la réflexion de Roberto Esposito*, Mimesis, Paris.

CALDARONE R., (2011), *Impianti. Tecnica e scelta di vita*, con una prefazione di Jean-Luc Nancy, Mimesis, Milano.
CAMPBELL T., (2012), *L'immunità come soglia. Dialogo con Timothy Campbell*, in R. Esposito, *Dall'impolitico all'impersonale: conversazioni filosofiche*, Mimesis, Milano.
CARBONE M., LEVIN D.M., (2003) *La carne e la voce*, Mimesis, Milano.
CARROL D. (1993), *Community after devastation: Culture, politics, and the "Public Space"*, in *Politics, Theory and Contemporary Culture*, POSTER M. (ed.), pp. 159–196, Columbia University Press, New York.
CAVARERO A., (1995), *Corpo in figure. Filosofia e politica della corporeità*, Feltrinelli, Milano.
CAVARERO A., (2003), *A più voci. Filosofia dell'espressione vocale*, Feltrinelli, Milano.
CIARAMELLI F., MORONCINI B., PAPPARO F.C., (1994), *Diffrazioni. La filosofia alla prova della psicoanalisi*, Guerini e Associati, Milano.
CHAMBERLAIN J. (1996), *Born free*, "Radical Philosophy", 79, pp. 52–53.
CIMATTI F., (2018), *Cose. Per una filosofia del reale*, Bollati Boringhieri, Torino.
COLANGELO C., (2015), *La ragione che veglia. Maurice Blanchot, la politica e la questione dei valori*, Orthotes, Napoli-Salerno.
COLEBROOK C., MAXWELL J., (2016), *Agamben*, Polity Press, Cambridge (USA).
CORNELL D. (1992), *The philosophy of the limit*, Routledge, New York an London
CORTELLA L., (1996), *La teoria critica dalla dialettica alla dialogica*, in «Fenomenologia e società», n. 1–2, pp. 210–230.
COURTINE J.F., (1990), *Heidegger et la phénoménologie*, Vrin, Paris.
COURTOIS S. E.A. (1997), *Le livre noir du communisme*, Robert Laffont, Paris.
CRITCHLEY S. (1993), *The ethics of deconstruction. Derrida and Levinas*, Blackwell, Oxford.
CRITCHLEY S. (1996), *Il y a - Holding Levinas' hand to Blanchot's fire*, in *Maurice Blanchot, The demand of writing*, BAILEY GILL C. (ed.), pp.108–22, Routledge, London and New York.
CRITCHLEY S. (1997), *Very little, almost nothing, Death, philosophy, literature*, Routledge, London.
CRITCHLEY S. (1999), *Ethics- Politics-Subjectivity: Essays on Derrida, Levinas and Contemporary French Thought*, Verso, London.
CROUCH C., (2011), *The Strange Non-death of Neoliberalism*, Polity Press, Cambridge 2011, tr. it. di M. Cupellaro, *Il potere dei giganti. Perché la crisi non ha sconfitto il neoliberalismo*, Laterza, Roma-Bari.
CROZIER M.J., HUNTINGTON S.P., WATANUKI J., (1977), *The Crisis of Democracy. Report on the Governability of Democracies in the Trilateral Commission*, © The Trilateral Commission 1975, tr. it. di V. Messana, *La crisi della democrazia. Rapporto sulla governabilità delle democrazie alla Commissione Trilaterale*, Franco Angeli Editore, Milano.
CURI U., (1995), *Endiadi. Figure della duplicità*. Feltrinelli, Milano.
D'ORS A., (1976), *Teologia politica: una revisione del problema*, in «Revista de Estudiox Politicos», n. 205, pp. 41–79.
DAL LAGO A., (1984), *"Politeia": cittadinanza ed esilio nell'opera di Hannah Arendt*, "Il Mulino", n. 3, pp. 417–441.
DAL LAGO A., (1989), *La città perduta*, in H. Arendt, *Vita Activa. La condizione umana*, Milano, Bompiani, pp. XVI-XIX.
DAL LAGO A., (1999), *Introduzione* a H. Arendt, *Tra Passato e futuro*, Garzanti, Milano.
DARDOT P., LAVAL C., (2009), *La nouvelle raison du monde. Essais sur la société néoliberale*, La découverte, Paris.
DAVIES P. (1996), *The work and the absence of work*, in *Maurice Blanchot. The demand of writing*, BAILEY GILL C. (ed.), pp. 91–107, Routledge, London and New York.
DE BENEDETTI R. (1996), *Comunismo come supplemento d'anima?*, "aut aut", 12, pp. 28–39.
DE CAROLIS M., (2017), *Il rovescio della libertà. Tramonto del neoliberalismo e disagio della civiltà*, Quolibet, Macerata.
DE FONTENAY E. (1987), *Fribourg-Prague-Paris. Comme l'être, la détresse se dit de multiples manières*, "Le Messager Européen", 1, pp.13–75.

DE GIOVANNI B., (2011), *Hegel e Spinoza. Dialogo sul moderno*, Guida, Napoli.
DEBORD G. (1992), *La société du spectacle*, Gallimard, Paris.
DELANEY C.F. (ED.)(1994), *The liberalism-communitarianism debate. Liberty and community values*, Rowman & Littlefield Publishers, Maryland.
DELEUZE G., (1992), *Nietzsche et la philosophie*, PUF, Paris 1962, tr. it. di F. Polidori, *Nietzsche e la filosofia*, Feltrinelli, Milano.
DELEUZE G., (1968), *Différance et répetition*, PUF, Paris.
DELEUZE G., (1969), *Logique du sens,* Les Éditions de Minuit, Paris.
DELEUZE G., (1979), *Un manifeste de moins*, Éditions du minuit, Paris.
DELEUZE G., (1993), *Pour en finir avec le jugement*, in Id., *Critique et Clinique*, Minuit, Paris.
DELEUZE G., GUATTARI F., (1980), *Mille plateaux. Capitalisme et schizophrénie*, Éditions de Minuit, Paris.
DERRIDA J. (1967a), *La voix et le phénomène*, PUF, Paris.
DERRIDA J. (1967b), *L'écriture et la différence,* Seuil, Paris.
DERRIDA J. (1967c), *De la grammatologie*, Minuit, Paris.
DERRIDA J. (1972a), *Marges de la philosophie*, Minuit, Paris.
DERRIDA J. (1972b), *La dissémination*, Seuil, Paris.
DERRIDA J. (1972c), *Positions,* Minuit, Paris.
DERRIDA J., (1972d), *La mythologie blanche*, in Id., *Marges - de la philosophie*, Éditions de Minuit, Paris
DERRIDA J., (1972e), *La pharmacie de Platon*, in *La dissémination*, Éditions du Seuil, Paris.
DERRIDA J., (1978), *Parergon*, in *La vérité de la peinture*, Flammarion, Paris.
DERRIDA J., (1980), *La carte postale. De Freud à Socrate et au-delà*, Flammarion, Paris.
DERRIDA J., (1986), *Forcener le subjectile*, in *Artaud. Dessins et portraits*, Gallimard, Paris.
DERRIDA J., (1987), Geschlecht. *Différence sexuelle, différence ontologique* (1983), in *Psyché. Inventions de l'autre. Tome 2*, Galilée, Paris.
DERRIDA J., (1987), *Lettre à un ami japonaise* (1985), in *Psyché. Inventions de l'autre. Tome 2*, Galilée, Paris.
DERRIDA J., (1987), En ce moment même dans cet ouvrage me voici. *Psyché. Inventions de l'autre*, pp. 159–202, Galilée, Paris.
DERRIDA J., (1987), *De l'esprit. Heidegger et la question*, Galilée, Paris.
DERRIDA J., (1988a), *Interview with Jean-Luc Nancy,* "Topoi", pp. 113–121.
DERRIDA J., (1988b), *Mémoires – pour Paul de Man*, Galilée, Paris.
DERRIDA J., (1988c), *The politics of friendship*, "The Journal of Philosophy", 85, 1, pp. 632–644.
DERRIDA J., (1989), *La démocratie ajournée*, in *L'autre cap*, Minuit, Parigi.
DERRIDA J., (1990a), *Heidegger et la question. De l'esprit et autres essais*, Flammarion, Paris.
DERRIDA J., (1990b), *Limited Inc.*, Galilée, Paris.
DERRIDA J., (1993a), *Spectres de Marx. L'état de la dette, le travail de deuil et la nouvelle Internationale*, Galilée, Paris.
DERRIDA J., (1994), *Politiques de l'amitié. Suivi de L'oreille de Heidegger*, Galilée, Paris.
DERRIDA J., (1995), *Je devrai errer tout seul*, in «Libération», 7 november
DERRIDA J., (1997), *Des tours de Babel* (1985), in Id., *Psyché. Inventions de l'autre. Tome 1*, Galilée, Paris.
DERRIDA J., (1997), *Le retrait de la métaphore* (1978), in Id., *Psyché. Inventions de l'autre. Tome 1*, Galilée, Paris.
DERRIDA J., (2000), *Foi et savoir* (1996) and *Le Siecle et le Pardon*, Seuil, Paris.ù
DERRIDA J., (2003a), *La main de Heidegger (Geschlecht II)* (1985), in Psyché. Inventions de l'autre, Tome II, Galilée, Paris.
DERRIDA J., (2003b), *Béliers. Le dialogue ininterrompu: entre deux infinis, le poème*, Galilée, Paris
DERRIDA J., (2006), *L'animal que donc je suis*, Galilée, Paris.
DERRIDA J., STIEGLER B., (1996), *Écographies de la télévision*, Galilée, Paris.
DERRIDA J. E VATTIMO G. (1996), *La religion*, Seuil, Paris.

DESCARTES R., (1969), *Meditationes metaphisiques*, in *Œuvres complétes*, t. V., Victor Cousin, Paris.
DESCARTES R., (1637), *Dioptrique*, in *Œuvres complétes*, t. V., Victor Cousin, Paris.
DI CESARE D., (2015), *Heidegger & sons. Eredità e futuro di un filosofo*, Bollati Boringhieri, Torino.
DI CESARE D., (2018), *Sulla vocazione politica della filosofia*, Bollati Boringhieri, Torino.
DI MARCO C., (1993), *Deleuze: lineamenti di una ontologia eventuale*, in «Fenomenologia e società», n. 2, pp. 27–41.
DI PIERRO M., (2019), *Il concetto di istituzione in Claude Lefort*, in E. Lisciani-Petrini, M. Adinolfi (a cura di), «Discipline Filosofiche», n. 2, pp. 99–120.
DONÀ M., (2004), *Sulla negazione*, Bompiani, Milano
DROIT R.-P. (2001), *La precaution et le destin*, Le Monde.
DUFRENNE M., (1991), *L'oeil et l'oreille*, Jean Michel Place, Paris
DURAS M., (1983), *La maladie de la mort*, in «Nuoveau Commerce», n. 55, pp. 29–46
ELSTER J. (1992), *Local justice*, Cambridge University Press, Cambridge.
ESPOSITO A., (2012), *Variazioni sul politico in Jean-Luc Nancy*, in U. Perone (ed.), *Intorno a Jean-Luc Nancy*, Rosengerg & Sellier, Torino.
ESPOSITO R., (1988), *Categorie dell'impolitico*, Il Mulino, Bologna 1999 (prima edizione).
ESPOSITO R., (1996), *Oltre la politica. Antologia del pensiero "impolitico"*, (a cura di), Mondadori, Milano.
ESPOSITO R., (1998), *Communitas. Origine e destino della comunità*, Einaudi, Torino 1998.
ESPOSITO R., (1999), *Polis o communitas*, in Simona Forti (ed.), *Hannah Arendt*, Mondadori, Milano.
ESPOSITO R., (2000), *Nichilismo e comunità*, in R. Esposito, C. Galli, V. Vitiello (ed), *Nichilismo e politica*, Laterza, Milano.
ESPOSITO R., (2000), *Libertà in comune*, in J.-L. NANCY, *L'esperienza della libertà*, Einaudi, Torino, pp. VII-XXXV.
ESPOSITO R., (2002), *Immunitas. Protezione e negazione della vita*, Einaudi, Torino.
ESPOSITO R., (2004), *Bíos. Biopolitica e filosofia*, Einaudi, Torino.
ESPOSITO R., (2004),*Il dono della vita tra "communitas" e "immunitas"*, in AA.VV., *Umano Post-umano. Potere, sapere, etica nell'età globale*, a cura di M. Fimiani, V.G. Kurotschka, E. Pulcini, Editori Riuniti, Roma, pp. 63–78.
ESPOSITO R., (2007), *Terza persona. Politica della vita e filosofia dell'impersonale*, Einaudi, Torino.
ESPOSITO R., (2012), *Dall'impolitico all'impersonale: conversazioni filosofiche*, Mimesis, Milano.
ESPOSITO R., (2013), *Due. La macchina della teologia politica e il posto del pensiero*, Einaudi, Torino.
ESPOSITO R., (2014), *Le persone e le cose*, Einaudi, Torino.
ESPOSITO R., (2016), *Da Fuori. Una filosofia per l'Europa*, Einaudi, Torino.
ESPOSITO R., (2016), *Il comunismo e la morte*, in G. Bataille, *La sovranità*, SE, Milano, pp. 9–35
ESPOSITO R., (2017), *In dialogo con Negri*, in E. Lisciani-Petrini, G. Strummiello (eds.), *Effetto Italian Thought*, Quodlibet, Macerata, pp. 23–32.
ESPOSITO R., (2018), *Politica e negazione, Per una filosofa affermativa*, Einaudi, Torino.
ESPOSITO R., (2019), *Pensiero istituente. Tre paradigmi di ontologia politica*, in M. Di Pierro, F. Marchesi (eds.), *Almanacco di Filosofia e Politica I. Crisi dell'immanenza. Potere, conflitto, istituzione*, Quodlibet, Macerata, pp. 23–40.
ESPOSITO R., (2020), *Pensiero istituente. Tre paradigmi di ontologia politica*, Einaudi, Torino.
ESPOSITO R., (2022), *Immunità comune. Biopolitica all'epoca della pandemia*, Einaudi, Torino.
ESPOSITO, R., (2023), *Vitam instituere. Genealogia dell'istituzione*, Einaudi, Torino.
FEDERN P., (2016), *La società senza padre*, Artstudiopaparo, Napoli.
FERRARI F., (1997) *La comunità errante. George Bataille e l'esperienza comunitaria*, Lanfranchi, Milano.
FERRARIS M., (1981) *Nichilismo e differenza. Una traccia*, in «aut aut», n. 181–182, pp. 105–126.
FERRARIS M., (2003), *Introduzione a Derrida*, Laterza, Roma-Bari.

FERRY L. e RENAUT A. (1988), *Heidegger et les modernes*, Grasset, Paris.
FINK W. (1995), *Vers un roman unidimensionnel. Aspects de la communauté utopique dans le roman allemand des XVIIème et XIXème siècles*, in Communauté et modernité, RAULET G. e VAYSSE J.M. (eds.), pp. 63–85, L'Harmattan, Paris.
FLEGO G. (1995), *Sujet et modernité*, in *Communauté et modernité*, RAULET G. e VAYSSE J.M. (eds.), pp. 218–228, L'Harmattan, Paris.
FOOT F. (1978), *Virtues and Vices and other essays in moral philosophy*, Basil Blackwell, Oxford
FORMENTI C., (2016), *La variante populista. Lotta di classe nel neoliberismo*, DeriveApprodi, Roma.
FORTI S., (1999), *Hannah Arendt: filosofia e politica*, in EAD. (ed.), *Hannah Arendt*, Mondadori, Milano.
FORTI S., (2017), *Strategie di decostruzione della nuda vita*, in E. Stimilli (a cura di), *Decostruzione o biopolitica*, Quodlibet, Macerata.
FOUCAULT M., (1970), *Theatrum philosophicum*, in, «Critique», n. 282, pp. 885–908, ora in *Dits et écrits. 1954–1988, Vol. II*, pp. 75–99.
FOUCAULT M., (1976), *La volonté de savoir*, Gallimard, Paris.
FOUCAULT M., (2004), *Sécurité, territoire, population. Cours au Collège de France 1977–1978*, Gallimard-Seuil, Paris.
FOUCAULT M., (2001), *La «gouvernementalité»*, in ID. *Dits et écrits (1954–1988)*, Gallimard, Paris, pp.635–657.
FOUCAULT M., (2009), *Le courage de la vérité. Le gouvernement de soi e des autres II. Cours au Collège de France 1983–1984*, Seuil/Gallimard, Paris.
FRANCK D., (1981), *Chair e corps. Sur la phénomenologie di Husserl*, Minuti, Paris.
FRANCK D., (1986), *Heidegger et le problème de l'espace*, Éditions de Minuit, Paris.
FRANCK D., (2004), *L'explication silencieuse. Heidegger et le christianisme*, PUF, Paris.
FRAZER E. (1999), *The problem of communitarian thought. Unity and conflict*, Oxford University Press, Oxford.
FREUD S., (1905), *Drei Adhandlungen zur Sexualtheorie*, Franz Deuticke, Leipzig und Wien.
FREUD S., (1921), *Massenpsychologie und Ich-Analyse*, in *Gesammelte Werke 13*, S. Fisher Verlag, Frankfurt.
FREUD S., (1948), *Selbstdarstellung* (1924), in *Gesammelte Werke 14*, S. Fisher Verlag, Frankfurt, Imago Publishing Co, London.
FYNSK C. (1993a), *Heidegger. Thought and historicity*, Cornell University Press, Ithaca and London.
FYNSK, C. (1993), *A note on language and body*, "Paragraph", 16, 2, pp. 192–201.
FYNSK, C. (1996), *Crossing the threshold. On 'literature and the right to death'*, in *Maurice Blanchot. The demand of writing*, BAILEY GILL C. (ed.), pp.70–90, Routledge, London and New York
GALIMBERTI, U., (1994), *Il corpo*, Feltrinelli, Milano.
GALLI, C., (1986), *Genealogia della politica. Carl Schmitt e la crisi del pensiero politico moderno*, Il Mulino, Bologna.
GALLI, C., *(2011)*, *Il disagio della democrazia*, Einaudi, Torino.
GARELLI, G., (2010), *Lo spirito in figura. Il tema dell'estetico nella "Fenomenologia dello spirito" di Hegel*, Il Mulino, Bologna.
GASCHÉ, R., (2007), *Without title*, in ID., *Views and interviews. Deconstruction in America*, Aurora, Davies Group.
GASCHE R. (1986), *The tain of the mirror: Derrida and the philosophy of reflection*, Harvard University Press, Cambridge.
GASCHE R. (1994), *Inventions of difference. On Jacques Derrida*, Harvard University Press, Cambridge.
GAUCHET M. (1985*), Le désenchantement du monde. Une histoire politique de la religion*, Gallimard, Paris.

GENEL K., DERANTY J.P., (2016), (eds.), *Recognition and Disagreement. A critical encounter on the Politics of Freedom, Equality and Identity*, Columbia University Press, New York.
GENTILI D., (2018), *La crisi come arte di governo*, Quodlibet, Macerata.
GIACCHETTA F., (2005), *Gioco e trascendenza*, Cittadella Editrice, Assisi.
GIL J., (2008), *O imperceptível devir da imanência*, Relógio d'Água, Lisboa.
GIRARD M., (2017), *L'art de la faute selon Georges Bataille*, Lignes, Paris.
GIVONE S., (1995), *Storia del nulla*, Laterza, Roma-Bari.
GOLDSCHMITT V., (1953), *Le système stoicien et l'idée de temps*, Vrin, Paris.
GRAMSCI A., (1977), *Quaderni del Carcere*, Einaudi, Torino.
GRANEL G., (1995), *Les années 30 sont devant nous*, in Id., *Études*, Éditions Galilée, p. 71–74.
GUANTI G., (1999), *Estetica musicale*, La Nuova Italia, Milano.
GUARESCHI M., (2001), *Gilles Deleuze popfilosofo*, Shake Edizioni Underground, Milano.
GUSFIELD R.J. (1975*), Community. A critical response*, Basil Blackwell, Oxford.
HABERMAS J., (1997), *Theorie des kommunikativen Handelns 2 Bände (*1981), Suhrkamp Verlag, Frankfurt am Main.
HABERMAS J., (1988), *Nachmetaphysisches Denken. Philosophische Aufsätze*, Suhrkamp Verlag, Frankfurt am Main.
HABERMAS J., (2005), *Zwischen naturalismus und Religion. Philosophische Aufsätze*, Suhrkamp Verlag, Frankfurt am Main 2005.
HABERMAS J., TAYLOR C., (1998), *Multiculturalismo. Lotte per il riconoscimento*, Feltrinelli.
HARDT M., NEGRI A., (2000), *Empire*, Harvard University Press, Cambridge (Massachusetts).
HARDT M., NEGRI A., (2009), *Commonwealt*, The Belknap Press of Harvard University Press, Cambridge (Massachussets).
HAUERWAS S. e MACINTYRE A. (1983), *Revisions: changing perspectives in moral Philosophy*, University of Notre Dame press, Indiana.
HAYEK F., (1973), *Law, Legislation and Liberty*, Routledge & Kegan, London.
HEELAN P.A., (1995), *Heidegger's Longest Day: Twenty-Five Years Later*, in B.E. Babich (ed.), *From Phenomenology to Thought, Errancy, and Desire*, Kluwer Academic Publishers, Dordrecht, Boston, London, pp. 579–587.
HEGEL G.W.F., (1807), *Die Phänomenologie des Geistes*.
HEGEL G.W.F., (1835), *Vorlesungen üer die Ästhetik*.
HEIDEGGER M. (1989), *Beiträge zur Philosophie (vom Ereignis)*, Vittorio Klostermann, Frankfurt an Main.
HEIDEGGER M., (1927), *Sein und Zeit*, © Max Niemeyer Verlag, Tübingen.
HEIDEGGER M., (1950), *Wom Wesen des Grundes* (1928), © Klosterman, Frankfurt am Main.
HEIDEGGER M., (1950), *Der Spruch des Anaximander* (1946), in *Holzwege*, in *Holzwege*, © Klosterman, Frankfurt am Main.
HEIDEGGER M., (1957), *Überwindung der Metaphysik* (1946), in Id., *Vorträge und Aufsätze*, © Verlag Günther Neske, Pfulingen
HEIDEGGER M., (1957), *Das Ding* (1950), in *Vorträge und Aufsätze,* © Verlag Günther Neske, Pfulingen.
HEIDEGGER M., (1957), *Was Heißt Denken* (1952), in *Vorträge und Aufsätze,* © Verlag Günther Neske, Pfulingen.
HEIDEGGER M., (1957), *Wissenschaft und Besinnung* (1953), in *Vorträge und Aufsätze,* © Verlag Günther Neske, Pfulingen
HEIDEGGER M., (1957), *Der Sats vom Grund*, © Verlag Günther Neske, Pfulingen.
HEIDEGGER M., (1959), *Unterwegs zur Sprache*, © Verlag Günther Neske, Pfulingen.
HEIDEGGER M., (1961), *Nietzsche*, © Verlag Günther Neske, Pfullingen.
HEIDEGGER M., (1969), *Die Kunst und der Raum*, © Erker Verlag, St. Gallen.
HEIDEGGER M., (1971), *Schelling: Vom Wesen der menschlichen Freiheit (1809),* © Max
HEIDEGGER M., (1976), *Vom Wesen der Wahreit* (1930), in Id., *Wegmarken*, © Klosterman, Frankfurt am Main.

HEIDEGGER M., (1983), *Die Grundbegriffe der Metaphysik. Welt – Endlichkeit – Einsamkeit*, (course of 1929–1930) copyright Klostermann Verlag.
HEIDEGGER M., (1985), *Nur noch ein Gott kann uns retten* (1966), © Klosterman, Frankfurt am Main.
HEIMONET J.-M., (1990), *Politiques de l'écriture. Bataille/Derrida. Le sens du sacré dans la pensée française du surréalisme à nos jours*, Jean Michel Place, Paris.
HENRY M., (2000), *Incarnation. Une philosophie de la chair*, Le Seuil, Paris.
HOFFE O. (1996), Der Kommunitarismus als Alternative?, "Zeitschrift Für Philosophische Forschung", 50, pp. 92–112.
HOLLIER D. (1979), *Le collège de sociologie 1937–1939*, Gallimard, Paris.
HOLMES S. (1993), *The anatomy of antiliberalism*, Harvard University Press, London.
HONNETH A., (1992), *Der Kampf um Anerkennung. Zur moraliscen Grammatik sozialer Konflikte*, Suhrkamp Verlag, Frankfurt am Main.
HONNETH A. (1996*), Communauté. Dictionnaire d'éthique et de philosophie morale*, CANTO-SPERBER M., pp. 270–274, PUF, Paris.
HUSSERL E., (1913), *Ideen zu einer reinen Phänomenologie und phänomenologische Philosophie* Husserliana, Gesammelte Werke.
HUSSERL E., (1931), *Cartesianische Meditationen und Pariser Vortrage*, Husserliana, Gesammelte Werke
HUSSERL E., (1936), *Die Krisis der europäischen Wissenschaften und die transzendentale Phänomenologie: Eine Einleitung in die phänomenologische Philosophie*, Husserliana, Gesammelte Werke.
HUSSERL E. (1991), *Rovesciamento della dottrina copernicana nell'interpretazione della corrente visione del mondo*, in "aut aut", n° 245.
HYPPOLITE J., (1946), *Genèse et structure de la "Phenomenologie de l'Esprit" de Hegel*, Aubier Montaigne, Paris.
IOFRIDA M., (2019), *Per un paradigma del corpo: una rifondazione filosofica dell'ecologia*, Quodlibet, Macerata.
JANICAUD D. (1989), *La politique introuvable. Phénoménologie et politique*, (Mélanges offerts à Jacques Taminiaux), pp. 333–362, Ousia, Bruxelles.
JANICAUD D. (1990), *L'ombre de cette pensée: Heidegger et la question politique*, Millon, Grenoble.
KAMBOUCHER D., (1983), De la condition la plus général de la philosophie politique,,in P. Lacoue-Labarte, J.-L. Nancy (dir.) *Le retrait du politique, Cahiers du Centre de recherches philosophiques sur le politique*, Éditions Galilée, Paris, pp. 113–158.
KANT I., (1902), *Gesammelte Schriften*, De Gruyter, Berlin-New York.
KAUL V., (2019), *Populismo, liberalismo e nazionalismo*, in «Politica e Società», n. 2, pp. 201–220
KELSEN H., (1934), *Reine Rechtslehre. Einleitung in die rechtswissenschaftliche Problematik*, Deuticke, Wien
KIRCHMAYR R., (2002), *Il circolo interrotto. Figure del dono in Mauss, Sartre e Lacan*, E.U.T., Trieste.
KIRCHMAYR R., (2002), *Jean-Luc Nancy e "l'esposizione" del soggetto*, postfazione a J.-L. Nancy, *Il ritratto e il suo sguardo*, Raffaello Cortina, Milano, pp. 69–105.
KOHN J., (1999), *Per una comprensione dell'azione*, in S. Forti, *Hannah Arendt*, Mondadori, Milano, pp. 155–176.
KOJÈVE A., (1933–39), *Introduction à la lecture de Hegel. Lecons sur la "Phénoménologie de l'esprit"* professées de 1933 à 1939 à l'Ecole des Hautes Etudes, ed. by Raymond Queneau, Gallimard, Paris 1979.
KRELL D.F., (1994), *The "Factical Life" of Dasein: From the Early Freiburg Courses to Being and Time*, in T. Kisiel, J. van Buren, *Reading Heidegger from the Start. Essays in His Earliest Thought*, SUNY Press, New York, pp. 361–380.
KUKHATAS C. (1996), *Liberalism, communitarianism and political community*, "Social Philosophy and Policy Foundation", 13, 1, pp. 80–104.

KYMLICKA W. (1990), *Contemporary political philosophy. An introduction*, Clarendon Press, Oxford.
KYMLICKA W. (1991), *Liberalism, community and culture*, Clarendon Press, Oxford..
KYMLICKA W. (1993), Community. *A companion to contemporary political philosophy*, R.E. Goodin e P. Pettit (eds.), pp. 366–378, Blackwell, Oxford.
KYMLICKA W. (1995), *Multicultural citizenship. A liberal theory of minority rights*, Clarendon Press, Oxford.
LACAN J., (1973), *Le séminaire livre XI. Les quatre concepts fondamentaux de la psychanalyse*, Seuil, Paris.
LACAN J., (1975), *Le séminaire. Livre XX. Encore (1972–1973)*, Seuil, Paris.
LACAN J., (1986), *Le séminaire livre VII. L'éthique de la psychanalyse*, Seuil, Paris.
LACLAU E., (2005), *On populist reason*, Verso, London.
LACOUE-LABARTHE P. (1973), *L'oblitération*, "Critique", 313, pp. 487–513.
LACOUE-LABARTHE P., (1981), *La transcendance finit dans la politique*, in *Rejouer le politique*, NANCY J.L.e.a., pp.171–214, Galilée, Paris.
LACOUE-LABARTHE P. (1986), *La poésie comme expérience*, Paris: Bourgois.
LACOUE-LABARTHE P., (1986), *L'imitation des Modernes. Typographies 2*, Galilée, Paris.
LACOUE-LABARTHE P., (1987), *La fiction du politique. Heidegger, l'art et la politique*, Bourgois, Paris.
LACOUE-LABARTHE P., (1992), *Il faut*, in «Modem Language Notes», n. 107, pp. 421–40
LACLAU E., MOUFFE C., (1985), *Hegemony and Socialist Strategy*, Verso, London.
LAPORTE R. (1994), *À l'extrême pointe. Bataille et Blanchot*, Fata Morgana, Paris.
LARMORE C. (1996), *The morals of modernity*, Cambridge University Press, Cambridge.
LEFORT C. (1978), *Sur une colonne absente. Ecrits autour de Merleau-Ponty*, Gallimard, Paris.
LEFORT C., (1981), *L'invention démocratique. Les limites de la domination totalitaire*, Fayard, Paris.
LEFORT C., (l986a), *Le travail de l'oeuvre machiavel*, Gallimard, Paris.
LEFORT C., (1986b), *Essais sur le politique, XIX°-XX° siècles*, Seuil, Paris.
LEFORT C., (1992a), *Ecrire. À l'épreuve du politique*, Calmann-Lévy, Paris.
LEFORT C., (1999a), *La complication. Retour sur le communisme*, Fayard, Paris.
LEFORT C., (1999B), *Retour sur le communisme*, "Esprit", 249, pp. 28–35.
LEVINAS E. (1953), *Liberté et commandement*, "Revue de Métaphysique et de Morale", 58, pp. 264–272.
LEVINAS E., (1968), *La substitution*, "Revue Philosophique De Louvain", 66, pp. 487–508.
LEVINAS E., (1971), *Totalité et infini. Essai sur l'extériorité*, Kluwer Academic, Paris.
LEVINAS E., (1972), *Humanisme de l'autre homme*, Fata Morgana, Paris.
LEVINAS E., (1976), *Difficile liberté. Essais sur le judaïsme*, Albin Michel, Paris.
LÉVINAS E., (1982), *De l'evasion*, Fata Morgana, Montpellier.
LEVINAS E., (1987), *Les droits de l'homme et les droits d'autrui. Hors sujet*, Livre de poche ed., 157–170, Fata Morgana, Paris.
LEVINAS E., (1991b), *L'ontologie est-elle fondamentale? Entre nous. Essais sur le penser-à-l'autre*, pp.12–22, Grasset, Paris.
LEVINAS E., (1993), *Dieu, la Mort et le Temps*, Éditions Grasset et Fasquelle, Parigi.
LEYENBERGER. G. e FORTE J.J. (1992), *Politique et modernité*, Osiris, Paris.
LIPOVETSKY G., SERROY J., (2013), *L'esthétisation du monde. Vivre à l'âge du capitalisme artiste*, Gallimard, Paris.
LINGIS A. (1994), *The community of those who have nothing in common*, Indiana University Press, Bloomington and Indianapolis.
LIPOVETSKY G. (1983), *L'ère du vide. Essais sur l'individualisme contemporain*, Gallimard, Paris.
LISCIANI-PETRINI E., (2001), *Il suono incrinato. Musica e filosofia nel primo Novecento*, Einaudi, Torino.
LISCIANI-PETRINI E., (2002), *Risonanze. Ascolto corpo mondo*, Mimesis, Milano.
LISCIANI-PETRINI E., (2002), *La passione del mondo. Saggio su Merleau-Ponty*, Esi, Napoli.

LISCIANI-PETRINI E., (2009), *Introduzione*, in V. Jankélévitch, *La morte*, Einaudi, Torino.
LISCIANI-PETRINI E., (2012), *Charis. Saggio su Jankélévitch*, Mimesis, Milano.
LISCIANI-PETRINI E., (2014), *La fine della vita eroica*, in «Filosofia Politica», n.1, 9–26.
LISCIANI-PETRINI E., (2015), *Vita quotidiana. Dall'esperienza artistica al pensiero in atto*, Bollati Boringhieri, Torino.
LIVIANA MESSINA A., (2017), *Apocalypse et croyance en ce monde. Monde, finitude et christianisme chez Nancy et Blanchot*, in J. Lèbre, J. Rogozinski, *Jean-Luc Nancy. Penser la mutation*, Presses Universitaires de Strasbourg, Strasbourg, pp. 153–168.
LIVIANA MESSINA A., TAUB L., (2016), *The apocalypse of Blanchot*, in «Philosophy Today», n. 4, pp. 877–892.
LOSURDO D., (1991), *La comunità, la morte, l'Occidente. Heidegger e l'«ideologia della guerra»*, Bollati Boringhieri, Torino.
LUCCI A., (2019), *Categorie italiane della filosofia. Sul posizionamento teoretico di Giorgio Agamben nel canone del pensiero italiano contemporaneo*, in «Lessico di etica pubblica», n. 1, pp. 40–50.
LYOTARD J.F., (1979), *La condition postmoderne. Rapport sur le savoir*, Minuit, Paris.
LYOTARD J.F., (1983), *Le différend*, Minuit, Paris.
LYOTARD J.F., (1988), *L'intérêt du sublime*, in *Du sublime*, COURTINE J.F. (e.a.), pp. 149–177, Belin, Paris.
LYOTARD J.F., (1988), *L'Inhumain: Causeries sur le temps*, Galilée, Paris.
MALABOU C., (1996), *L'avenir de Hegel. Plasticité, temporalité, dialectique*, Librairie Philosophique J. Vrin, Paris.
MARTONE A., (2001), *Un'etica del nulla. Libertà, esistenza, politica*, Liguori, Napoli
MAYNÉ G., (2003), *Georges Bataille, l'érotisme et l'écriture*, Descartes & Cie, Paris.
MEAZZA C., (2018b), (a cura di), *Le retrait*, in «Phasis», n. 1.
MEHLMAN J., (1984), *Legs de l'antisémitisme en France*, Denoël, Paris.
MERLEAU-PONTY M., (1942), *La structure du comportement*, PUF, Paris.
MERLEAU-PONTY M., (1945), *Phénoménologie de la perception*, Gallimard, Paris.
MERLEAU-PONTY M., (1947), *Humanisme et terreur*, Gallimard, Paris.
MERLEAU-PONTY M., (1948), *Sens et non-sens*, Nagel, Paris.
MERLEAU-PONTY M., (1953), *Éloge de la philosophie*, Gallimard, Paris.
MERLEAU-PONTY M., (1955), *Les aventures de la dialectique*, Gallimard, Paris Sugar.
MERLEAU-PONTY M., (1960), *Signes*, Gallimard, Paris.
MERLEAU-PONTY M., (1964), *L'œil et l'esprit*, Gallimard, Paris.
MERLEAU-PONTY M., (1964), *Le visible et l'invisible*, Gallimard, Paris
MERLEAU-PONTY M., (1968), *Résumés de cours au Collège de France(1952–1960)*, Gallimard, Paris.
MERLEAU-PONTY M., (1969), *La prose du monde*, Gallimard, Paris.
MERLEAU-PONTY M., (1974–76), *Philosophie et non-philosophie depuis Hegel*, "Textures", n° 8–9 and 10–11; after in), *Notes de cours 1958–1959 et 1960–1961*, Gallimard, Paris.
MERLEAU-PONTY M., (1996), *Notes de cours 1958–1959 et 1960–1961*, Gallimard, Paris.
MCQUILLAN M., (2011), *Decostruzione e globalizzazione. Il mondo secondo Jean-Luc Nancy*, in M. Senatore, F. Vitale (eds.), *L'avvenire della decostruzione*, Il Melangolo, Genova, pp. 59–86.
MORA F., (2019), *Martin Heidegger. Pensare senza fondamenti*, Mimesis, Milano.
MORONCINI B., (1998), *Mondo e senso. Heidegger e Celan*, Cronopio, Napoli.
MORONCINI B., (2001), *La comunità e l'invenzione*, Cronopio, Napoli.
MOUFFE C., (2018), In *For a Left Populism*, Verso, London.
MOUFFE C., (2000), *The democratic paradox*, Verso, London - New York
MULHALL S. e SWIFT A. (1996), *Liberals and communitarians*, Blackwell, Oxford.
MÜLLER H. (1995), *Sur quelques usages de la notion de communauté*, in Communauté et modernité, RAULET G. e VAYSSE J.M.(eds.), pp. 13–29, L'Harmattan, Paris.
NEGRI A., (1995), *La crise de l'espace politique*, in «Futur antérieur», n. 23.

NEWMARK K. (1992), *L'absolu littéraire*, "MLN", 107, 5, pp. 905–930.
NIETZSCHE F.W., (1872), *Die Geburt der Tragödie aus dem Geiste der Musik*, Verlag Von E.W. Fritzsch, Leipzig.
OLAFSON F.A. (1998), *Heidegger and the ground of ethics. A study of Mitsein*, Cambridge University Press, Cambridge.
PANIZZA F., (2005), *Introduction. Populism and the Mirror of Democracy*, in ID. (ed.), *Populism and the Mirror of Democracy*, Verso, London and New York.
PERNIOLA M., (2011), *L'estetica contemporanea. Un quadro globale*, Il Mulino, Bologna.
PETERSON E., (1935), *Der Monotheismus als politisches Problem*, Hegner, Leipzig.
PHILLIPS D.L. (1993). *Looking backward. A critical appraisal of communitarian thought*, Princeton University Press, New York.
PORTINARO P.P., (1987), *La politica come cominciamento e la fine della politica*, in R. ESPOSITO (a cura di), *La pluralità irrappresentabile. Il pensiero politico di Hannah Arendt*, Edizioni QuattroVenti, Urbino, pp. 29–46.
POSSATI L.M., (2013), *La ripetizione creatrice. Melandri, Derrida e lo spazio dell'analogia*, Mimesis, Milano.
RAFFOUL F. (1995), Otherness and individuation in Heidegger. *Man and World*, 28: 341–358.
RAFFOUL F. (1998), *Heidegger and the subject*. New York: Humanity Books.
RANCIÈRE J., (1996), *Mallarmé: La politique de la sirène*, Hachette, Paris.
RANCIERE J., (1998), *Existe-t-il une esthétique deleuzienne*, in E. Alliez (ed.), *Gilles Deleuze, une vie philosophique*, Institut Synthélabo pour le progrès de la connaissance, Le Plessis-Robinson, pp. 525–536.
RANCIERE J., (1998), *Deleuze, Bartleby et la formule littéraire*, in Id., *La chair des mots*, Galilée, Paris, pp.179-203.
RANCIERE J., (2009), *Malaise dans l'esthétique*,Galilée, Paris 2004, tr. it. di P. Godani, *Disagio dell'estetica*, ETS, Pisa.
RASMUSSEN D. (ed.) (1990), *Universalism vs. communitarianism*, in *Contemporary debates in ethics*, MIT Press, Cambridge.
RAWLS J. (1971), *A theory of justice*, Oxford University Press, Oxford.
RAWLS J. (1996), *Political liberalism*, Columbia University Press, New York.
REESE-SCHÄFER W. (1994), *Was ist Kommunitarismus?*, Campus Verlag, Frankfurt.
REGAZZONI S., (2010), *Derrida. Biopolitica e democrazia*, il melangolo, Genova.
REGAZZONI S., (2011), *Esoterismo pop e democrazia. Le confessioni della decostruzione*, in F. Vitale, M. Senatore (eds.), *L'avvenire della decostruzione*, il melangolo, Genova, pp. 101–123..
RESTA C., (2003), *L'evento dell'altro. Etica e politica in Jacques Derrida*, Bollati Boringhieri, Torino.
RICHARDSON W. J., (1968), *Heidegger's Critique of Science*, in «The New Scholasticism», n. 42, pp. 511–536.
RICOEUR P., (1975), *La Métaphore vive*, Éditions du Seuil, Paris.
RIGOTTI F., (2007), *Il pensiero delle cose*, Apogeo, Milano.
RIGOTTI F., (2013), *Nuova filosofia delle piccole cose*, Interlinea, Novara.
RIZZO G., (2002), *Pensare senza balaustre. Saggio su Hannah Arendt*, Mimesis, Milano.
RODOTÀ, S. (2006). *La vita e le regole. Tra diritto e non diritto*. Milan: Feltrinelli.
ROGOZINSKI J. (1988), *Le don du monde*, in *Du sublime*, COURTINE J.F. (e.a.), pp. 179– 210, Belin, Paris.
ROGOZINSKI J. (1995), *"Etranger parmi nous": la Terreur et son ennemi*, "Césure. Revue De La Convention Psychanalytique", 9, pp. 125–164.
ROGOZINSKI J. (1999), *Le don de la loi. Kant et l'énigme de l'éthique*, PUF., Paris.
ROUSSEAU J.J. (1762), *Du contrat social ou principes du droit politique (et autres)*, in *Collection complète des oeuvres*, Genève, 1780–1789, vol. 1, in-4°
ROVATTI P.A., (1987), *La posta in gioco. Heidegger, Husserl, il soggetto*, Bompiani, Milano.

ROVATTI P.A., (1994), *Abitare la distanza. Per un'etica del linguaggio*, Feltrinelli, Milano. SADE D.A.F. de (1994), *La philosophie dans le boudoir*, Bookking international, Paris.
RONCHI R., (2015), *Gilles Deleuze. Credere nel reale*, Feltrinelli, Milano.
SAIDEL M.L., (2012), *Roberto Esposito nell'ambito del pensiero politico contemporaneo*, introduzione a R. Esposito, *Dall'impolitico all'impersonale: conversazioni filosofiche*, Mimesis, Milano, pp. 9–45.
SANDEL M.J. (1982), *Liberalism and the limits of justice*, Cambridge University Press, Cambridge.
SANDEL M.J. (1996), *Democracy's discontent. America in search of a public philosophy*, The Belknap Press of Harvard University Press, Cambridge.
SARTORI G., (1995), *Elementi di teoria politica*, Bologna 1987, III edizione.
SARTRE J.-P. (1936), *L'imagination*, Alcan, Paris.
SARTRE J.P., (1960), *Critique de la raison dialectique*, Gallimard, Paris.
SARTRE J.P., (1943), *L'Être et le Neant*, Gallimard, Paris.
SCHMITT C., (1932), *Der Begriff des Politischen* (1927), München Leipzig.
SELZNICK P. (1992), *The moral commonwealth. Social theory and the promise of community*, University of California Press, Oxford.
SERRATORE C., (2012), *La comunità come concetto ontologico. Dialogo con Constanza Serratore*, in R. Esposito, *Dall'impolitico all'impersonale: conversazioni filosofiche*, Mimesis, Milano, pp. 65–76.
SEVERINO E., (1980), *Destino della necessità. Katà tò chreon*, Adelphi, Milano.
SHEEHAN T., (2014), *Making Sens of Heidegger. A Paradigm Shift*, Rowman & Littlefield International, London-New York.
SIEGFRIED H., (1978), *Heidegger's Longest Day: "Being and Time" and the Sciences*, in «Philosophy Today», n. 22, pp. 319–331.
SIMMEL G., (1957), *Die Großstädte und das Geistesleben* (1903), in Id., *Brücke und Tür*, © K. F. Koehler, Stuttgart.
SMITH D.W., (2003), *Deleuze and Derrida, Immanence and Transcendence: Two Directions in Recent French Thought*, in P. Patton, J. Protevi (eds.), Between Deleuze and Derrida, Continuum, London-New York, pp. 46–66.
SOULEZ P., (1983), *La mère est-elle hors-jeu de l'essence du politique*, in P. Lacoue-Labarthe, J.- L. Nancy, (dir.), *Le retrait du politique*, Cahiers du Centre de recherches philosophiques sur le politique, Éditions Galilée, Paris.
STEINER G., (2002), *Grammars of creation*, Yale University Press, New Haven.
STIMILLI E., (2011), *Il debito del vivente. Ascesi e capitalismo*, Quodlibet, Macerata.
SURYA A., (1992a), *La communauté des amis. Georges Bataille, La mort à l'œuvre*, pp. 378–384. Gallimard, Paris.
SURYA A., (1992b), *De la communauté de l'impossible à l'impossible de la communauté. Georges Bataille, La mort à l'oeuvre*, 385-7, Gallimard, Paris.
SWIFT S., (2009), *Hannah Arendt*, Routledge, New York.
TAMINIAUX J., (1985), *Arendt, disciple de Heidegger?*, in «Études Phénoménologiques», n. 2, pp. 111–136
TARIZZO D., (2003), *Il pensiero libero. La filosofia francese dopo lo strutturalismo*, Raffaello Cortina, Milano.
TASSIN É., (1999), *L'azione "contro" il mondo. Il senso dell'acosmismo*, in S. Forti (a cura di) *Hannah Arendt*, Mondadori, Milano.
THORSTEINSSON B., (2007), *La question de la justice chez Jacques Derrida*, L'Harmattan, Paris.
TORTOLONE G.M., (1988), *Il corpo tentato. Per un discorso sull' uomo*, Marietti, Genova.
TRAVERSO E. (2001), *Le totalitarisme. Le XX° siècle en débat*, Seuil, Paris.
URBINATI N., (2012), *Liberi e uguali. Contro l'ideologia individualista*, Laterza, Roma-Bari.
URBINATI N., (2019), *Me the People: How Populism Transforms Democracy*, Harvard University Press, Cambridge.
VV. AA., (1987), *Bataille. Il politico e il sacro*, (a cura di J. Risset), Liguori, Napoli.

VV. AA., (1999), *Bataille-Leiris. L'intenable assentiment au monde*, Belin, Paris
VV. AA., (2000), *Nichilismo e politica*, a cura di R. Esposito, Laterza, Roma-Bari.
VV. AA., (2002), *Bataille/Sartre: un dialogo incompiuto*, (a cura di J. Risset), Artemide edizioni, Roma.
VV. AA., (2004), *Scenari dell'alterità*, (a cura di P.A. Rovatti), Bompiani, Milano.
VAN DEN ABBEELE G., (1997), *Lost horizons and uncommon grounds: for a poetics of finitude in the work of Jean-Luc Nancy*, in D. Sheppard, S. Sparks, C. Thomas (eds), *On Jean-Luc Nancy. The sense of philosophy*, Routledge, London, New York, p. 15–21.
VAN GINNEKEN J., (1984), nel suo *The Killing of the Father. The Background of Freud's Groupo Psychology*, in «Political Psychology», n. 3, pp. 391–414.
VATTIMO G., (1984), *Introduzione* a M. Heidegger, *L'opera d'arte e lo spazio*, Il melangolo, Genova, pp. 7–12.
VATTIMO G., (1988), *Le avventure delle differenza*, Garzanti, Milano.
VATTIMO G., (1989), *Ermeneutica e teoria dell'agire comunicativo*, in L. Sciolla - L. Ricolfi (ed.), *Il soggetto dell'azione*, Franco Angeli, Milano, pp. 233–245.
VATTIMO G., (1991), *La fine della modernità*, Garzanti, Milano.
VATTIMO G., ROVATTI P.A., (2009), (eds.), *Il pensiero debole*, Feltrinelli.
VERCELLONE F., (1992), *Introduzione al nichilismo*, Laterza, Roma-Bari.
VILLA D., (1996), *Arendt and Heidegger. The Fate of the Political*, Princeton University Press, Princeton.
VILLA D., (2000), *The Cambridge Companion to Hannah Arendt*, Cambridge University Press, Cambridge, pp. 130–147.
VILLACAÑAS BERLANGA J.L., (2015), *Populismo*, La Huerta Grande, Madrid.
VISKER R. (1998), *Levinas, le multiculturalisme et nous*, in *Questions au libéralisme*, Dillens A.- M. e.a., pp. 47–59, Facultés Universitaires Saint-Louis, Bruxelles.
VISKER R. (1999), *Truth and singularity. Taking Foucault into phenomenology*, Kluwer Academic Publishers, Dordrecht.
VITALE F., (2018), *Biodeconstruction. Jacques Derrida and the Life Sciences*, SUNY Press, New York.
VITIELLO V., (1979), *Dialettica ed ermeneutica. Hegel e Heidegger*, Guida, Napoli.
VITIELLO V., (1973), *Scienza e tecnica nel pensiero di Heidegger*, in «Il pensiero», n. 1–3, pp. 113–148.
VITIELLO V., (1991), (ed.), *Hegel e la comprensione della modernità*, Guerini e Associati, Milano
VITIELLO V., (1992), *Topologia del moderno*, Marietti, Genova.
VITIELLO V., (1997), *Filosofia teoretica. Le domande fondamentali: percorsi e interpretazioni*, Mondatori, Milano.
VITIELLO V., (2001), *«Abgeschiedenheit», «Gelassenheit», «Angst». Tra Eckhart e Heidegger*, in «Quaestio», n. 1, pp. 305–316.
VOLPI F., (1987), *Il pensiero politico di Hannah Arendt*, in Id., (ed.), *La pluralità irrappresentabile. Il pensiero politico di Hannah Arendt*, Edizioni QuattroVenti, Urbino, pp. 47–72.
VIRNO P., (1999), *Il ricordo del presente. Saggio sul tempo storico*, Bollati Boringhieri, Torino.
VIRNO P., (2003), *Quando il verbo si fa carne. Linguaggio e natura umana*, Bollati Boringhieri, Torino.
WAHL J., (1929), *La conscience malhereuse dans la philosophie de Hegel*, Les Éditions Rieder, Paris.
WALLACH J.R. (1987), *Liberals, communitarians and the tasks of political theory*, "Political Theory", 15, 4, pp. 581–611.
WALL T.C., (1999), *Radical Passivity. Lévinas, Blanchot, and Agamben*, State University of New York Press, New York.
WEBER M., (1920–1921), *Gesammelte Aufsätze zur Religionssoziologie*, Tübingen, Mohr.
WHITEHEAD A.N., (2007), *The concept of nature* (1920), Cosimo Inc, New York.
WITTGENSTEIN L., (1922), *Logisch-philosophische Abhandlung*, Routledge, London.

WOLIN S.S., (2008), *Democracy Incorporated. Managed Democracy and the Specter of Inverted Totalitarianism*, Princeton University Press, Princeton.
YOUNG I. M. (1986), *The ideal of a community and the politics of difference*, "Social Theory and Practice", 12, 1, pp. 1–26.
YOUNG I. M. (1990), *City life and difference. Justice and the politics of difference, pp. 226–56, Princeton University Press, Princeton, New Jersey.*
YOUNG-BRUEHL E., (1982), *Hannah Arendt: For Love of the World*, Yale University Press, New Haven-London.
ZANATTA L., (2013), *Il populismo*, Carocci, Roma.
ŽIŽEK S., (2000), *Enjoyment as a political factor*, © Slavoj Žižek.

Printed in the USA
CPSIA information can be obtained
at www.ICGtesting.com
CBHW051602051124
16949CB00002B/7

9 783031 754005